The Heartland Chronicles

University of Pennsylvania Press
Series in Contemporary Ethnography
Dan Rose and Paul Stoller, General Editors

A complete listing of the books in this series appears at the back of this volume

The Heartland Chronicles

Douglas E. Foley

Winesburg Ohio?

— Interviews of women?

— Stories of racial injustice + misunderstanding

University of Pennsylvania Press

Philadelphia

Copyright © 1995 by the University of Pennsylvania Press
Printed in the United States of America

Library of Congress Cataloging-in-publication Data
Foley, Douglas E.
   The Heartland chronicles / Douglas E. Foley.
      p.   cm. — (University of Pennsylvania Press series in
contemporary ethnography)
   Includes bibliographical references and index.
   ISBN 0-8122-3326-3 (cloth : alk paper). — ISBN 0-8122-1562-1
(pbk. : alk. paper)
   1. Tama (Iowa) — Race relations.   2. Fox Indians — Iowa — Tama.
I. Title.   II. Series: Series in contemporary ethnography.
F629.T36F65   1995
305.8'0097756 — dc20   95-16951
                                                                 CIP

Contents

Introduction

This is a tale about Indians and whites living together in a small Iowa community. It is also about an anthropologist returning to his hometown and boyhood memories. The idea for this book came to me during my twenty-fifth high school reunion. Upon hitting town, I discovered that the Mesquakis had started a high-stakes bingo operation. This turn of events really piqued my imagination. How ironic that the longsuffering Mesquakis were making money on the whiteman's vices. There was even speculation about a future gambling casino that would employ hundreds of whites. Such a turn of events sounded like quite a story.

But, being an academic, I could not write a journalistic account about the great Mesquaki gambling caper. My study had to flow from my professional specialization. Having spent fifteen years studying Hispanic-white relations in South Texas, I am supposedly an expert on American race relations. In South Texas one incident in particular planted the seed for this study. During a dinner party an outspoken Chicano "radical" castigated me, "You'll never understand us. If you want to be a civil rights crusader, appease your white guilt by writing about racial injustice in your community." That confrontation was repeated several times over, and I left South Texas wondering about my own racial past.

In South Texas I often found myself mentally comparing the way white Texans and Iowans treated "their minority." Southern whites told me that was a typical guilty Northerner's trick. They said that Northerners like to pretend that things are better up North. I ended up writing that South Texas racism was built on a system of cheap vegetable and cotton pickers. South Texas whites thought of themselves as the successful, superior people who ran the economy and the local government. They thought Mexicanos were inferior because they were just laborers. The Mexicano workers supposedly lacked the get up and go of white folks.

Several years later, I ran into the same attitude in a small Mississippi town. Mississippi whites also felt that their economic success somehow made them morally superior to their poor black neighbors. Even more incredible, these whites imagined themselves spiritually superior because a treacherous black man Cain slew Abel, a good and noble white man. These experiences left me wanting to know whether Iowans looked down on nonwhites for such strange religious and economic reasons.

In many ways studying race relations in my hometown is terribly difficult for me. My memories of growing up on an Iowa farm are very positive. I still tell stories about haymaking that extoll my noble heartland origins. My urban, academic friends chastise me for romanticizing rural life. They say I have consumed too much foreign food and films to ever return. Yet, for all my travels and fancy education, I still feel these Iowa roots.

To pry open my racial memories, I went back to my hometown and spent a year rooting around. I interviewed old friends, read old newspapers, went to tribal council meetings, powwows, adoption ceremonies, burials, basketball practices, school board meetings, casino feeds, and family gatherings. That is what an anthropologist does. She or he goes around talking to people and attending as many public and private meetings as possible. Every night, I wrote down what I saw and heard. I could not write down everything, but these notes help me remember the year I spent there. The idea of this type of study is to become a part of the community and get to know as many people as possible. Since I already knew many people, I was able to talk to hundreds of people during my stay in Tama.

There has already been a great deal written about the Mesquaksi. In truth, I had no idea how many other academics and journalists had preceded me. It turned out that the University of Chicago sent thirty-five anthropology students to the Mesquaki settlement from 1948 to 1959. Professor Sol Tax, a noted anthropologist of his times, created a field school for training anthropologists on the Mesquaki settlement. These student anthropologists were supposed to be learning how to be anthropologists while they helped the Mesquakis solve some of their community problems. This unique approach to training anthropologists became known as "action anthropology." More important for my purposes, the original fieldnotes from Tax's "Fox Project" to study and help the Mesquakis were deposited in the Smithsonian archives. Those old fieldnotes contained an amazing record of what the whites and Indians whom I grew up with thought about each other. As I read these historical documents and talked to people, my memories of growing up in that era finally came alive.

After anthropologists collect such materials, they write an "ethnography" about their temporary stay somewhere. There is currently considerable debate over what an ethnographic study really is. Some still think of ethnographies as objective scientific studies. Others, like me, have lost faith in this grand ideal. I now think of ethnographies more as personal encounters. I make no claims that the tale I am about to spin is absolutely true. I have worked hard to make it more fact than fiction, but as in all so-called factual books, I am characterizing people as I see them. I am also reporting the events and stories that I found most interesting and revealing. Others might put a very different face on these people and events.

Some readers might rightly ask why a book like this is needed. Above all, I would like to tell a story that teaches whites and Indians a little something about each other. I left town in search of interesting, different cultures only to find such a culture in my hometown. I invite whites to cross that cultural border and be real neighbors with the Mesquakis. Others will ask, "Is not this book written for more than just the people you grew up with? Surely you hope that someone will turn it into a movie and make you rich?" Of course anyone who writes a book hopes to garner a national audience. But nonfiction books on serious topics never make the best seller lists or much money.

While on the issue of financial gain, I must make clear to the Mesquakis that I received $4,500 from the Spencer Foundation to collect materials at the Smithsonian. Otherwise, I financed the entire study myself. On that score, I owe Tom Hill, a University of Northern Iowa anthropology professor, my gratitude. He helped me secure a one-semester teaching position near the settlement. I also owe my aunt, Gertrude Clark Timm, a ton of gratitude for housing and feeding me for the past four summers.

My main reward for this labor will be seeing what I wrote taught in college classes. It may help chip away at popular stereotypes about the Mesquakis and their white neighbors. I also have a wildly optimistic idea that many old friends will read this book as easily as they watch their favorite TV show. But, when I come down to earth, I figure no more than a handful of locals will read this. Even more perplexing, some will read only the parts about themselves. Others will read only the parts that confirm their prejudices.

I also need to explain for local readers why most of the people in this study have been given pseudonyms. The only real names used in this version are those of individuals no longer living. Originally, the plan was to use everyone's real name. After writing the manuscript, I circulated it to forty of the main characters and, in two grueling weeks, collected their comments and criticisms. Nearly everyone liked the manuscript with real names, but a few people, including my publisher, wanted me to use pseudonyms. The epilogue chronicles that review process and the general reactions of local reviewers to the original manuscript.

For those readers sensitive to ethnic terms, I should add that I use the term Indian rather than Native American as a general ethnic label. A few local white teachers used the term Native Americans, but after several years on the settlement, that term sounds a little affected. It is the politically correct term on university campuses, but most Mesquakis refer to themselves as Indians. Ultimately, I decided to use the term that the Mesquakis use.

I should close this introduction by saying that this book is dedicated to the Clark women: Hazel Clark Rockwood, who brought me into this world; Mary Elizabeth Boyer Clark, who raised me; and Gertrude Clark Timm, who has always taken care of Grandma and me. They are the best of the heartland, the best of me. They cannot be held responsible for my views, but if I have an ounce of decency in me, I got it from them and from the Clark men, Grandpa Glenn and Uncle Cal. They taught me all about hard work and frugality—and maybe even a little bit about spinning tales—especially Cal, a real talker if there ever was one.

Chapter 1
Home to the Heartland

*Contrast new
old — now
then —*

On the heels of a snowstorm, I set off for my first Iowa winter in thirty years. Thanks to Professor Tom Hill at the University of Northern Iowa (UNI), I had landed a teaching job forty miles from the Mesquaki Settlement. Since the settlement is just outside my home town of Tama and UNI is my alma mater, this would be a double homecoming.

The drive up from Texas was pretty uneventful. Anyone who has driven I-35 North has yawned through inconspicuous towns and death-defying chain restaurant stops. As I came upon the Iowa border, the state welcome sign smiled out, "Come Explore the Heartland." Very neighborly. Very Iowan. A heartland explorer — now there is an interesting thought. So part of a title was born, and it just stuck. It seemed appropriate then and still seems appropriate.

Here I was in search of America in its red and white people. I must get my graduate assistant a postcard of that sign. Being an Ivy League type, she has shown little appreciation for rural Iowa. It was hard to get a commitment from her to collect materials for the project. Iowa and the Mesquaki Indians were not exactly her idea of big-time anthropology in some far-away exotic culture. If she visits the settlement, I cannot wait to see whether she falls for cousin Dave's "dumb farmer" routine. Anyway, onward to the great American heartland.

After settling into a UNI apartment, I set up my Tama household at Aunt Gertrude's and headed for the settlement. The Mesquaki settlement is five thousand densely wooded acres cut from the gently rolling hills of surrounding farms. Anyone who knows the central Iowa landscape would be struck by such a large stand of timber. The only open part of the settlement is the flat river-bottom land that accommodates the tempestuous Iowa river. A gravel road snakes through the settlement and provides people with three portals to the outside world. A railroad track serving the surrounding towns also rips through the Mesquaki homeland. There used to be two railroads, but only one and some bitter memories remain.

Two state highways enclose the settlement on the north and south, and the tiny hamlet of Montour and the towns of Tama and Toledo come within two or three miles of the eastern and western borders. A couple of inconspicuous highway signs have always quietly announced the settlement. Now new trading post and casino signs boldly invite white passersby to stop. The center of the settlement has also been transformed. A old cluster of buildings that included the Redman's Grocery, Kapayou's barbershop, and the Legion Hall is gone. So is the communal TV that used to bring the Saturday night Gillette fights. So is the University of Chicago house, which accommodated a steady stream of anthropologists.

The settlement's religious buildings have also changed dramatically. The once imposing Presbyterian mission church building and childcare center has been abandoned to local vandals. Self-appointed graffiti artists have decorated the gaping holes left by marauding cars. The crumbling church is a stark reminder of the mission's failure on the settlement. Meanwhile, several new clan ceremonial centers, built by clan leaders, and a Drum Society center, built with Methodist contributions, have sprouted in private wooded areas. The few peyotists left hold their ceremonies in private houses.

The new tribal center, built in the late 1970s, is far more physically impressive than the makeshift stores of the 1940s. The spacious center with vaulted ceilings contains a health clinic, council chambers, kitchen, gym, commodity foods program, and maintenance shop. The center now employs fifty new tribal bureaucrats. Accountants, bookkeepers, alcohol counselors, community workers, nurses, maintenance men, and janitors keep expanding tribal affairs going. With the coming of a gaming operation, there are also an enterprise committee and several grant writers. Everything has become much more modern and more organized. The new center also includes a senior citizens' housing project and dining hall. Although many of the apartments are filled with young families, the dining hall puts on an active lunch and social program for seniors.

Down the road, the old tribal school is still more or less as it was. The building went up in 1937, and was almost instantly—and still is—a firetrap. The battle to replace it, to be recounted later, has raged for forty years. Like the new tribal center, the school houses several new grant writers and now has Mesquaki aides for all the white teachers. There are a couple of certified Mesquaki teachers at the kindergarten building next to the senior citizens' dining hall. The tribal school also houses the dreaded Bureau of Indian Affairs (BIA) agent. He implores students to go to school but delivers their scholarship checks six months late. Life on the settlement is inconceivable without a BIA agent to kick around.

All in all, the settlement has made real material improvements since World War II. Many people have moved from small houses in the flood plain to newer style houses in the higher, hilly areas near the new tribal center. Some are in open subdivision-like areas, but many family compounds of houses and trailers are set off the road in well-kept clearings. The whole family mows and weeds these clearings as dutifully as any suburban family.

The only thing different and "Indian" about these family compounds are the round wickiups used as summer houses. Canvas covers have replaced the old woven cattail covers, but the frames are still made of saplings and the floors are earthen. Piles of firewood for cooking and religious ceremonies still accompany the wickiups. One is struck by the collage of modern houses and cars and lawn mowers and these ancient wickiups. Picnic tables have replaced blankets and reed mats. The menstrual huts for women no longer exist, and sweat lodges are rare, but such practices still go on.

When I was growing up, the settlement contained little more than eighty single-wall houses that whites ungraciously referred to as "shacks." There was no modern tribal center and gym, apartment complex, modern houses and trailers, or sewage plant and water system. "Pitiful," my grandpa used to say. "Those Indians are living in pitiful conditions." But times have changed. There are at least fifty newer style houses and almost as many trailers, and the population has exploded (one thousand settlement dwellers) to the point that two hundred and ten Mesquakis now live in my hometown. In the 1950s no more than a handful of Mesquakis lived in town. Despite all the new units, many Mesquakis are forced to rent in town. And some things never change. Now that housing is generally better, many whites say, "It is pitiful how fast they tear up the free houses the government gives 'em."

Welcome to a Cultural Borderland

And white people still remember the settlement as a mysterious, forbidden place. It was a scary place that was supposedly full of violence and strange goings-on. Kids were told to stay away from "those Indians." One of my classmates, now a prominent businessman, remembered it like this:

It was this dark, scary place, kinda like a forest. My parents warned me to never ride my bike out there, but me and my buddy just couldn't resist. One day we snuck out there, just took off. I remember being scared as hell. People used to say that the Indians cut white people up out there. They used to say it was a dangerous place after dark with all the drinking and fighting and all the knives and guns.

I heard many scary stories about the settlement, but one version, told to me by a white woman married to a Mesquaki, stands above all others. Her scary story was about a white boy who got castrated for messing around with an Indian woman. As she told it, I suddenly remembered the first time I heard reference to this shocking story. I was sixteen and was watching Jay WhiteHawk and Lujack GreySky playing pool. This white guy asked them, "Is it true that a guy could lose his nuts on the reservation?" The Mesquaki boys, both excellent athletes, laughed slyly and said, "Maybe." Maybe? I wondered what the hell maybe meant.

This whiteman's nervous question springs from a well-traveled tale that we all heard growing up. There are many versions of this story, allegedly based on a true incident, and they all start with Mr. Z out on the settlement late one night. He is parked with this "squaw," whom he picked up in a local bar. Mr. Z is trying his best to get her drunk so he can bed her. While they are drinking and necking, a group of "bucks" sneak up and drag him out of the car. They scream at the woman to go home where she belongs and beat him within an inch of his life. He fights back as best he can, but the Indians stick together like a pack of wild dogs. They are all hootched up and lusting to get even with whites, so in the end they castrate him with a rusty beer opener.

That is the story hidden within my friend's innocent story about bicycling on the settlement. Young white males were brought up listening to this horror story about losing their balls on the settlement. The settlement was a dark place where revenge hung heavy from the boughs of sacred pine trees. A place where young men riding on bicycles might pay for the sins of their older brothers. A place where a young white boy might cross the most tempting border of all and have sex with a wild Indian woman. Such were the fears and fantasies of some of the young white men that I knew growing up.

And from the other side comes the voice of Jean GreyEagle, the only Mesquaki cheerleader in the history of Tama High. Jean graduated a few years after I did, so I asked her what she learned about the town while growing up. Her reply was not unlike that of many other Mesquakis:

You learned that you were Indian, and they were white. When you're growing up we were really poor, no electricity and running water. That sticks with you. Town was a kinda scary place. It seemed like people stared at you. We kept to ourselves. We heard teachers were mean. Some people taught their kids that whites would hurt them. It was a place to go to movies and shop. You didn't talk to nobody when I was growing up. We didn't go to their houses. We'd see 'em, but you weren't friends enough to spend the night at their house. Some white kids weren't that friendly.

Other Mesquakis said they too were taught to be careful in town. Town was a strange white place run by rich people who thought they were better than Indians. To protect their children, Mesquaki parents taught them to ignore the white clerks, who followed them around as if they were thieves. They taught them to avoid the police, who were quick to arrest them. As you can see, the border between the town and the settlement is a state of mind born of fear and mistrust. Much more about all of this later.

Anyway, on this first day back, I arrived at the tribal center in time to catch the tribal director, Claude Windsong. I had talked to Claude and several old classmates the previous summer. At the time, Claude mused that there had not been a study for quite some time, so maybe it was time. Some of my old classmates also said that they would help me write my book. Today I just want to check in with Claude and tell him I am ready to start. He probably never figured I would come back. Whites are constantly pestering him for information. White people come and go on the settlement. They are like cutworms that get into your sweet corn patch. Modern-day Indians have to learn how to deal with this onslaught of journalists, dissertation researchers, anthropologists, social workers, folklorists, art collectors, linguists, and historians. Everyone wants to write about the strange and exotic Indians. So Claude, like most Mesquakis, shrugged a knowing shrug and said, "Sure, do your study of us."

I got my first inkling of how different researching Indians would be when Claude gave me an initiation lecture. To really appreciate this encounter, a little background on Claude is necessary. He is what some whites call a "militant" or "over-educated Indian." Claude, of course, takes that as a great compliment and so much racist babble. Such white dislike and envy only confirm the justness of his cause, and he never lets whites forget it. He has led several battles to reform the white schools, and I like to think of him as the "Richard Nixon of Mesquaki politics." Like Nixon, Claude is a terribly important but controversial politician. He has been a force in post-World War II Mesquaki politics and has returned from several political defeats to doggedly pursue his ideal of educational self-determination.

One day I shared my Nixon analogy with Claude, and in the twinkle of an eye, he did a wierd little tricky Dick head bob and flashed the victory sign. Anyone who can parody Nixon and himself that well cannot be such a bad guy. But on this day he was hell bent to start yet another dumb anthropologist off on the right foot. If he had to put up with my silly questions, he was going to point me in the right direction.

Before going in to see him, I had stopped by the house of Ryan Grey-Eagle, an old classmate and friend, who had encouraged me to do this study. I asked Ryan to accompany me to see Claude. When we arrived, Claude seemed surprised to see us, and I announced, somewhat breathlessly, that I was back to study Mesquaki-white race relations. Claude smiled and handed me a copy of Fred McTaggart's dissertation. For him this study, which became the book *Wolf That I Am* (1976), was exemplary. Later I will go into some detail on this and other writings about Mesquaki culture, but it suffices to say that McTaggart wanted to collect the "winter stories" that teach spiritual beliefs. Very few people would share these stories, so he went away with a healthy appreciation for the fabled Mesquaki circumspection and secrecy about their religion. In the book, Claude and his family were characters who guided him to a greater respect for Mesquaki culture. So lesson number one was be like McTaggart and keep your nose out of our religion.

Lesson number two was even more unexpected. A question about Sol Tax's action anthropology project provoked a long discussion on cultural assimilation. Claude disliked the project for several reasons, but he found value in the assimilation concept. With great solemnity, he began drawing a diagram of Mesquaki culture — the naming, ghost feasts, adoptions, mourning, and burial ceremonies. He wielded white anthropological discourse about "the Mesquaki core ritual complex" with real facility. These ritual celebrations of birth, ancestors, and death are still widely practiced on the settlement, but some Mesquakis are much less active than others. As Claude talked, I could see him mentally recording who was a traditionalist and who was an assimilated back-slider. How strange to meet a "native" who speaks the academic dialect so well and uses it for very practical purposes.

During the lecture on assimilation, my companion Ryan suddenly chipped in a story that his dad told him when he was a boy. Apparently his dad caught him killing a snake, so Ryan got a lecture on the basic goodness of snakes. Ryan continued, "But one day a bull snake that looked little and harmless came into our yard and started eating birds and chickens. No one was paying attention to the snake, so it just helped itself."

It would seem that not all bull snakes are good and trustworthy. I thought to myself: I am sitting between one Mesquaki who talks like an anthropologist and another who talks in animal stories. What could all this possibly mean?

Months later I came to understand this conversation a bit better. Ryan laughed heartily as he explained that the bull snake story was meant for all politicians. At election time politicians are all shiny and clean, but once in office they are like the bull snake who eats what it wants. As Claude lectured us on surveilling "acculturated Indians," Ryan, a practicing Christian, was answering his veiled challenge in an indirect, circumspect way. So there I was, the bewildered anthropologist ensnared in all the communicative subtleties of Mesquakis arguing about who is a real Mesquaki. On one hand, there was Claude the traditionalist and clan elder chastising Ryan in white anthropologese. On the other hand, there was Ryan the Christian responding with a Mesquaki animal story parable.

So who was the real traditional Indian here? The one who goes to tribal ceremonies and speaks like a white, or the one who goes to a white church and speaks like an Indian? So much for simple, essentialist cultural traits or practices that firmly locate Mesquakis in either the Indian or the white world. This was my first inkling that all Mesquakis live in some kind of cultural borderland that traverses both worlds. They slip in and out of white jobs and ways of talking. As we shall see, the boundary between white and Indian culture is often distinct and antagonistic but hardly impermeable. People from both races live in this complex racial borderland that partakes of both cultures. Later we will meet some Indians and whites who cross the racial border regularly.

At any rate, after Claude's orientation lecture I went looking for someone less intimidating and a little more reassuring. The first person on my list of old sports buddies was Lone TrueBlood, whom I remembered as a tall, powerfully-built athlete. He was the best softball pitcher around and much more likeable than his wicked, rising fastball. People told me that he had built himself a house deep in the woods on a high hill. He lives there with his white wife and helps take care of her ex-husband's son's three kids. The ex-husband's son and his brother fix cars, so used cars and car parts adorn the hillside leading to the house. My pickup barely made it up the winding, sandy driveway, but there Lone was, fixing his motorcycle. I jumped out of the truck and shouted,

"Hi Lone. Do you know who I am?"

"Sure Doug, played any basketball lately? What are you doin' back here? I heard you went off to Texas. I read it in the paper or something. What'ca doin' back here hangin' around with us Indians?"

Up close I could see that Lone had not changed all that much, save some extra pounds and gray hair. He works as a security guard at the tribal center, and more important, is part of the Mesquaki royal family and next in line to be the hereditary chief. Since 1896, the tribe has been politically split between supporters of the royal family and of the elected tribal council. Various TrueBloods, including his father, had taken their claim to the BIA and the federal courts, only to be rebuffed again and again. In 1937 the tribe officially voted to legally abolish the hereditary chieftainship under the Indian Reorganization Act. The election was hotly contested, some say rigged. So creating an elected tribal council, as we shall see later, did not end this political controversy.

Without getting too deeply into Mesquaki politics, it suffices to say that Lone shows no signs of claiming his chieftainship. He is too busy taking care of his aging mother and three grandchildren. When he can find time, he enjoys a little fishing and his tiny terrier dog. As we talked a little about politics, he said jokingly, "I am too dumb to be the chief, Doug. I don't know nothin' about that stuff the council is always trying to pull. I'm just the security guard around here." This "Aw-shucks-I'm-just-a-dumb-Indian-routine" is very reminiscent of cousin Dave's dumb farmer routine. When I read the Fox Project fieldnotes, I found many Mesquakis pulling that same routine on the student anthropologists. Some of these young anthropologists seemed to see through it and some did not.

One thing I do know about Lone's intelligence is that he is the only person, Indian or white, who noticed when I changed my glasses and when I replaced my pickup tires. He also seemed to notice my every mood change. I was quite impressed with his observational powers. So one day I told Lone that he was a keen observer and mentioned these incidents. With a twinkle in his eye, he put his hand over his eyes, feigned peering into the woods, and said, "You mean like those Indians who can see a deer coming? I guess I must be a real Indian, huh, Doug?" I had no quick comeback for this little slice of Indian humor. Stereotypes of eagle-eyed Indian woodsmen aside, Lone really was an astute observer of people.

So my first day ended with several mind-benders. One Mesquaki speaks anthropologese and the other tells bull snake tales, and my favorite softball pitcher is a reluctant hereditary chief married to a white woman. It had been quite a first day on the job. I headed back to town with my head full of questions about Mesquaki culture and politics.

Welcome Home, Mr. Anthropologist

In the next few weeks I also began talking to people in the white community. I started with old classmates and friends and quickly expanded to other businessmen, teachers, farmers, high school students, and whites married to Mesquakis. Before arriving, I imagined myself talking to old white friends freely about their views of Indians. I figured that Iowans would speak plainly and to the point. It would be un-Iowan, or at the very least unneighborly, to hide what they think. I confided my optimism to a certified Mesquaki pessimist, and he retorted with another of those all-knowing wise Indian shrugs. It turns out that he had a point. Some old friends were pretty good at hiding their views. One classmate and her husband invited me to their farm for a little chat. Afterward she told my aunt that I had "done real good." I asked good questions and seemed to know what I was doing.

The only disconcerting thing was her husband's silence. Mr. Y is a big, rawboned guy who was a redneck in his high school days. He is also quite a talker and makes an effort to know what is going on. When I folded up my notebook, he chirped in, "Well, I guess you didn't get much out of us. Anyway, we don't know nothin' much sittin' out here." Right. I thought to myself, What am I, a vacuum cleaner salesman trying to sell you something? Meanwhile, this book gets written without your opinion, pal. Although I had never met Mr. Y's son, he turned out to be much more open than his father. We shall meet this son later in the racial barroom fights that marked the 1970s. Anyway, there I was "interviewing" these old friends. I asked the questions. They answered politely. I wrote down their answers. We all played our parts brilliantly.

Other old white friends were much more open, but it was never as predictable as I imagined. One aging Lothario who used to try and get Indian women drunk acted as if he were a racially concerned citizen. One former classmate turned businessman was as blunt and opinionated as he always was. He was not about to try to impress me by putting flowers on local race relations. He did, however, express some fears that I might write some biased, crusading civil rights expose. He hoped that I was "not as dumb as some of these Des Moines *Register* reporters are. At least you grew up here. You ought to know better." An old baseball teammate was even more suspicious. During a conversation in his store, he asked to see my tape recorder. He was certain that I was hiding one in my shoulder bag.

My relatives had a range of reactions to having an anthropologist living in their midst. Aunt Gertrude just said, "Don't you dare go putting anything I said in that book of yours." Sorry Gert, here you are, if only for a moment. Cousin Dave cut right to the bottom line and asked how much money I was going to make on this book. He wondered why anyone would read a book about a little burg like Tama and its Indians. Some other family members wondered if I was always recording what they said, even during the family Fourth of July celebration. If I was spying on them, they seemed willing to live with it. Like many whites, they were not ashamed to act and talk the way they always have.

Most people seemed willing to tell me what they knew, but one of my best high school buddies, Larry Simmons, always the skeptic, wondered how I was going to "separate the bull from the truth." Unlike many whites, he has actually spent some time on the settlement and has a half-breed son. Now a postman, Larry has heard just about every tall tale ever told about whites and Indians. He and others figured that most Indians would exaggerate how bad whites mistreated them. He also figured that it might take a few Old Milwaukees to loosen some white tongues. Some whites gave me pointers on which Indians to talk to and which were the rabble-rousers. Given the recent casino controversy, everyone seemed to have an Indian informant on settlement politics. Some whites were constantly trying to pump me for information to see if my information squared with theirs.

I was particularly curious about what whites would think of my doing a study on the Mesquakis. Initially, I got the "Well-that-is-interesting" response. An awkward silence usually followed, and no one ever volunteered more opinions. But these "pregnant silences" spoke volumes. For the readers who do not speak Iowaese, "Well-that-is-interesting" is a polite way of saying, "Well, that is the craziest idea I've ever heard," or "Well, if you are dumb enough to waste your time, go ahead." A few liberal white teachers saw it a little differently. They felt that my study might publicize inequities and help solve the town's minority problem.

Another old friend offered the following opinion:

What is there to study? Oh I suppose they have a colorful history, but really, their culture is pretty much gone now. If you have ever gone to the powwow, you can see that being Indian is pretty much a show for the white tourists.

He went on to tell a story that many white folks told about Indians in the good old days. His father used to farm near the settlement and always knew some of the old leaders.

Those old Indians were so trustworthy that a person could leave machinery and tools out in the fields and nothing would ever be stolen. In those days they still retained some of their old ways. An Indian's word was as good as gold. Nowadays the drinking, gambling, and unemployment has ruined them. They aren't much better than poor white trash now.

So the idea of studying a supposedly extinct culture did not make much sense to this white, or to many others that I interviewed.

Most local whites find the typical liberal view that Indian cultures are a national cultural treasure pretty bizarre. For many locals, the Mesquakis are a defeated race. Worse still, they have been ruined by the government's welfare policies. The white community always looked on the Mesquakis as an economic burden, since they supposedly "pay no taxes." Outside of a few teachers and over-educated types, no one is interested in preserving and knowing more about Mesquaki culture. Even if you grant that the old culture survives, it is supposedly not different and exotic enough to be interesting. That point was driven home with a vengeance by one young white. He told me this story about when he "finally met some real Indians" on a Navajo reservation:

I was real impressed with the way the Navajo live. Those people still ride horses and herd sheep for a living. I've lived here all my life, but those were the first real Indians I'd ever seen. I was pretty impressed with what good people they are too, real hard working like farmers are.

Since the Navajo made more Indian handicrafts and still rode horses, they were more "real" than the Mesquakis. Although he did not put it this way, he seems to be saying that the Navajos live closer to a state of nature, thus are more natural and "savage" and less modern and "civilized."

Given this view of Mesquaki culture, many whites are pretty indifferent about Indians. Another old friend, now a community leader, put it like this:

To me Mesquakis aren't anything special. They are not a particularly talented bunch that has made something of themselves. Some of them are good in art, but you never see one become a well-known commercial artist and make a living at it. I don't think of them as particularly good or bad. Very few really ever get out of here and make something of themselves. After school, they seem to pretty much hang around out there, and eventually some get into trouble with the law.

For this individual it was a matter of having the drive to achieve something. Since they were not high-achievers, what could you say that is special about them? What is there to write if they do not individually excel at something?

So there you have it — a race of people who have lost their ancient, noble culture and achieve little as individuals. Worse still, since the civil rights movement the Mesquakis have increased their demands on mainstream society. My friend who questioned the authenticity of the powwow asked jokingly one day, "Well what are the 'Squawkies' squawking about now?" He sees Indians as doing little for themselves but demanding much from the federal government. "Squawking. Whining. Complaining. Feeling sorry for themselves. Trying to get something for nothing." For him the modern Mesquaki has lost that noble, rugged individualism of earlier Indians and white frontiersmen.

Searching for My Racial Memories

From the moment I began hearing whites talk about the Mesquakis, I started remembering what I learned about Indians as a child. My first recollection of seeing a non-white comes from a story Grandma used to tell about me. We were waiting in the car for Grandpa when an African American woman walked by. I apparently shouted, "Grandma, Grandma, look, there's a nigger!" Confronted with a scowling black face, she tried to hush me up and said, "Shush, don't you say that to anyone! That's not a nice thing to say! That lady will get real mad at us. See her looking at us. Be quiet, now!" Grandma used to tell that story with considerable delight — how she had saved her naive little grandson from a serious racial beating. She was a former rural school teacher who was always dreaming about visiting far-off lands. Raising six kids and running a farm only left her time to travel in the evening. She was a voracious reader and visited many places in her beloved historical novels and travelogues.

In retrospect, she probably had more sympathy for minorities than the men in our family. She used to say things like, "Oh they aren't that bad, Glenn. Some Negroes are just as good as a lot of white folks." On one trip to Kansas City to sell cattle, I remember going to a movie house. We were all scared silly that the African Americans milling around on the streets were going to do us in, but Grandma kept saying, "Oh they won't do anything to us if we act decent to them." When someone would complain about Indian children roaming the streets of Tama on Saturday night, she would say, "Well, they have to come to town and buy things just like we do." Grandma was no ardent crusader for Indian rights, but she often found herself defending the rights of minorities to do simple everyday things.

My mother also found herself defending the rights of Indians to drink alcohol. In the late 1940s she ran a beer tavern in Tama for a couple of years. When I visited her on Saturdays, she allowed me to roam freely with the "trashy" white and Indian kids in her bar. I say trashy because that is what my grandpa and uncle, both respectable farmers, thought of people who let their kids hang around bars. During my high school days, the mayor and city council tried to prohibit Mesquakis from drinking in the local bars. When I read the passionate pleas of tavern owner Red Crawford against the prohibition (Tama *News Herald* [TNH] June 30, 1960), I actually heard my mother's voice.

Mom was particularly vocal on the Indian temperance issue. Being a fairly wild youth, and not much of a church-goer, I remember her staunchly defending the rights of Indians to drink. I can still hear her saying that Indians held their liquor just as good as whites; that Indians were no bigger deadbeats than whites about paying. She thought the town fathers were pretty much full of themselves. Once she spouted off, "What a bunch of goddamn hypocrites those little goody two-shoes are!" Hearing her views on this issue and being allowed to play with Indians probably made me a little more open to Mesquakis.

The other major thing that shaped my views of Indians as a youth was the *Leatherstocking Tales* of James Fenimore Cooper. My rural school library had several of his romantic books about the frontier and Indians. The one I read many times was *The Last of the Mohicans*. Although scholars (Berkhofer, 1978) have pointed out how paternalistic these portrayals of Indians are, they made me imagine Indians — and the white frontiersmen who were Indian-like — as extra-ordinary, dashing, heroic figures. Indeed when I saw the new movie starring the Irishman Daniel Day Lewis, it brought back a flood of memories. Indians were incredible physical specimens of manhood who could run forever, leap across cliffs, swim miles, canoe down impossible rivers, deftly kill with knives and tomahawks, and survive winter snows, bears, wolves, and all manner of forest dangers.

I do not honestly remember thinking Indians were no-good, drunken bums. When we went to town on Saturday nights, I saw Mesquakis on the streets in front of the taverns. I also heard whites make disparaging remarks, but I had a romantic Leather-Stocking-Tale view of Indians. Indians were a big part of my male fantasies. By comparison, Hollywood's singing cowboys like Gene Autrey and Roy Rogers were big sissies in silly white hats. The best cowboys were Red Ryder, who stepped out of a book with Little Beaver, and the Lone Ranger, who had Tonto. In retrospect, my two favorite cowboys were paternalistic white guys with child or child-like Indian sidekicks, but in my childhood mind Tonto was never a white-man's lackey. He used his people's superior survival skills in the fight against evil. Being like Indians was a good thing because they were honorable, natural athletes, fighters, and real men.

Moreover, being a farm kid, I was also treated like an outsider in my own town. My first year in Tama High School was pretty unpleasant. Some kids called me nasty names and I got into several fights. Initially I gravitated toward the white kids from "smokey row" (the poor side of town near the railroad tracks) and the Indian athletes I admired. Eventually I became good in sports, thus more accepted, but I never ran around with the rich, popular white kids from "the hill." After interviewing many former high school classmates about race relations, I still could not recall much open racial hostility. Nearly everyone, even many Mesquakis, gave a fairly rosy picture of race relations in Tama High in the 1950s.

Everyone except Ryan GreyEagle. He told me the story of how Rich Sears elbowed him during football practice. Later that day in the locker room Chester Moline and Jay WhiteHawk confronted Sears about picking on an Indian more his size. Ryan was a skinny, quiet, friendly kid, and Sears was a 250 pound, tough-guy tackle. After hearing these two accounts, I do remember that day. I remember sitting there in the locker room with two other sophomores afraid to go in and help defend Ryan. I felt sorry for Ryan. He was a far nicer guy than Sears, but I was afraid of this big white bully. He picked on me during football practice, too.

The striking thing about this story is how hard it was to remember. Only after listening to Ryan's life story for hours could I visualize the locker room incident again. That incident was one of those moments of truth that the novelist Joseph Conrad writes about so eloquently. When Ryan needed help, I was no more able to stand up to Sears than other whites were. Some readers may think this is a story to soothe my guilty conscience. Perhaps. But I see it as the perfect metaphor for well-intentioned but timid whites. Many whites do not condone racism, but we find it hard to stand up to our rednecks. It is hard to do the right thing.

High school was my first serious contact with Mesquakis. I remember the Mesquakis as alternately quiet and withdrawn and very outgoing and funny. In class they always sat at the back, and they rarely asked or answered questions. On the other hand, they hung together in groups outside class and constantly horsed around and played jokes on each other and any whites who joined them. Mesquaki teenagers did not generally participate in school social life like the prom and homecoming dances. Except for the athletes, they kept to themselves. Being an athlete, I got to know a number of the Mesquaki boys, but never any of the girls. They seemed particularly shy, and interracial dating was generally frowned on in the 1950s.

The one exception during my high school days was a controversial romance between two student leaders, Billy Warrior and Madge Smith. Billy, an all-state athlete and son of a tribal leader, and Madge, a would-be actress and daughter of a prominent businessman, had a scandalous romance. Some whites accepted this relationship because the Warriors were a "good Indian" family. Billy's father was even an officer in the Boosters Club. After a time Madge was sent off to a private girls' school to break up the relationship. Billy went to college, married another white woman, and became a businessman, and Madge finished college and became a New York stage actress. Old classmates still cite this incident as an example of how restricted racial dating was in the 1950s.

Encounters with Anthropological Ghosts

Not being a "Native American specialist," I have neither read many books on Indians nor heard many Indian jokes about anthropologists. Nancy Lurie's (1988) history of relations between Indians and anthropologists chronicles how difficult it has become to write about Indians. My introduction into this fraternity of anthropologists came during a visit to Sol Tax. Tax is a retired University of Chicago professor who ran an anthropological field school on the settlement for eleven years. His "Fox Project" also developed a variety of "action anthropology" activities. Fox is another name scholars use for the Mesquakis. Tax and his students wanted their Fox Project to do more than study the Mesquakis. They wanted to help solve social, economic, and educational problems on the settlement as well. After leaving the settlement, Professor Tax continued to work for Native American causes. He helped form the American Indian Congress (AIC) which spawned a wave of pan-Indian activism in the 1960s era.

After seeing a 1933 picture of Tax doing fieldwork on the settlement, I was surprised how frail this jaunty adventurer in khaki shorts had become. Despite his eighty-five years, he was still quick of mind and memory, but I took him by surprise: "And you were a teenager when the Fox Project was going? Now you are an anthropologist at the University of Texas? Are you a full-time faculty member? You teach at the university there? You grew up in Tama?"

Before him was a Tama native-turned-anthropologist who wanted to follow in his footsteps. Not an altogether improbable turn of events, but his incredulity made me feel like I was on an impossible search for the Holy Grail of anthropology.

Then some primal anthropological gene kicked in and he began inducting me into his fraternity. He outlined all the Indian organizations that dedicated Native Americanists must join. Still the action anthropologist, he advised me to "Go slowly. Do your study over a number of summers. Don't get a grant and finish in a year. There is just too much to learn." It was good advice. Four years after this conversation, I still feel like a rookie on the Native American beat. Even more important than his encouragement was the treasure trove he left in the National Anthropological Archives at the Smithsonian. Twenty-two boxes of diaries, interviews, and historical documents. Thousands of pages of observations by thirty-five student anthropologists. I spent a month reading these papers, which turned out to be good baseline data and a mirror for my reflections.

How strange it was to read an interview done in the Tamahawk Sweet Shoppe with one of my Indian teammates. Perhaps it was done right under my nose while I sipped a cherry coke. Perhaps I even saw one of these earnest young anthropologists pumping Mesquaki teenagers for information. It would have been strange for some college-type to be talking to one of "our Indians," but I do not recall it. And the deeper I plunged into these boxes, the stranger it got. One box contained psychological test profiles. A folder listed my Mesquaki classmates' scores from the draw-a-man IQ test. A number of the characters you shall meet did pretty well on this silly psychological test.

To be fair, much of what action anthropologists wrote was of high quality and perceptive. They kept elaborate fieldnotes that often revealed a deep commitment to helping Mesquakis adapt to the white world. But reading someone else's fieldnotes about your hometown is a very strange experience. You begin to see how anthropologists use rather limited, casual observations to create stories about people. The diaries contained facile characterizations of various individuals I knew personally. For example, there was a long discussion of one Mesquaki who I know fairly well. Their profile of him as a rake and life of the party fits fairly well, but the file also claimed to probe his dark side as well.

According to the report, Mr. X laughed and joked a lot because he had suicidal tendencies. One day he told this earnest young anthropologist about his suicidal feelings. Knowing Mr. X, I thought this little speech sounded suspiciously like a put-on, but his story was dutifully recorded. In the end he was portrayed as a deeply troubled, insecure person trapped between two cultures. Is this the guy that I get such a kick out of? Forty years later, he had apparently laughed his way through several steady jobs and a couple of divorces and raised a family. He never did himself in, and his life seems to have turned out fairly well — certainly better that their gloomy portrayal of his suicidal tendencies.

There is also the problem of treating some people as experts, or "informants," as anthropologists are fond of saying. For example, three different student anthropologists considered a squirrely little white guy who lived near us a valuable source of information. My family always thought he was a decent enough guy but a bit of a busy-body. In these "scientific documents," he was speaking for the white community, giving the "white view." Of course other white views were collected, but it was disconcerting to see how dutifully and uncritically his views were recorded regularly.

And the notes were full of fragmented conversations and tantalizing tidbits: a fleeting chat with a taxi driver who quipped, "I take more drunk Indians home than you can shake a stick at"; a quickie interview of a redneck paper mill supervisor who said, "Oh, some of my best workers are Indians"; a chance meeting with traditionalist Adel TrueBlood who swore, "No, I don't know nothin' about that old stuff. I'm too busy workin' at the hatchery to care about those superstitions." Do people always wear masks and say the opposite of what they believe? At times the anthropologists collecting these comments seemed to see through the masks. At times they seemed to take what was said very literally.

Seeing how these anthropologists worked mirrored the inevitability of my making the same mistakes. At times during the fieldwork I felt like the brooding Captain Kurtz in the movie *Apocalypse Now*. He eventually goes stark raving mad when he realizes that he has no control over the dirty little war he is conducting. Our ethnographies, like Kurtz's war, are often adrift. We have little control over what "informants" tell us, and we often feel lost. Sometimes all we can do is flee from the field.

Fred Gearing's *Face of the Fox* (1970) is full of tortured ruminations about being an estranged white who cannot penetrate the inscrutable mind of the Mesquaki. Gearing ends up telling a very unusual departure story. Anthropologists usually say their grateful goodbyes and ride into the sunset with their data. But Gearing left at midnight on an impulse because

some unspoken premonition made me know that some [Mesquakis] would come around to say good-bye, that no one would know what to say or how to say it, that it would be awkward — not painful, certainly not tearful, just awkward. We left at midnight to avoid that awkward situation. (1970,139)

Prior to this sudden departure there had been a party and people had even given them gifts and made short speeches, but it all made Gearing feel even more estranged. So he and his wife slipped out under cover of darkness.

When I retreat to my library, what story will I tell about my departure? And how will I assemble all the tidbits and fragments that I collected? This lament about doing fieldwork is not intended to be disrespectful to the settlement's anthropological ghosts. These intrepid anthropological travelers left a record that both haunts and informs me. As you shall see, the story I chose to tell bears their mark in many ways.

Encounters with New-Fangled Mesquakis

Having introduced the settlement's anthropological ghosts, I must highlight a few Mesquakis whom I encountered that first summer. Anthropologists are taught that their earliest encounters and flashes of insight are special. Convention has it that everything and everyone seems most strange and different upon first taste. So if you are trying to capture the "difference" between peoples you must religiously record those first experiences and impressions before time erodes them. After you have seen and heard it all many times, what was initially a wondrous cultural difference becomes predictable routine. What was once a magical character becomes another John Doe.

Picking out memorable characters on the Mesquaki settlement is no simple task. I met many memorable people, but those who impressed me initially were people who gave me ideas for portraying life on the settlement. They also made me question myself and my motivations. Without opening up too big a can of worms, I think of myself as a pretty good anthropologist and a decent writer. To be honest, I am a would-be novelist in an anthropologist's skin. I have been reluctant to actually write fiction, but I fancied myself on the verge — until I met Ted Pipestar, who really is a creative writer. There I was flying along in my little Piper Cub fantasy about writing fiction, and the Ted Pipestar storm blew in. It was one of those scary but wonderful moments when your fantasy meets reality.

I first ran into Ted at South Tama County High School (STC). He was finishing up a one-month stint teaching creative writing as a humanities scholar in residence. Hearing it was his last day at the school, I rushed to catch him before he left school. "Are you Ted Pipestar?" My eagerness seemed to startle him a little, maybe even irritate him. He said yes, and there I was face-to-face with this stocky, short little guy who was scowling at me. I say little because I am six-foot-three and Ted is about five-foot-seven. I say scowling because he has a fairly serious, almost stern face. Having just started my fieldwork, I was still giving a pretty generic introduction of myself and my purpose. Ted nodded through my monologue and said charitably that my study sounded interesting.

I may have sounded a little condescending when I asked him, "You have published two books of poetry? Books that you can buy in a book store? You are working on a novel? You grew up here on the settlement and went to South Tama County schools?"

My initial reaction to Ted was probably a little like Sol Tax's initial reaction to me. He never expected to meet an anthropologist from Tama. I never expected to meet a nationally known writer in Tama or on the Mesquaki settlement. Things like that take you by surprise. After a brief exchange, we agreed to talk later about his work, which I confessed to not having read. Not very good field technique, but I had thrown caution to the wind to meet him.

When I did finally read Ted's two books of poetry, I was astonished at their power and beauty. He was breaking all the time and space dimensions we take for granted. People turned into animals. Dreams turned into everyday events. It was very challenging stuff, very creative. I have written a number of unpublished poems, and I fantasize about writing the great novel, but his poems left me feeling a little pretentious. Two years later his first novel came out to rave reviews in the *New York Times* and the *Los Angeles Times*. The book was a thinly-veiled autobiographical account of growing up on the settlement that sets quite a standard. After reading it, I wondered how I could possibly write something as insightful about the Mesquakis. I was faced with a Mesquaki who can write better than I can, one who has already written this fascinating book about the settlement.

But my lesson in humility does not end there. Within those first few months I began meeting a host of other Mesquakis who, in their own ways, seemed just as impressive as Ted. There were so many active young Mesquakis that I began formulating a theory. Unlike the action anthropologists, I wanted to argue that the post-war civil rights era had spawned some new "organic intellectuals" or home-grown leaders. This new group of political, cultural, and educational leaders, many of whom you will meet later, were taking the tribe in some new directions. I found myself gravitating toward these people and wanting to highlight their political activities and cultural writings.

I must hasten to add that the Mesquakis have a highly egalitarian political system, and that they are quick to cut self-appointed leaders down to size. So portraying a new generation of Mesquaki leaders is a white's way of talking about these matters. I honor their individual achievements, but my praise has little to do with how they are honored in their society. I can only hope my portrayals of these Mesquakis as "leaders" will not evoke envy or resentment from fellow tribesmen.

Having made my apologies, I must recount my initial encounters with two other individuals who helped me discover the main theme of this book. The first is Jonas CutCow, the new tribal historian. I met Jonas at a powwow fundraiser shortly after meeting Ted. Several white friends had mentioned him as a talented young Mesquaki who had a history degree from the University of Iowa. They all said, "You have to talk to Jonas. He is very knowledgeable and very easy to talk to." Some added, as if this was the true source of his knowledge, that his father was white.

Indeed, Jonas's half-breed status became the target for a crusading journalist (Cedar Rapids *Gazette,* June 21, 1987). As Jonas said, "This guy made a big thing out of the fact that the tribe only recognizes off-springs of enrolled Mesquaki males." The article juxtaposed Jonas's story with that of Hal Miller, a disgruntled half-breed living in Cedar Rapids. It left the impression that this soft-spoken, educated young man, who still faithfully practices his clan religion, also felt mistreated. In truth, Jonas never complains about losing the benefits that enrolled members have. He is grateful for "being allowed to live on the settlement" and raise his children as Mesquakis.

Like Ted, Jonas is a part of a new generation of college-educated Indians who help run the tribal social service and gaming operations. But he is no politician or professional. Rather than parlay his history degree into a high school teaching job, he has choosen to write a history of the tribe. To this end, his small trailer is stuffed to the gills with nearly every article and book written about the Mesquakis. For the past ten years, he has labored in absolute obscurity on his book. He has none of the usual academic incentives — a permanent teaching position, grants, and graduate assistants. His study is strictly a labor of love, a gift to his people from their half-breed guest. On seeing his library and hearing him talk about Mesquaki history, I knew instantly that I would never spend the time and energy he had learning about his people. So now I had met a better writer *and* a more dedicated scholar than I. What could possibly be next?

The "what next" was an interesting guy who brashly announced to me that he wanted to be an anthropologist. About the only thing that the Mesquakis do not have is a home-grown anthropologist. I met their would-be anthropologist in the basement of the STC elementary school. Don Johnson, a high school teacher who had worked for ten years among the Sioux, told me, "I know a Mesquaki that you ought to interview. Go see Tom Warrior. He's a janitor at the elementary school. He's real sharp, and he'll tell you what he thinks. He's a real sleeper."

By sleeper Don meant an unknown, a guy who did not have a college degree or publications but who knew a great deal — a guy whites thought of as "just" a dependable, hard-working, ex-Viet Nam vet who cleaned up their elementary school. But Don fancied himself a shrewd judge of Indian talent, so I headed for the elementary school.

Tomas greeted me with a broad smile and said, "I've been wondering if you would show up to talk." I had met him earlier during the West Bend powwow. He seemed curious about what I was doing but we had never found the time to talk. As we discussed tribal politics, Tom sounded even more like an anthropologist than Claude Windsong had. Here he was giving me this treatise on the evolution of tribal leadership patterns and how the old hunting-gathering society that needed strong leaders was gone. "What we have today is a lack of people who are willing to take responsibility and make decisions. The tribal council has too many dummies on it."

Don was right. This guy is outspoken. He went on to say that he could never get elected to the tribal council because he "had too big a mouth."

Later in this conversation he came out with the real zinger, "When my kids get older and I can afford it, I want to go back to a good college, maybe Grinnell, and become an anthropologist." It is not every day that one of the "natives" you are interviewing says, in effect, "Hey, I want to do what you do. I want to go around interviewing people and writing books about Indians. It doesn't look that hard." I thought to myself, sure why not. Then his boldness made me pause. Having already met a better writer and a more dedicated scholar, I wondered whether maybe my days as Tama's only anthropologist were also numbered.

The main idea Tomas impressed on me was that Indians are rarely portrayed as ordinary people. He complained that even the articles and books and movies of sympathetic whites often romanticize Indians.

It is always the sensational stuff like eating dogs, or their magical practices, or the drunk Indian raising hell. They never show any Indians with normal families and jobs. Indians who go to work, raise their kids, pay their bills, and stay out of trouble. I want to read something that shows us as people just like everybody else.

That should not be a tall order for anthropologists and journalists, if they stay on the settlement long enough to get to know a number of families.

Digging Up the Temperance Tempest

Before I end this chapter, I want to give a little slice of 1950s race relations that shows the Mesquakis beginning to assert themselves against racism. My old classmates remembered this era as very peaceful compared to the turbulent "sixties" era. Aside from the incidents with Ryan and Billy, that is how I remembered it too. We were just kids then, and no one was particularly sympathetic to minority causes. The newspaper archives contained stories that whites have long since forgotten. So, in the interest of historical accuracy, I want to present a sad tale about local race relations that still sticks in the craw of most Mesquakis. The white temperance campaign against Indian drinking begins in earnest around 1940 and finally ends around 1960.

Relations between the races apparently started heating up in the early 1940s when local county officials refused to give four unwed and abandoned Indian mothers federal ADC (Aid to Dependent Children) benefits (TNH, May 18, 1944). The board of supervisors feared that paying these four women would make the Indians eligible for all types of county relief aid. One board member said,

I've seen the time when practically all of them were on relief of one sort or another. When we start collecting levies from the Indians, the Indians will be ours and not the federal government's. I feel that the government owes them a lot more than Tama County does. The whole thing boils down to this. We are being asked to assume a potential burden of eighty or ninety children in order to get aid for thirty or forty of our own. I don't think anybody will contend that is a good deal for us.

During this incident white officials portrayed the Mesquakis as "non-taxpayers" and potential "welfare cheats." After much unfavorable publicity, the state welfare officials ordered Tama county officials to give these women the same federal assistance that they gave white women. As I recounted this forgotten story to a Mesquaki, he noted that during this time fifty-two Mesquaki men were fighting in the armed forces and many more Mesquaki women were working in war plants. With considerable irony he said, "We fought for them, but, the whiteman couldn't give four needy Indian women fifteen dollars a month." For him this story showed that the whiteman's soul was made of money and greed.

The other negative white image of Indians was as "irresponsible drunks." Prior to World War II, an Indian Agency newspaper, the *Mesquaki Booster*, constantly moralized about stamping out bootleggers and booze on the settlement. During the annual August powwow celebrations, the local papers also commented regularly about the "progress" being made to control Indian drinking. The local paper began to moralize about the "Indian drinking problem" regularly after World War II.

The first sign of a new, tougher white attitude towards drinking was expressed by Jack White, a crusading county attorney. The county attorney and the federal peace officer had been making unsuccessful raids into Mesquaki houses in search of bootleg whiskey. They were never able to find the fabled illegal still (TNH, July 6, 1944). Frustrated, the county attorney initially championed an Indian court as a solution for the settlement's law and order problem (TNH, September 14, 1944). Unfortunately the Indian Court became embroiled in the Youngbear-Oldbear political dispute and lasted less than six months. It collapsed when Judge George Youngbear tried to fine an alleged still operator from the Oldbear faction.

Having failed to find an Indian-led solution to the law and order problem, the merchants association and the county attorney initiated a full-scale temperance movement against the Mesquakis. They began to wage a heated rhetorical battle in the local newspaper from the mid-1940s on. The paper was full of lurid stories of drunken Indians being run over on the railroad tracks, of teenage drinking and crime rampages, and of white men fornicating with Indian women.

Apparently the final straw for whites was the savage beating of an elderly white man who had been fishing on the settlement (TNH, October 6, 1947). The article emphasizes that the attackers were wild teenagers who were drinking home brew and had been in trouble before. The settlement was portrayed as a place filled with fights, break-ins, and beatings of defenseless women. Without an Indian court and Indian police, the county attorney lamented that "trouble might spill over into the white community."

Shortly after the elderly white man was attacked, County Attorney White formed a county grand jury to investigate "lawlessness on the Tama Indian Reservation." That grand jury quickly concluded that, "A gross lack of law and order is fast becoming detrimental to the Tribal Indians as well as very troublesome to non-Indians and to the law enforcing officers of Tama County."

The report claims that the tribal council and Sac and Fox Indians have shown no desire for law and order on the settlement (TNH, October 30, 1947). To remedy the situation, the grand jury drew up a resolution requesting the federal government to grant the state of Iowa and local law enforcement agencies the right to enforce Iowa laws on the settlement.

By December the county attorney was already testifying before the House Indian affairs subcommittee (Des Moines *Register*, December 10, 1947). Although the local papers never reported it, the Fox Project fieldnotes indicate that Bertha Waseskuk, secretary of the Oldbear faction, also testified at these hearings. The Tama *News Herald* did report White's testimony before Congress in great detail, however. White regaled the members of Congress with a scathing grand jury investigation that included stories and pictures of rampaging Indian youths, drunken orgies and burning houses, and drunken males beating up women and elders (TNH, December 18, 1947). The image conveyed was that of a violent, anarchistic tribe that needed sensible whites to protect them from themselves.

In the spring Congress passed a law turning police jurisdiction over to the local authorities (TNH, March 18, 1948). Thus ended a long rhetorical white media campaign to portray Indian wildness and drunkeness spilling over into the peaceful white community. From my reading, Tama civic leaders created what sociologist Stuart Hall (1978) calls a "moral panic" among the white population. Once a situation is defined as a moral crisis, that justifies strong government intervention. In this case, the law and order bill stripped Mesquakis of some of their political sovereignty.

In the post-World War II era, white and Indian veterans came home to a booming economy. Before the advent of super highways, chain stores, shopping malls, and all-night TV, small Iowa towns were still lively social and commercial centers. The town had main-street band concerts, a movie house, a night fast-pitch softball league, and a dozen bars. Farmers flocked to town on Saturdays to buy supplies. They socialized in the stores and bars while their kids filled the sweet shops and the movie house. I remember the street concerts and carnivals, and the death-defying double feature movies. Tarzan the ape man. Buster Crabbe adventurer. Lash Larue and his bull whip. Hawkeye the Indian-raised frontiersman. I grew up feeling proud of tiny Tama (3,000) the railroad town with good football teams, tough street fighters, and wild beer taverns.

But this post-war economic paradise had its problems. Nearly every able-bodied Mesquaki male went overseas to fight. But when these loyal American citizens returned home, they were prohibited from drinking in the bars and in the Veterans of Foreign Wars (VFW) Club. Despite such restrictions, the Mesquakis came to town to buy booze, and the worst fears of whites who had championed the law and order bill came to pass. One elderly merchant recalled, "Too many drunk Indians staggering around in front of the stores just didn't look right. It drove decent people away. We had to do something."

The local merchants feared that the town's "image problem" would kill their Saturday night golden goose. In response, they vowed to clean up "their Indian drinking problem." The Merchants Association persuaded Mayor E. C. Carnal to pass a city ordinance prohibiting Indians from drinking in the local bars (TNH, June 16, 1960). Since the federal government declared the Indian prohibition law unconstitutional in 1957, they were forced to base their ordinance on an old state law forbidding the sale of liquor to Indians. What follows is a sad little episode that has the makings of a good Gilbert and Sullivan comic opera.

More Great White Fathers of Prohibition

To fully appreciate this story, you need a little background on Mayor E. C. Carnal. "Dopey" Carnal was a popular, colorful character who ran a local barber shop. On and off, he was the mayor for twenty-seven years. People say he was a workingman's politician, a Roosevelt Democrat. Few knew why he was called "Dopey," but his obituary explained the nickname as a result of his always having ready answers and information about the town's history. He had the "dope" on what was going on (TNH, July 25, 1968). We kids thought this tiny, large-headed man was called Dopey because he looked like one of Walt Disney's seven dwarfs.

The earliest reference to the mayor and Mesquakis was in a 1929 *News Herald* story (June 6). For many years, the Mesquakis had their own traveling team and played exhibition games during the annual powwow celebrations. Several of their players were good enough to be coveted by the local white teams, and the paper mill team invited them to play. As commissioner of the summer baseball league, "Czar Carnal" barred the Mesquakis from playing in the white league. The article suggests that his motivation was not racism but the desire to weaken the powerful mill team so that his favorite team could win.

We may never know the truth of this accusation, but by the 1960s Mayor Carnal became a lightning rod for Des Moines *Register* (DMR) stories on the downtrodden Tama Indian. One article (DMR, Dec. 31, 1967) portrays him as the enforcer of a blatantly racist credit system among local merchants. Instead of keeping Mesquaki debts in a regular book of accounts, the local merchants had Mesquaki borrowers sign a bank check for the amount borrowed. The merchants interviewed gave the unpaid checks to Mayor Carnal to "get a little more leverage" for repayment. Although most Mesquakis had no money in the bank, many apparently felt that they could be fined or imprisoned for not paying off the checks.

A second article (DMR, June 7, 1967) explores Mayor Carnal's justice of the peace decisions on intoxication charges. After examining one hundred and twenty cases and comparing them to four hundred Des Moines cases, the reporter concluded that Indians received rougher treatment than whites. The mayor was quoted as saying, "I get all the money I can for the city of Tama." He also liked to portray himself as "too soft-hearted to be a good judge." Other whites portrayed the mayor as a kindly man who often put drunk Indians in a cab and sent them home. The article ends with the mayor saying, "They talk about the white man taking advantage of the Indian. Here it is the other way around. I see a lot of Indians in my court. I've faced more Indians than General Custer!"

If there was ever a sound bite destined for local immortality, it is the mayor's quip about being like General Custer. For different reasons, both Mesquakis and whites get a real kick out of that story.

The local image of how the mayor handled the Town's "Indian problem" is eloquently expressed by the following headline (TNH, November 28, 1957): "Troublesome Indian is Evicted From Home on Settlement. Mayor Restores Peace." The article goes on to say, "With the wisdom of a Solomon, Mayor E.C. Carnal Monday dispossessed one Indian from another Indian's house on the settlement and restored peace and tranquility once again."

In this case Julius Cesar, a Pawnee married to a Mesquaki, is described as a "big husky Indian." He was apparently an uninvited resident in the house of his wife's half-brother, who is described as "a feeble, nearly blind" elderly man. Under the new law and order bill the mayor, if requested, could adjudicate such domestic squabbles. The mayor is portrayed as defending the tribe's feeble against its bullies. He is the wise, sensible white man restoring harmony among the squabbling, child-like Indians.

In a related Chicago *Tribune* article (reprinted in TNH, January 28, 1965) the mayor lays out his "affection" for the Mesquaki in colorful language

I'll tell you how relations [between whites and Indians] are. Do you know that my theme song as mayor was "The Indian Love Call?" Why I even used to be the pitcher for a traveling Indian baseball team. For years I danced at Mesquaki pow-wows. Pretty good, I was, too. They gave me an Indian name. Pashewatha, they call me. That means, "Man afraid of his squaw." They have a great sense of humor.

They surely do, Mayor, and the joke is on you. The mayor acted out his paternalism most dramatically in the 1959 Frontier Day parade. That day he dressed up as Yancy Derringer and led the parade with his faithful Indian companion Pakoa, played by Tom Scott (TNH, August 13, 1959). This event took place around the same time that the local merchants and the mayor were planning a local ordinance to keep the bars safe for whites.

The final battle in this futile, comic attempt to restrict Indian drinking in the local bars ended almost as quickly as it began. Mayor Carnal started the ball rolling by announcing (TNH, June 16, 1960) "If we want to get rid of the Indian trouble we will have to pass an ordinance barring Indians from buying beer within the city limits." He went on to estimate that about forty or fifty Indians made up 75 percent of the trouble and claimed that most tavern owners had no objection to losing the Indian business. Most tavern owners claimed that they lost white trade when the Indians "took over and became bothersome."

Not all whites agreed, however, and white tavern owner Ray Crawford protested that the law punished a whole race for the offenses of a few (TNH, June 30, 1960). After only a week of the ordinance, the paper reported "considerable indignation among whites and Indians alike." A delegation from the settlement asked the city council what citizenship meant and pleaded that the council work with the tribe. Ultimately, Mayor Carnal was forced to retract an earlier sweeping statement that "Indians were not gentlemen." He quickly clarified that only drunk Indians, like drunk whites, were not gentlemen. Although the local paper never reports the end of this sad little tale, City Attorney Jim White recollects that the ordinance died a quick, quiet death.

Throughout the temperance movement, one voice consistently articulated opinion in the white community. While County Attorney White was constructing evidence through a grand jury investigation that roused public sentiment, Tama *News Herald* owner and editor John Hynek took it upon himself to write a series of editorials on the virtues of Indians as a race. During the debate over the law and order bill he deflected Mesquaki criticism of the press campaign against them as follows (TNH, April 18, 1948):

The Indians here also complain about the publicity given on criminal cases by the newspapers. They say that when an Indian gets in trouble the newspapers make sensational stories and make it a point to explain that he is an Indian. The Indians say that the Indians are about on an equal with whites in criminal matters, that as many white men get drunk as Indians. They say that whites fight among themselves as much as the Indians, but when an Indian pounds somebody up he gets a lot of publicity. . . . Whites, who are friends of the Indians, agree on this publicity but nobody seems to have a remedy. The Indian is a romantic and historical figure, and whatever he does makes good copy. He is a good subject for sensationalism. Newspaper reporters jump at the opportunity to write about him, and they undoubtedly always will . . . the Indians are too sensitive. Indians seem to forget that there has been a lot of publicity in praise of the Indian. . . . The News-Herald particularly has printed much about the strong qualities of the Indian.

So what did Hynek write in praise of the Indian? In "Reservation in Early Spring" (TNH, March 6, 1947), he waxes lyrical about trees and wildflowers blooming and a group of Tamaites who derived much happiness from observing the vegetation on Indian land. He ends wistfully with the hope that younger whites will renew the practice of visiting the reservation.

In "Our Indians" (TNH, March 20, 1947) he says that few Tama people know the real quality of the Indian and praises Indians for their poetic abilities and their determination to resist slavery, "The white man could never make a slave of the North American Indian. The white could enslave the black man, but the North American Indian would die before he would work for the white man."

In "Is the Indian Civilized?" (TNH, July 10, 1947), Hynek praises Tribal Council Chairman Edward Davenport, a man with white and Indian blood in his veins, as a leader and thinker who could live in the city and enjoy all the comforts but "prefers to live with those he considers his people, the Indians." Later in the article, he philosophizes about the wisdom of Indian civilization and the West's barbaric world wars. In "The Indian" (TNH, July 24, 1947), he adds that the Mesquakis returned to their beloved Iowa hills to take up the white man's civilization and jobs, yet remain true worshippers of nature.

In "Indians as Workers" (TNH, May 15, 1947) Hynek praises Indians for going off to war and for working in the war plants, and he chastises whites for thinking that the Mesquakis are all "lazy loafers." He goes on to say that "Having obtained jobs, the Indians have spruced up. Our Indian maids now get their hair do and rival our white girls in makeup and dress, and the boys show us that they know how to dress up."

In this article Hynek confesses that Americans got the best land, but he absolves his countryman of any guilt by arguing that America put its Indians on reservations, not in concentration camps the way Hitler did. He adds that "those activities are water over the dam. Now we whites know and respect the Indian."

Hynek exemplifies the romantic, paternalistic Indian-as-noble-savage perspective. The thing that he most admires about Indians is that they fought enslavement, which makes them a cut above blacks and South American Indians. For him the Indians are still not civilized and advanced but are nevertheless virtuous because they worship nature. He even exhorts whites to go out to the settlement and enjoy the trees and wildflowers the way the childlike Indian does. Despite their closeness to nature, Indians must, nevertheless, take up white ways and become civilized.

Sadly, many contemporary whites who also imagine themselves "friends of the Indian" still talk this way. Hynek was good at philosophizing about the noble savage, but he never raised his pen against everyday injustices. He was silent when white county officials refused Mesquaki women ADC payments and when white merchants refused Mesquaki war veterans a drink. As my Grandpa might have said, his editorials praising Mesquakis were mostly hot air.

You have to wonder why whites exaggerated the threat of Indian drinking so much. Whites made law and order and drinking a huge morality issue. They went to great lengths to misrepresent, persecute, and restrict the constitutional rights of Mesquakis. Having lived through all this white moralizing, and having lost their sovereignty, why would any self-respecting Mesquaki feel good about his white neighbors? All the negative images that whites created about "their Indians" just lay there festering.

As you can see, the newspaper archives of the 1940s and 1950s completely fascinated me. I lived through all these events and must have read some of the stories about lawlessness and the drinking ordinance. Yet I have no recollection of these controversies. I remembered none of the events, nor any feelings about Mayor Carnal or Editor Hynek as paternalistic and unfair toward Mesquakis. I now find myself astonished at how adults that I respected behaved.

As I interviewed Attorney White and some of the merchants of this era, it was clear that their views have softened. Some still believe that recent racial confrontations stem from "giving the Indian liquor," but most remember fondly Mesquaki friends who were "good, hard-working Indians." They remember the times when the townspeople and Mesquakis cooperated to put on the annual powwow. As angry young Mesquakis sprouted in the 1970s, these old-timers were left searching their memories for older, more accommodating Indians.

Looking Back over My First Summer

So the first summer of heartland research had come to an end. I had dipped into my racial memories and found myself seeing the 1950s with rose-colored glasses. When I started rummaging through old newspapers and listening to Mesquaki talk, I heard a rumbling that childhood ears had missed. I read newspaper archives filled with battles over the tribal school, ADC payments, and alcohol. I also read a little Mesquaki history about the French policy of genocide and the American policy of removal. Clearly the Mesquakis used to give their enemies, white and Indian, hell (Edmunds and Peyser, 1993). I began seeing them as more feisty and enterprising than action anthropologists had portrayed them (Gearing et al., 1960; Gearing, 1970).

I also ended that first summer with a glowing feeling about coming back to Iowa. This probably sounds hopelessly gushy, but it was good to be home. I had gone back to the farm where I grew up. The one-room school house of glorious box socials, sledding, and softball was gone. But the creek with crawdads and the hills with Indian arrowheads were still there. All those rolling hills with spider-web creeks still spin endless corn rows. The smell of clover and corn fermenting on humid Iowa days still perfumes the air. The sweet corn is the sweetest in the world, and city folks kill for our tomatoes. This Iowa heartland of grain elevators and sale barns and small towns remains a good place to grow up. It produces sturdy, sensible people to work in nervous cities. I have been reinventing this mythical place for years. Now I am finally tasting my black-dirt heartland anew and discovering its red earth people.

Chapter 2
AIM Arrives and "Things Got Rough"

During the 1960s I never went home to Tama. I was busy seeing the world via the Peace Corps and going to graduate school. After I finished my studies, my family and I came through Tama on the way to Texas. At the time, I had two little mixed-blood (Filipino) kids and was sporting a long pony-tail. Uncle Phil greeted my Stanford look with, "By golly you look like a girl. Is that how they dress out in California?" The only person who said anything remotely political was an old classmate. He and his wife made sure to document my fall into hippiedom with a snapshot. Then he asked, "Are you going to see your old buddy Nathan Bearchild? I hear he's one of those AIM [American Indian Movement) radicals now." That should have piqued my curiosity, but I was rushing off to find Chicano activists in South Texas. Looking back, this was around the time that some Mesquakis wanted to burn down the county courthouse.

No one was quite sure how it began, but whites remember angry young Indians storming city hall and walking out of the schools in the 1970s. Many felt the way this teacher did, "That AIM bunch riled 'em up. Around the time of that Wounded Knee thing, things got rough 'round here." As I read about it in the old newspapers, memories of the "sixties" came rushing back. Like many other American youth, I was involved in anti-war protests, civil rights marches, and like President Clinton, I never inhaled pot. The sixties were memorable times for me. I think of them as the time when I grew up politically, but I never realized that the sixties visited my hometown, too.

I began to understand how turbulent things got when I read an Iowa Civil Rights Commission Report entitled *Race Relations in Tama County* (1981). The local papers gave extensive coverage on the commission's two public hearings (Toledo *Chronicle,* January 20, 1970; TNH, January 25, 1970). Although very few whites showed up for either presentation, it sounded like an important event, so I asked at least fifty townspeople what they thought of the report. Hardly anyone remembered seeing the report. A typical comment was,

Oh yeah, these outsiders came in and asked questions. Mesquakis who like to complain like the Windsongs complained. The outsiders went away and wrote this report, a bunch of bull about how bad whites treat Indians. Yeah, that happened, I guess. I don't really remember. Was it important? I don't think it changed anything around here.

It was as if this six-month-long survey and the public meetings had vanished into the quicksand of local opinon — lost somewhere among TV ads, blaring headlines, and a million other bits of floating information.

The local editor admonished the commission to look further and not accept half-truths of alleged discrimination. He urged concerned citizens of both sides to air their grievances regularly rather than having "state and federal agencies interfering with our lives" (TNH, February 1, 1979). When the final report actually surfaced, the editor called it fair but played down its harsh tone. He claimed that the report found no definite civil rights problem or serious discrimination (TNH, August 20, 1981). Another white businessman remembered being angry about the report and asked to see my copy. After rereading it he said, "It is as biased as I remembered it. They came looking for how bad whites are to Indians, and that is what they found." I tried to get him to take issue with specific findings about discrimination by police, teachers, and local employers. No response. It was just more outsiders trying to exaggerate things. No comment.

Anything generating such studied indifference makes me intensely curious. Unlike the local editor, I thought the report was a strong indictment of the town, but it did a poor job chronicling what happened and people's views. So I began searching the newspaper archives for what the report omitted. Once I knew the main events and actors, I collected people's recollections of those times. What follows is my reconstruction of the time that the "Tama Indians" got fed up with Tama — and the feeling was mutual.

AIM Brings Martial Law to Town

The real racial battleground was in the local bars. Many townspeople do not frequent bars, and they find this entire scene a "sorry way to spend your time." Nevertheless, the bar scene was one place where whites and Mesquakis met regularly. Several older merchants lamented the failure of the Indian prohibition law. Their worst nightmare had come to pass. On the other hand, most white working stiffs who frequented the drinking scene were less critical: "It's no big deal, just a bunch of guys who liked to drink and fight, always has been, always will be."

By the 1970s at least two "Indian bars" had developed. This is not to say that Tama's bars were strictly segregated. Some Mesquakis drank in white bars, but certain bars became Indian hangouts. A few of the white barroom brawlers recalled going into the Indian bar, "just to stir up some trouble." Mesquakis also remember going into white bars looking for action. Otherwise, people generally frequented certain bars with their buddies. When I was a kid there were no Indian bars and racial street fights, so this entire scene surprised me.

People recalled racial fights in the bars "practically every week-end" but no particular starting point for "all the trouble." Judging from the local papers, race relations hit a low in the summer of 1973 (TNH, July 5, 1973). The city council was forced to curb "a lawless group trying to take over the city." The story portrays the events as an

uprising that left three unconscious Indians in front of a main street tavern after being attacked by six or more whites, "motorcycle-riding-types," armed with baseball bats and clubs. Indians used broken pool cues from a club across the street, and Indian woman tried to help their men.

The local police reportedly stopped two fights but were unable to catch those involved in the beating. Apparently the crowd dispersed and friends carried off the victims.

At least for a few days, the baseball bat beating of two Mesquakis created a very tense atmosphere. Rumors were flying that AIM was sending an armed group for a final showdown. Law enforcement authorities were caught off guard by local criticism and by the Mesquakis' aggressive reaction. City Attorney Jim White was quoted as saying that "people were up in arms over what happened," and he urged people to testify before the grand jury to get this "renegade group." He went on to say that "townspeople were afraid to get involved for fear of retaliation from a dozen gutless hoodlums," so he advised the council to hire auxiliary police from a private firm in Cedar Rapids (TNH, July 5, 1973).

The following week, twelve AIM members visited the county courthouse and demanded that the county attorney prosecute the white offenders. A showdown was apparently imminent when "seven carloads of out-of-town Indians converged on the city hall" (TNH July 12, 1973). Meanwhile, the city council closed down the bars for the weekend and suspended carry-out beer sales. Within a week after the incident, a grand jury met and indicted three white men. Ultimately only one, Tom Smith, was sentenced to two years for assault with a deadly weapon. The grand jury also reported a lack of manpower, training, professionalism and morale among the police, which the mayor strongly denied (TNH, July 19, 1973).

When I read about this event, I decided to interview participants in AIM and in the motorcycle gang as well as the city officials. During this era, Editor Hynek portrayed a growing lawlessness among white youth with stories about drug parties. In addition, a motorcycle gang was supposedly terrorizing everyone, especially Mesquakis. When I recounted this image of a white motorcycle gang, several whites scoffed at Hynek's and White's portrayal. One made the following sardonic crack, "These guys must have watched too many old Marlon Brando motorcycle movies." So was there a white supremacist gang or not?

One Mesquaki brawler put it this way. "Those guys had sort of a motorcycle group like white supremacists. They had colors and called themselves the Town Pump Angels. To me they were a gang, but they weren't as tough as they thought." The Town Pump was the main white bar where this group hung out. One Gang member recalled,

We all got us a cycle, rode together on weekends and other guys from Belle Plaine, and this bunch from Omaha, would come for parties — a hog roast. Back then everybody had long hair and head bands. It didn't matter if you had a Yamaha or a Harley. We had colors, and we'd take up the side of a street, drinking, fooling around, having a good time.

This all sounds like what sociologists might call a "weekend gang," a small town imitation of hardcore groups like the Hell's Angels. As for them being white supremacists, several whites proudly called them "puckie pounders." (Puckie is a local racial slur against Indians and is analogous to "nigger" or "spick.") The white joke about AIM was that it stood for "Assholes in Moccasins." In this climate, scuffles between individuals quickly turned into racial street fights. One young Tama businessman who frequented the bars remembers it as

a scary time. It was pretty ferocious. You had to be careful to not lip off, even among whites. It fed from AIM, the whole neurosis of it. That was the fun of it too. It brewed upon itself. You never knew when it would explode.

He went on to recount the special animosity whites had toward AIM's cause celebre, John Nighthawk. Nighthawk was a big, muscular Mesquaki who was said to have castrated and drowned a little white guy in one can of beer after another. AIM was protesting how the police were railroading Nighthawk, but it was gospel that Nighthawk was "a murdering SOB."

The local paper echoed this theme, "Jones was slightly built" and "Nighthawk was tall and strongly built with a barrel chest and narrow waist" (TNH, August 9, 1973). Once again, it was the proverbial big mean drunken Indian picking on the innocent little white guy.

The Mesquakis had their own version of this incident. For them the big bad Indian was really the defenseless victim. According to several Mesquakis, both men got drunk and fell asleep along the railroad tracks. While they slept a group of malicious whites came along and murdered the white boy, and when Nighthawk woke up the police were there to frame and arrest him. Whatever the truth of these stories, AIM eventually staged a rally at the county courthouse demanding Nighthawk's release. Nighthawk ultimately pleaded guilty and went to prison on a second-degree murder charge.

Most whites accused AIM of stirring up racial trouble. One business-man even blamed the VISTA workers on the settlement. This talk re-minded me of what whites said about Chicano "militants" in South Texas (Foley et al., 1988). Whites were determined to find an outside devil that made their happy Mexicans revolt. They were convinced that the Chi-canos were allied with Fidel Castro and hell-bent on revolution. Appar-ently some whites in my hometown engaged in similar red-baiting. They tried to explain away Mesquaki racial discontent as the work of outside agitators.

One businessman reported that John Birchers showed several white civic leaders Russian AK-47s that were allegedly used at Wounded Knee. They gave their usual fanatical line that civil rights groups were really communists seeking to overthrow the government. In fact, AIM never had any connection with the international communist movement. More-over, they never had much direct influence on settlement politics. The tribal council never applauded their demonstrations against the police and for Nighthawk. Perhaps Councilman Claude Windsong said it most eloquently: "AIM came to the Settlement once, but like the mosquito, they came in, looked and left" (Toledo *Chronicle*, January 25, 1979).

Nevertheless, AIM had an inspirational effect on many young Mes-quakis. Their self-determination and red-power message struck a chord with a whole generation of students and young adults. Rex Slickroad Jr. and Jay WhiteHawk were often mentioned as "hardcore AIM," but most Mesquakis denied being members. There was never a well-organized chapter on the settlement, or widely-acknowledged leaders. There were, however, a number of Mesquakis fighting for their civil rights. Most cur-rent Mesquaki leaders fondly remember meetings at the old stone house, protest rallies, and the barroom fights. They still celebrate the impact that AIM had on making them more assertive. Some say that AIM arrived armed to the teeth. "It got pretty tense after those guys baseball-batted Eddie. We were ready to blast anybody who tried that stuff again." Driving around Tama with a trunkload of automatic weapons was pretty heady stuff. For many young Mesquakis, the time had come to fight back, and the white motorcycle gang was a perfect target for their anger.

The Barroom Scene

But what was it like in the bars? What were Mesquakis and whites doing that aroused such passions? There is nothing particularly exceptional about Tama bars. Most of them are what so-called decent people call dives. Most are dingy, smoky, and sparsely furnished. They generally have a stand-up bar, some tables, and a juke box with country western and rock and roll music. Unlike many English pubs, they are not family-oriented places that serve good food. Nor are they like urban singles' bars where yuppies sip wine and pick up dates. Mostly working men, and some women, frequent these bars to let off steam after a hard day in the fields or factories. They are ordinary people looking for some fun, people who care little what church and chamber of commerce types think.

When Indians drank in the white bars they did so at their own risk. The common complaint of the white patrons was that "Indians tend to take over the place, if you let them." The whites like to paint an image of their peaceful bars being invaded by rude Indians. The typical story told about Mesquaki drinkers was that they were "mouthy":

They get a few beers in 'em and all that hard-luck stuff starts coming out. It is discrimination this and discrimination that. You stole our land. You won't give me a job. You did this. You did that. Ya' get sick of all their belly aching.

The other main theme was that Indians were "moochers":

When they get a little drunk they aren't like whites. They gotta start bothering you. You know, mooching drinks and cigarettes, slobbering all over you like you were their best buddy. If they'd stick to themselves and just drink, it wouldn't be so bad, but I can't stand 'em acting like you are their good friend and mooching drinks and smokes.

On the other side of it, Mesquakis reported suffering many indignities in white bars:

If you sit there long enough, whites will start feeling their oats and will start talking. "Indians don't belong here. The best thing to do is line 'em up and shoot em, ha ha ha." That joking shit can go on and on. "The only good Injun is a dead one, ha ha ha." Sometimes they will let you alone, but some drunk asshole always has to get his two cents worth in about no-good Indians. If you got any self-respect, you eventually have to do somethin' about that stuff.

A Mesquaki woman said that women had to put up with another kind of white aggression:

If a woman goes out on Friday or Saturday night to a bar all I ever heard growing up was that Indian girls were good to screw. The first line is usually, "Are you part Indian? Oh, which part is the Indian part?" Big joke, right? Then practically the next line is "Would you like to go to bed with me?" Some of these white guys are so crude you have to wonder how they were brought up. No Mesquaki guy would say the crap that they think they can say. They act like animals.

The racial feelings in these stories are obvious. The bars were rough places where people said racist and sexist things to each other. Bars were places where, as one old friend cautioned, "lots of Old Milwaukee is doin' the talkin'." So fights happened between all kinds of people, but especially between strangers who invaded each other's cultural spaces. Much of this hostility stemmed from a long history of racial separation and suspicion, but there were also some interesting differences in each group's drinking and socializing styles.

I never had the opportunity to participate in what Mesquakis call "forty-nining," but I collected many stories about these all-night drinking sessions. Forty-nining is when Mesquakis get together and drink and sing Indian love songs or "forty-niners." Most people say these drinking and powwowing songs originated from the Kiowa. There were Mesquaki composers of these songs, but I never taped any of them. In these collective drinking events everyone chips in and buys a case or keg, and people wander in and out as the singers beat on drums, trash cans, or car hoods and sing "snagging songs." Songs to snag a woman might go something like this, "Hey ya hey ya, gonna go to Tama and get me a honey, gonna take her for a ride in my one-eyed pony, hey ya hey ya," and on and on.

When Mesquakis drink and socialize together, they do it very communally. There is a great deal of sharing of drinks, smokes, food, and songs. Whites also buy each other rounds and share, but probably not to the degree that the Mesquakis do. Mesquakis are also very open about their personal views, their problems, their political views — whatever is on their mind. Contrary to the popular image of Indians as stoic and taciturn, Mesquakis often seemed more open and talkative about personal feelings than whites.

It is conventional wisdom that people go to bars to drown their sorrows and tell sad tales. Country western music has made a fortune telling lost-love tales. So whites like to go to bars and drown their sorrows too, but only with their buddies. It is bad form to talk too much personal stuff or politics with strangers. That can easily be misinterpreted as being "mouthy" and invading another person's privacy. Being too open or bumming too many beers and smokes might also be seen as "mooching." Probably some of the friction between Mesquaki and white drinkers stems from the different ways they learn to share drinks and feelings with fellow drinkers. And racist feelings magnify these cultural differences.

As I listened to both sides, my anthropological imagination took me back to what I learned growing up. Where does such racial hate come from? Going to a little one-room country school, I never experienced what town kids did. The son of my tight-lipped farmer friend laid it out more honestly than most,

It all started in grade school. You'd get a green teacher who'd never seen a minority, and they'd let them get away with kid pranks. One principal was always praisin' Indians. We felt they were teachers' pets. Then I remember them jumping you for money when the odds were in their favor. Younger kids would go to the grocery store and buy candy, and these older Indian kids would jump them and take it. Pretty soon, when we got a littler older and bigger, we started liking the idea of pounding 'em. There was fights every day. I got so I liked beating up Indians. They deserved it. They are always crying discrimination even though they get all this government welfare and free houses. Then they turn around and pick on little kids.

It may not be in the school curriculum, but some Tama whites learn to like "pounding puckies" in grade school. Both white and Mesquaki boys are organized into groups that provide plenty of practice for joining the adult barroom scene.

And from the other side, a Mesquaki who often fought whites recounted what it was like to come into town and go to the white schools,

I had some problems with my teachers and the white students. My grandparents were trying to teach me the traditional ways. Everyday I went to the long house and prayed before the sacred fire and made offerings to four directions. So I always had the smell of the sacred tobacco on my clothes. I had this gym teacher who'd smell the smoke, and he called me a "stinkin' Indian." So then some of these white kids started calling me "stinky." Then there were other names that they called us like "puckie" and "Injun." Have you ever went to a basketball game and heard people giving out war whoops and stuff like that? You get tired of all that "How, chief" crap, so you either clam up or you fight back. We used to like to sit in the halls and give whites some grief when they walked by.

Different people told variations of these stories, but they all made the same basic point. Most whites and Mesquakis came to school expecting the worst. They had heard endless discrimination stories from older siblings and parents. Initially the younger children got along fairly well, but around fifth or sixth grade racial peer groups formed that began picking on each other. They took each other's candy and pencils. They called each other names. Every transgression lead to a payback, and every payback lead to another payback. Meanwhile, both races invented stories about how bad the other race was. After several years of squabbling and stereotyping, the next generation of barroom battlers is born.

The Great Mesquaki Pig Heist

The other racial fight story that caught my eye involved AIM activist Jay WhiteHawk. Jay's story is the story of many young Mesquaki males. Jay would never call himself a leader, but the scrapes he got into and out of expressed what many young Mesquaki males felt. The only difference might be that Jay was a little more angry and fearless. He terrorized the local whites and local cops a little more, and his exploits made better newspaper copy. In those days he was considered a real "hell-raiser," and he became a symbol for Mesquaki discontent.

Today Jay is what you might call a respectable small businessman. He and his family run a traveling Indian taco stand that sells at small-town celebrations. To dispel the local paper's stereotype of him as a wild, drunk, law-breaking Indian, I would like to tell why he became an AIM activist and barroom brawler. Although I played football with this guy, I never knew what made Jay, or for that matter most Mesquakis, tick. Then I stumbled across an old interview in the Fox Project fieldnotes. Jay met a young anthropologist in the old Clifton Hotel and told him the story about how "they" killed his mother. Later, I asked Jay what happened to his mother, and to my surprise, he began to cry. He would only say that he knew who left her to freeze to death in the snow and that someday they would pay. What could all this possibly mean?

I eventually found a newspaper story of his mother's death (TNH, February 14, 1957). Forgive me for speaking of your deceased mother, Jay, but no one will understand why you heisted the pigs without this story. The headlines blared out, "Three Coats Wrapped Around Body of Indian Woman a Mystery; Govt. Attorney Orders Autopsy; Questioning." They found her frozen body in a corn field on the Indian settlement. The story plays up the intrigue and mystery of who left this drunken Indian woman to freeze? Did the tear in her jacket mean her body had been dragged? And why was she wrapped in three coats? Had some guilty companion come back and tried to save her? Was it her young companion, a known hell-raiser? In those days the local paper made a habit of turning Mesquaki misfortune into a spectacle for curious white readers. This big murder mystery was another confirmation of the awful things that go on "out there." Her death was eventually ruled accidental.

The newspaper story jogged my memory that Jay had just graduated from high school and was going to Chicago to work and fight professionally. The next thing I heard was gossip like, "Jay is starting to drink just like the rest of 'em and isn't going to amount to a hill of beans either." I could not believe it. Jay, our star half-back and clean-cut fighter a drunk? But I never asked him what happened, so I never knew that he was grieving for his mother. Jay still believes that the white authorities are covering up for the whites who got her drunk, the white taxi driver who dumped her out on the settlement, and the whites and Indians who left her to freeze like a wounded animal. Living in a society where such things happen regularly makes you want to drink and fight. It is hard to stay out of trouble and jails.

After his mother's death, Jay left Tama and tried to make it on the loading docks and in the ring. But life in Chicago was hard, and after eight years he moved back to the settlement. He remembers being "disgusted with the way it still was. It was still just like when I was a kid with Indians getting beaten up in bars and not fighting back and always accepting what the cops told them that they were guilty."

So he began fighting back and became known as a "troublemaker" who liked to drink and fight. AIM appealed to Jay because they were Indians who fought back against racism and police brutality. He complained that the cops not only harassed Mesquakis in the bar scene, they also illegally entered the settlement to make arrests.

Of course Jay has forgotten his history here. The county sheriff and deputies have a right to arrest Mesquakis on the settlement because local white leaders legally stripped the Mesquakis of their policing powers in the 1940s. Like most Mesquakis, Jay has a long list of grievances against the local police. Mesquakis claim that the white police have a quota of Indian drunks to pick up. So the police "wait outside the bars like vultures" and descend on Mesquakis driving home to the settlement. They also claim that the police often beat up Mesquakis whom they arrest and throw in jail. There are many stories circulating about policemen who put the bodies of drunken or beaten Indians on the railroad tracks to "accidentally" die.

Such is the context for Jay's hell-raising days and his great pig heist. The night before the heist Jay and several guys had been drinking at the powwow grounds. Come morning, Eddie Fudd was playing around with this rifle that he was going to pawn in town. They ended up on old highway thirty horsing around at the moment when two young white guys, who sold dope on the settlement, came by with a pickup truck full of pigs. Jay and Eddie wanted to see if they had any dope, so they pulled their car across the road and stopped the two white boys.

According to the newspaper account, "Three Indians had set up a roadblock on the highway and were stopping traffic. Eddie Fudd had a rifle and was drunk and laughing like it was a big joke" (TNH, October 17, 24, 1974). The story continues based on interviews of the white guys:

According to the driver, they asked if the gun was loaded and Fudd fired it in the air and then pointed it through the window saying he was going to shoot the driver. The driver reported saying that he wanted no trouble. He got out and gave Eddie the keys and took off running and hid in the ditch.

Jay remembers watching the white guys take off "like scared rabbits." Apparently their hasty retreat was so funny that he and Eddie decided to take the truck for a little ride and listen to the pigs squeal. They wobbled and weaved down the winding settlement road until they ended up in the ditch. By then the two white boys had called the sheriff, and his deputies were in hot pursuit. When the law arrived, Jay and Eddie were laughing and having a good time, but things ended badly when Jay resisted arrest and punched out the county deputy.

The newspaper story tends to portray the whole incident as a sign of escalating Mesquaki militancy. The image is one of wild Indians waylaying innocent white motorists near the settlement. Stealing a truck and assaulting a police officer are serious offenses, but this story begs to be put in a historical context. The previous summer, a group of whites baseball-batted Eddie Fudd and another Mesquaki senseless, forcing the town to close down the taverns. Barroom fights were a weekly event, and AIM had staged several protests on police brutality. Given these political events, Jay and Eddie's heist seems more like a prank than an organized criminal or militant political act. *play down*

Mesquakis like Jay and Eddie were primed to give whites who wandered onto the settlement a taste of what they got in town. They also loved to play on fears that the settlement is a good place to get ambushed. Scaring the pants off two young white guys, who may have been selling dope on the settlement, would have been both a good payback and very funny. Whatever it really was, Eddie got several years for theft and Jay eventually got a deferred sentence for aggravated assault. As Jay ended his story he said laughingly, "Just another day of being an Indian around here. So are you going to make me a movie star with that story?" No Jay, not a big-time movie star—just an anthropological symbol of Indian anger and AIM militancy.

More Trouble on the School Front

While some Mesquakis were battling in the local bars, others were busy trying to create a whole new kind of school system. The prime mover behind educational reform was Claude Windsong. In retrospect, many whites and Mesquakis were reluctant to give him credit, and they labeled him "moody," "arrogant," "hateful," and "full of big words." Whether you like him or not, Claude was clearly ahead of his times on the Indian education issue. After helping force the BIA to keep the tribal school open in 1968, Windsong joined the Coalition of Native Americans for School Improvement in Denver. They organized a network of activists from 160 tribes to implement the Indian Self-Determination Act of 1972. He was the only Mesquaki involved in this pan-Indian movement to create tribal school boards and tribally run schools. After a year or two, Claude returned home to try to implement this new approach.

The tribal school was in dire need of reform, but neither the local whites who ran the school nor most Mesquaki parents were interested in a bilingual-bicultural approach. Most Mesquakis still thought that culture and language should be taught in the home only. Consequently, most Mesquaki children (75 percent) were attending the white schools. These Mesquaki parents felt that the white school was better academically, was less politicized, and helped their children adjust more quickly to the white world. The white schools offered no special language and cultural programs for Mesquakis. As a result, Mesquaki youth were fast becoming what linguists call "passively fluent." They could still understand Mesquaki but spoke English more easily than their native language. Claude Windsong and others wanted to arrest this alarming trend.

But, as Claude soon discovered, reforming the Mesquaki school system was extremely difficult. Initially, he was elected to the tribal council and headed its educational committee. He admits "stacking the committee" with people who preferred a tribally run school, and they quickly obtained $20,000 in BIA planning money to build a new $3 million K–8 tribal school (TNH, August 9, 1973). Within a year, however, strong opposition developed toward Windsong's educational committee and its grand scheme. What follows is the saddest tale I collected during my time with the Mesquakis.

On the one hand, Claude and his followers contended that their opponents were assimilated Indians who bowed to the whitemen. He alleges that the Presbyterian mission church hosted meetings for this group and powerful local whites, including the South Tama superintendent of schools. Local whites supposedly opposed his school because they feared the loss of Indian impact aid money. According to Claude, they were obsessed with destroying the tribal school and culturally assimilating Mesquakis.

On the other hand, what Jonas CutCow (CutCow, ND) calls the "We-Love-South Tama-Group" remembered these events quite differently. They strongly denied that the church and whites were behind their petitions to stop the school. They also claimed to be for a new tribal school. What they objected to was one family having too much control over the school. They feared that Windsong's educational committee would run the school in a dictatorial manner. After the initial planning money was spent, a petition drive developed to block the tribal council from obtaining the $3 million construction grant. This bitter tribal dispute reached its zenith during a Mesquaki walkout in the white schools.

The School Walkout at South Tama County High

While the council debated the tribal school issue, racial tempers were heating up in the white schools. As the 1975 school year ended, Mesquaki high school students staged their first walkout. Some members of the tribal council accused Windsong of using the walkout to get back at them for killing his plan for a new tribal school. Windsong had publicly accused one council member of practicing witchcraft and others of various improprieties. In response, the embattled tribal council chairman implied that Windsong was provoking Mesquaki youth to walk out, "there was an evil force sitting here snickering, who put the racist note" (TNH, May 25, 1975). The infamous note that sparked the walkout read "Due to overpopulation of Mesquakis, the federal government has declared open season on Puckies."

Various white teachers were convinced that Windsong was an AIM operative bent on stirring up racial conflict. Mesquaki students saw Windsong's role in all these events quite differently. Windsong was their behind-the-scenes advisor, and he urged them to stand up to white racism. The students reported that Windsong opposed AIM, and that redneck whites really had written the inflammatory note. Things came to a head one Thursday when a number of Mesquaki high school and middle school students decided to walk out. The following day student walkout leaders, Jonas CutCow and Billy Blackhat, presented various issues to the high school staff as outsiders and reporters looked on (TNH, May 15, 1975). Superintendent John Nicks remembers the outsiders as AIM activists and concerned Mesquaki parents. Tensions were high, so TV cameramen were barred from the meeting.

Student leader Jonas CutCow was quoted as saying that the walkout was peaceful and "If it had been Sioux, they would have burned down the building." He challenged teachers to come and live with him for a year on the settlement. The vocational teacher responded that he and other teachers agreed with their cause but not their methodology. He claimed that not a single white teacher intentionally stepped on Mesquaki toes. Then he asked if they knew how it made him feel when Mesquakis talked in their native tongue instead of speaking to him in English.

Various participants remembered this initial meeting between the staff and Mesquaki protesters as tense and angry. The superintendent cited examples of Mesquaki sports stars to prove that coaches did not discriminate against Mesquaki athletes. One white teacher present felt that the staff response was very defensive and patronizing. Several Mesquakis recalled this meeting as "one white after another denying that racism existed." That weekend several STC school administrators attended meetings on the settlement with concerned parents and students. By Monday, settlement tempers were rising, and approximately seventy adults and students visited the high school and demanded to meet with teachers. According to them, they "got the run-around."

When no meeting materialized the group decided to "camp in" at the high school. They planned to stay there until the school board, meeting in a closed session, received them. One woman at the camp-in remembered it like this:

I put on dress pants to look good. The TV cameramen were there. These Indian women were ready to fight. They were saying mean things like this white teacher was fondling Indian girls. It was exciting, AIM people were on the way. Police were there. We wouldn't let them in or leave, but we let deputy Mike Quigley in with messages. The school board wouldn't talk to us that night, but they agreed to meet with Indian students the next day. You couldn't get nothin' without a protest.

Runners went back and forth between the two groups until 2:00 a.m., and the school board relented. They would hear the Mesquaki student representatives in a special meeting. Mesquaki parents recalled dispersing with great anticipation. The next evening, student leader Billy Blackhat presented the following demands to the school board: (1) a Native American club, (2) teacher in-service training, (3) a grievance committee of students, (4) a Native American history course, (5) a review committee on all employees, (6) excused absences for walkout participants, and (7) expulsion of the students responsible for the note. The school board president responded that walking out would not solve the problems, but that they would consider the demands (TNH, May 15, 1975).

In the aftermath, a Native American club was formed, but the other demands were never really addressed. For a time there were occasional guest speakers from the settlement. Mable Moon presented a few Mesquaki words and a demonstration on fry bread. A few generic lessons on Indians were also added to the junior high social studies curriculum guide. But no Native American history course ever developed because, according to the social studies teachers, no white teacher felt qualified to teach it. As for teacher training, five white teachers were sent to Haskell for a one-week summer training institute. One participant remembered it as "a lot of brow beating of whites. I was shocked at how rabid some of the Indian speakers were."

Perhaps the biggest change was to hire several Mesquaki teacher's aides in the elementary and middle schools and a para-professional counselor for the high school. For the first time, Johnson-O'Malley federal funds were used to hire Mesquakis. Not surprisingly, four of the six people hired were from the group who opposed Windsong's tribal school plan. Superintendent Nicks remembers that group as "the integrationists. They were generally cooperative with the schools; their kids were on the athletic teams. They were well adjusted to the schools — didn't have fears. They were more open people." Being more cooperative, they eventually got the new staff jobs for Mesquakis. The walkout did generate a few basic staff changes and minor curriculum changes. A veteran white teacher summed up the walkout aftermath this way, "Not much to write home about got changed." Given the educational needs of Mesquakis, the reforms instituted were tepid at best.

Worse still, the political fallout from the walkout left the Mesquakis in a much more subordinate position. First, the new Title IV funding committee publicly apologized for the walkout in the local paper (TNH, May 22, 1975). They said that no student had asked their help for the minor incident that occurred:

Indian cultural studies need not be taught at STC. Our Indian beliefs begin at home. Mesquakis were not born with a white mind. We grew up on our cultural beliefs, and it is very sacred. Let this be an apology to you all, and we are not rivals to anybody.

They went on to say that many Mesquakis had had the opportunity to graduate with high honors and participate in sports. The general tone of their presentation was quite conciliatory, and racial problems were downplayed.

Within two months of this speech the tribal council was requesting STC to operate the tribal school (TNH, July 17, 1975). The white school board agreed to reopen the tribal school, but the STC superintendent requested a provision that the tribal council was responsible for educating any Indian student who disrupted the STC schools. The local newspaper (TNH, August 24, 1975) noted that "this provision was obviously designed to head off any unrest like last spring."

In effect, the tribal council said, we are sorry for our noisy walkout. We just killed a $3 million plan for a new tribal school, so please run our old tribal school for us. In response the white school officials basically said, we will help our red brothers, but no more squawking. No more walkouts. Given the sequence of events, this ending sounds like a total Mesquaki capitulation. Not only did they lose the funds for a new school, they also ended up with local whites running their old school. Claude Windsong's grand plan for a K–12 bilingual/bicultural tribally-run school had disappeared in a bitter inter-tribal squabble. The immortal words of the cartoon character Pogo seem appropriate here, "We have met the enemy, and he is us."

A Longer View of the Mesquaki Schooling Issue

After researching the walkout and tribal school fiasco, I became convinced that schools were a key site of racial conflict. One cannot truly understand the angry battles over education without a little history on

Bias?

BIA education policy. So we must backtrack here and portray how whites have always used the schools to destroy Mesquaki culture (Almquist, 1972; MacBurnie, 1974; Jones, 1931).

The Mesquaki educational problem began in the late nineteenth century. In those days Indian agents were trying to open, not close the tribal school. Late nineteenth-century Mesquakis were suriving without the benefit of any formal education. They were hunting and fishing and doing some day-labor for the local farmers. The most colorful account we have of the Mesquakis early indifference toward the whiteman's education is Alli Busby's *Two Summers Among the Mesquaki* (1886). Busby was a white teacher who found the Mesquakis loath to attend their modest one-room day school. A handful of kids straggled in for a few days and then just disappeared. Traditionalists told Busby and every visitor since, myself included, that three things would ruin the Indian — education, jobs, and money. Conversely, most whites wanted to save the Indian from savagery with large doses of education, jobs, money, and Christianity. So in those days the school building and the church mission often sat empty.

This idea of using public education to assimilate the Mesquakis forcibly arrived in earnest with Indian Agent Horace Rebok. Rebok, a native of Ohio and a former school teacher, was also the editor of the Tama County *Democrat,* and he wrote a history of the Mesquakis entitled *The Last of the Mesquakies* (1900). Like James Fenimore Cooper, he fancied himself a true "friend of the Indian," and he started an Indian Rights Association of local educational and religious leaders. In 1896 Rebok and his association got the U.S. Congress to allocate $35,000 to build a vocational boarding school near the settlement.

Like editor Hynek, he often extolled the virtue of the noble red man, and he was utterly convinced that only white education would save the Indian. Rebok expressed his general views confidently, if somewhat nostalgically, on the first Congress of American Indians held in Omaha:

On these Western plains and in these valleys he has fought his last battle in the contest with a superior race for the survival of the fittest. Here he has made his last but hopeless stand. Here he has been vanquished in the unequal contest for the sovereignty of the land over which he roamed. Here he as been compelled to swear an eternal and perpetual peace, as a subject or citizen of a nation dominated by another race." (Rebok, 1900, 58)

He goes on to portray how the six hundred Indian delegates from thirty different tribes marveled at the expositions of transportation, weapons, textiles, housing, and foodstuffs. For Rebok they were "learning new lessons" that would "fit him for the part he is destined to play in the life of the future, if he survives" (1900, 64).

The Mesquakis were politely but firmly against Rebok's school. One hundred parents refused their annual annuity payment if it meant putting their children in the new boarding school. Chief Pushetonequa initially said, "You may come and kill us, but we will not give you our children" (MacBurnie, 1974, 71). But he was eventually offered $500 annually and recognition of his chieftainship to cooperate. One story that circulates on the settlement is that Pushetonequa was blackmailed when the BIA police implicated one of his sons in the death of another tribal member. The school also hired Mesquaki laborers and constantly courted parents until they got the enrollments up to fifty (Caldwell, 1900; MacBurnie, 1974).

But Rebok's grand scheme came unraveled when a teenage girl named Le-lah-puc-ka-chee left school without permission. The incident illustrates nicely the overzealous tactics that Agent Rebok used to get Indian students for his school. Caldwell reports that

When the children were orphans, he had applied to the court of Tama County for the appointment of a guardian and then procured the consent of the guardian to the placing of the children in school. In most instances, he had W. G. Malin, who afterward succeeded him as agent, appointed as such guardian. (1900, 37)

After Le-lah-puc-ka-chee left, the tribal council took Rebok to federal court. At the trial the girl claimed to be eighteen and the wife of Ta-ta-pi-cha, a powerful Oldbear traditionalist, thus hardly an under-aged orphan in need of an appointed white guardian.

The federal court ultimately ruled that the state courts had no authority and right to appoint guardians for Indian children. Nor could they compel Mesquaki children to go to school by withholding annuities or by using the state's compulsory education law. Caldwell (1900) acknowledges that this ruling destroyed Rebok's vocational school, and he then gives an account of Rebok's other attempts to control the tribal traditionalists. Agent Rebok also charged the Mesquaki medicine man with practicing medicine in the state of Iowa without a permit. The medicine man brought suit against Rebok, and the courts handed him another defeat, ruling that the medicine man was improperly charged and arrested. So the white who started the first Indian rights association became an unpopular violator of Indian rights.

After Rebok's vocational boarding school fiasco, the Indian service retreated to a policy of developing day schools on the settlement. After twenty years of providing day schools, the agency then began conspiring to turn Indian education over to the local white officials (Toledo *Chronicle*, March 41, 1929). Agent Jacob Breid officially closed the tribal day school and pressed for state legislation to let local districts educate Indians

(Toledo *Chronicle,* January 24, 30, 1929). By 1931 the BIA had contracted with the nearby Montour schools to provide schooling for the tribe.

In response, the tribal council quickly passed a resolution against sending their children to the Montour schools. After a year-long school boycott and considerable wrangling, in 1937 the tribe forced the bureau to build the present K–8 day school. Meanwhile, the few Mesquakis who attended secondary schools were beginning to attend Tama High School. Having accepted white education on the settlement, the tribe preferred the local white high school over the loneliness of distant federal Indian boarding schools.

Meanwhile, the bureau quietly searched for a way to shift its educational obligations to local whites. In 1952 a fire partially destroyed the tribal school, and the bureau quickly sent Mesquaki seventh and eighth graders to the town schools. They then informed the tribal council of their revived plan to turn the day school over to the state. Rumors were flying that the tribal council had made a secret deal with the Indian service and the locals to close the school (Toledo *Chronicle,* July 17, 1952). Once again the Mesquakis fought back.

At this point, the University of Chicago anthropologists became involved, and Sol Tax urged the BIA to let the tribe, not local whites, run the school. Once again the Iowa Department of Education backed away from taking the school over, and the BIA was forced to retreat. But history has a way of repeating itself. For the next few years, the bureau avoided confronting the tribe directly. Instead, they quietly transferred more and more Mesquaki students to the local white schools. By 1968 the bureau had whittled the tribal school down to grades K–4 and declared the tribal school too small and unsafe to be viable. They initiated action to close the tribal school and send the remaining students to the South Tama County schools.

As before, this drew a quick response from the Mesquakis. For a few days Mesquaki students boycotted the STC schools (TNH, September 5, 1968). The tribal council also sought an injunction against the BIA in federal district court. On the publicity front the tribal chairman, Claude Windsong, and Petra White testified before the Kennedy Senate subcommittee hearings on Indian education, and the Des Moines *Register* published a series of sympathetic articles (September 1, 5, 28, 1968). Tribal Chairman Kingfish also sent a frantic telegram to an old ally: "Sol Tax, come quick. The BIA is closing our school, again." Other sympathetic whites from the Quakers and Drake University urged the Mesquaki to run their own school (TNH, December 5, 1968). The council even developed plans for a tribally-run school. In October a federal district judge conducted a one-day hearing and ordered the tribal school reopened.

In response, the BIA rejected the idea of a tribally run school and contracted with the STC schools to run the tribal school (TNH, October 3, 1968). STC officials admitted that they had no provisions for teaching any specific type of Indian culture or the Mesquaki language. Their excuse was that no Indian teachers applied for jobs (TNH, September 4, 1969). At this point, the tribal council stopped pressing the local school district to provide special Mesquaki language and culture programs. From 1928 to 1968, the tribe fought many battles to preserve the tribal school, but the bureau still refused to let Mesquakis run their own school. Nevertheless, some traditionalists say that the 1968 battle was a real turning point.

Who Is Getting Terminated Here?

One story that apparently never made the white newspapers is what happened to the BIA messenger who came bearing the latest termination message. This story, which still circulates on the settlement, illustrates the deep sense of vindication that Mesquakis felt upon saving their tribal school. During the council meeting to close the school, many people accused Agent Sam Brady and the bureau of lying. They demanded to know where the democracy was in arbitrarily terminating their school. At one point Brady apparently took great umbrage to these charges and shouted, "I can terminate you guys right now! I can terminate this school!" The traditionalist who battled with Brady that day retorted, "Only the Manitou (God) that created us can terminate us."

The meeting ended on a sour note, and Brady took his small plane back to Minneapolis. But according to the Tama *News-Herald* (November 2, 1967) he never made it. The story told on the settlement is that a farmer from Montour saw his plane fly into an approaching black cloud. When the plane came out of the black cloud it just exploded and blew into a million pieces. "I guess that was what he meant by termination, huh?" said the man who first told me this story. Verifying this story was a little beyond my investigative powers, but the Mesquakis took Brady's death as a sign of divine intervention against a white who wished their school ill will.

What I find interesting about this story is not whether the manitous really did Brady in, but that Mesquakis have such a strong sense of their destiny. Agent Brady, AIM activists, anthropologist Tax, Mayor Dopey Carnal—they are all mosquitos just passing through. All these bloodsuckers want a little snort of divine Mesquaki blood, but that is all they will get. And the Mesquakis will go on. This might be a tough pill for whites to swallow, but that is how Mesquakis see it.

Squabble Here, There, and Everywhere

As the 1970s shaded into the 1980s, the glory days of racial barroom brawls came to an end. The Town Pump Angels and the AIM faded away within a couple of years, but they were replaced by a new wave of barroom fighters. The Rathman brothers, the Stanley boy, and other whites carried on the tradition of "puckie pounding." New Mesquakis — the BrownBear brothers, the WalkingTall brothers, and assorted Firstleys and Robbins — pounded a little white flesh in return.

Everyone had his or her own favorite war stories and as Sean Rathman and I talked at the Eagles Bar I found myself comparing him to the tough guys of my era. Sean did what he called "nigger work" at the packing house. He had a huge gunshot scar in his left bicep. On his right shoulder he had a tattoo that said "white power." He rode a Harley and had lived with an Indian woman for fourteen years. Sure he fought Indians, especially, he said resolutely, "Those AIM assholes! They were troublemakers being protected by the cops. They got out of a lotta' shit and made Jay WhiteHawk an important person."

Sean recounted proudly that he fought anybody, especially the cops. Talking to these guys brought back bitter memories of the tough guys in my era. Scott reminded me a little of big Ron Stone, a star football player. The University of Iowa wanted all 250 pounds of him, but Ron liked to drink and fight too much to study. Then there were the tough little guys like Bobby O'Brian. He was an all-state half-back always looking for a fight, always ready to swing first and ask questions later.

At our thirtieth high school reunion he was as belligerent as ever. He asked me "What the hell are you really doing here? Are you really writing about those damn Indians. What the hell for?" As he became increasingly drunk, he started challenging people to fight. Here Bobby was, beer gut and all, itching to fight a bunch of old coots with dentures, toupees, and falling arches. At this point, none of us are macho enough to care who is the toughest. We just want to have a beer and shoot the breeze.

And that was pretty much how most white and Mesquaki barroom battlers saw it. Nearly everyone has mellowed with age. One white said, "I get along good with Jay today. Sometimes we have a beer and laugh about the time we got into a scrape."

Another Mesquaki concurred, "I don't have no problems with Rathman anymore. I saw him at the rodeo parade on his bike. He asked me how I was doin'."

Of course racial hatreds do not melt magically, but when the body goes, people mellow a little. These aging warriors have settled down into farms and jobs and families. Drinking, fighting, and chasing women have become fond memories. And the merry-go-round of life turns in mysterious ways. "Ex-puckie pounder" Sean Rathman now tends bar in a place that used to ban Mesquakis. A white and Mesquaki from the casino own the place and Sean serves up a few brews to his old adversaries.

Outside the contentious bar scene, racial incidents continued to occur with regularity. The paper screamed out more headlines like, "Indians Harass Whites on School Buses" (TNH, August 24, 1978). Two white families charged that the bus driver did nothing to stop Indian children from hitting and putting gum in the white children's hair. They claimed that Mesquaki children also refused to "double up" and sat one to a seat to prevent whites from sitting together. In response, the tribal council director said that a few ill-mannered kids were the problem. He chastised the committee and newspaper for using the general term "Indian" rather than naming individuals, thus further perpetuating stereotypes.

Within a few months another white bus driver made the headlines, this time for being abusive with Mesquaki children. The driver was initially suspended for "roughing up several Indian kids" (TNH, November 16, 1978). The tribal council and a parent education group appealed to the school board to conduct an open investigation. After a series of meetings, the driver was eventually fired for misconduct. Apparently this incident compelled the tribe to request an Iowa Civil Rights Commission investigation.

In addition, the issue of controlling Mesquaki hunting and fishing kept popping up. Whites generally resent the fact that Mesquakis hunt and fish and trap whenever they feel like it on the settlement. Whites grumble about this and about "that damn spear fishing thing in Minnesota." They like to forget that our government signed treaties giving all Native Americans these rights. Whites are obligated to honor these treaties, but periodically some zealous game warden just has to toss out this political football.

The first story that caught my eye was Obi Firstley's frozen squirrel. The game warden apparently barged into his house and searched the freezer. He found a frozen squirrel that he claimed was shot out of season. Game wardens are a hardy breed with a mission. Their charge is to regulate "scientifically" the amount of game for sport hunters. The county attorney offered the outrageous opinion that "If hunting isn't controlled, there wouldn't be a live animal out there." The whole silly case was dragged into county court, then thrown out because the warden had no jurisdiction (TNH, October 17,1968).

A few years later it was Gordon Lightheart's deer skin. Seeing a deer skin curing outside, the game warden demanded to inspect Gordon's freezer for illegal deer meat. Gordon testified that a relative gave him the venison in his fridge, and that dogs had dragged the deer skin into his yard (TNH, March 28, 1974). The county tried to argue that the Mesquakis were immigrants from New York state, not aborigines, and that they had purchased settlement lands, thus holding no greater rights than other landowners. Once again, the court dismissed the case for lack of jurisdiction on the settlement.

Finally, there are aggravating things that Mesquakis do to local whites who provide them county services on annual contracts. The tribe does not always pay its bills on time for fire and ambulance service. Mesquakis could purchase their own fire truck and ambulance, or they could volunteer to serve on these underfunded local services. But they have done neither. Regrettably, they are like most white citizens. They want lots of government services for little taxes and no effort. This attitude rankles local white county and city officials. They have come to accept that Mesquakis do not volunteer to help, but the very least they could do is pay their bills on time.

The other major irritation many whites mentioned was the difficulty of getting Mesquakis to show up for meetings. When angry about something, Mesquakis were quick to protest, but Mesquaki representatives on ordinary civic groups tend to operate on "Indian time." They show up late and attend meetings sporadically. Conversely, most white officials hate going to tribal council meetings. The council is notorious for not meeting regularly and for starting late and running into the early morning hours. Whites are frequently made to cool their heels waiting to get on the program. Since meetings also switch back and forth from English to Mesquaki, whites must sit there confused. Meetings with the new college-educated leaders have gotten considerably easier. But Mesquakis just do things differently, and it continues to exasperate many local whites. In short, although race relations have calmed down considerably, living and working together is still no picnic.

The Mesquaki Popular Memory of Resistance

While collecting all these stories of racial and cultural clashes, I wondered whether these confrontations had rekindled ancient tribal proclivities to fight back. This concluding discussion is dedicated to the white educator who told me, "The Mesquakis are a defeated people. It is sad to say, but I think we broke their spirit. Now the problem is they lack self-esteem." Since this so-called educator has never bothered to read any Mesquaki history, he cannot grasp that the Mesquakis believe they are a special people.

As we shall see, the Mesquaki sense of destiny and tribal history runs deep. The only thing defeated about the Mesquakis is that they lack the numbers to drive the whiteman back into the sea. As Chicano leader Reis Tijerina used to say, "When you can only be a fly in the ear of the elephant, all you can do is buzz around and irritate the hell out of the elephant." So the Mesquakis must be sensible and lie low. They must wait for their day of deliverance.

Indeed, such a world view is exceedingly difficult for the average American to comprehend. We live in a big powerful empire that continually intervenes into other sovereign countries. If we do not like the government in tiny Grenada, we send in the marines to replace it. Then Clint Eastwood makes a marine movie, *Heartbreak Ridge,* which portrays how heroic and noble we are to save Grenada from the communists.

Now that the evil Russian empire is gone, we have declared a "new world order" in which we send troops here and there to protect our economic interests. Saddam Hussein became a new "Hitler," and we saved an autocratic Kuwaiti royal family and our oil supply from him. It was all on CNN — direct reports from the Baghdad Hilton, smart bombs, and stormin' Norman. The TV coverage was so extensive that it must have killed the movie market. Given all this, how is the average American going to understand a tiny little group of "conquered Indians" who think they have more manifest destiny than we have?

Still being cursed with a little of that mentality, I was initially surprised when Jonas CutCow explained why the Mesquakis would someday reclaim all their lands. "Because it is prophesied that we will."

He said it with such conviction that I was a little taken aback. I hit back with a heavy dose of white realism, "Do you really think that your people will get back all of Iowa, all of these farms and businesses, all these towns?" Without batting a eye, Jonas said in his quiet, matter-of-fact tone, "Yeah. That is what is said. That is what our elders say." End of the debate. No more discussion is necessary.

I was unable to say anything else against such taciturn conviction. It almost seemed sacrilegious to speak of it again. But others told me the same prophecy in the same way. No one went into great detail, so I cannot repeat it like some juicy folktale to be contrasted to other Algonquin prophecies. All I know is that many Mesquakis believe they will eventually regain what was lost to the whiteman.

The tribal history that Mesquakis pass on to their children conveys many signs of their destiny. One story that gets told often is how they escaped total annihilation by the French. All Mesquakis are brought up knowing that they refused to gather furs for the French. Mesquaki children are told that they were so warlike and uncooperative that the French decided to kill every man, woman, and child. Using French colonial records, David Edmonds and Joseph Peyser (1993) have told the gruesome, heroic story of the Mesquakis' struggle against the French.

Even white journalists have heard of the Mesquakis' great escape from the French and their Ottawa, Chippewa, Menomini, and Winnebago allies in 1730. Donald Zorchert of the Des Moines *Register* (ND, Des Moines Public Library Mesquaki file) tells how an army of four hundred Frenchmen and eleven hundred Indians pursued a fleeing Mesquaki nation. The French and their Indian allies had waged constant war on the Mesquakis since the late seventeenth century. Their numbers already depleted, the Mesquaki were forced to stop and fight from a temporary fort of poles. After twenty-two days of siege, they tried to escape on a fog-filled night. The French account of Governor General Charles de La Boische Beauharnois emphasized that the following day the Frenchmen and their Indian mercenaries killed or enslaved two hundred Mesquaki warriors and slaughtered six hundred women and children.

What this white historical account leaves out, however, is why the tribe miraculously escaped (CutCow, ND). According to Mesquakis, their Creator, Giche Manitou, gave them the fog. This allowed the red earth people to slip away from their enemy. The point is that, even though many were lost, a hundred Mesquakis were spared that they might join the Sacs and replenish their numbers.

This long and distinguished history of survival against the French, English, Americans, and many other tribes stretches far beyond my little study. The tribal historian Jonas CutCow (ND) has chronicled that history. When he asked me to read his manuscript and offer some suggestions, I advised him to cut out some of the boring military history. A year later his University of Iowa Press editor repeated my "advice." In retrospect I see why this is difficult for him to do. Every battle did not produce a divinely guided escape, but every battle is a sign of the Mesquakis' burning desire to survive as a people.

Most Indian tribes can probably tell similar tales about surviving white and Indian wars. All I know is the Mesquakis love to talk about their glorious past. They see themselves as a tiny, ferocious little group that no one, white or Indian, could kill off. One day Tomas Warrior asked me if I had seen the displays of different Indian groups at the Chicago's Field Museum of Natural History. I had not, so he said,

Go look at them. You will see that the only one portrayed as a warrior ready to fight is the Mesquaki. The Mesquaki figure is in a loin-cloth, not a fancy dance costume, and he is crouched with a knife in hand ready for hand-to-hand combat.

Tom may be right that only the Mesquaki is portrayed as a fierce warrior. If so, the white guy who created the museum display may have heard the rousing war stories Mesquakis still tell to their children.

The historical story that most Tamaites, and perhaps most Iowans, like to recount is the Mesquakis' return to Iowa from their Kansas reservation in 1857. After the Black Hawk Wars ended in 1842, the Mesquakis were sent to a fifty-five-thousand-acre federal reservation in Kansas. Part of the tribe went to Kansas reluctantly, and others remained in Iowa illegally. By 1857 approximately three hundred and fifty tribal members resettled in Iowa. When whites tell this story, they usually emphasize how the Mesquakis yearned for their beloved Iowa homeland. In the white version, the generous whites passed a state resolution to let the tribe buy some land and stay.

In the Mesquaki version they are the only tribe that defied the federal government and left their assigned reservation lands. Their return-to-Iowa story generally emphasizes heroic resistance rather than servile gratitude to generous whites. In contrast, the displaced Sacs and Kickapoos stayed on their Oklahoma and Texas reservations. Even though the Federal government holds their new homeland in trust like other "reservations" (Ferguson, 1981), the Mesquakis distain the term reservation and call their lands a "settlement." They take great pride in having bought back their present-day lands from whites.

There are other miraculous moments in Mesquaki history that every Mesquaki learns. They all boil down to the same thing. The Creator has never let the sacred fire of the Mesquaki burn out and never will. Mesquakis believe that an unforeseen apocalypse will eventually drive the white invaders from the Mesquaki homeland. Only then will the terrible diaspora suffered by the Mesquaki be reversed. The descendents of Mesquakis forced into slavery and sent to the Caribbean and the western United States will return and join those who have stayed. Most white readers will find this prophecy hard to believe. I find it hard to believe. But what matters is that most Mesquakis believe it.

Summing Up: The Seventies as a Political Watershed

When Sol Tax's student anthropologists arrived on the settlement in the late 1940s, the tribe was apparently at a low point in its history. The battle over reinstating the hereditary monarchy was still raging. Many of the returning veterans were readjusting to civilian life poorly. The settlement had little political autonomy, no economy, and few college-educated leaders. Even traditional tribal elders painted a grim picture of cultural decline. Consequently, these action anthropologists left a rather gloomy picture of post-World War II Mesquaki society and politics (Gearing et al., 1960; Gearing, 1970).

But events of the turbulent 1970s provided a spark that rekindled old historical fires. The civil rights era provided tribal leaders with some unexpected empowering federal legislation. Mesquakis who came of age doing battle in the bars and schools understand these events as skirmishes in a long tradition of cultural and military resistance. More important, these new moments of rebellion signal an underlying cultural and political process of regeneration. The rest of my tale will concentrate on how the tribe is creatively fusing white political and economic practices with ancient cultural traditions. Before portraying the new assertiveness in Mesquaki politics and culture, however, we must explore the other main site where the races often mingle — the schools and sports scene.

Chapter 3
Living with Mukuman Schools and Sports

I initially planned to spend a great deal of time in the classrooms of South Tama County schools. Unfortunately, I never had the time, staff, and grant money to replicate my South Texas study (Foley, 1990). Moreover, I felt a little old to hang out with teenagers again. In lieu of extensive observations, I interviewed approximately eighty current and former teachers, administrators, and students. These are some of the stories people told about their school experiences.

The Myth of the White Taxpayers' Burden

One of the most misunderstood educational issues I came across was the controversy over federal Impact Aid. When federal military bases or Indian reservations send students to a local school but pay no property taxes, that district is entitled to impact aid. In theory the program sounds fair, but you would never get that idea from local talk. Whites firmly believe that the Mesquakis are a "financial burden" to the district because they pay no school taxes. Conversely, Mesquakis believe that whites make large sums of money from the federal Impact Aid — enough to keep their tax rates lower and to build the town's new high school fieldhouse.

After hearing a great deal of sour grapes from whites and Indians, I interviewed the school administrators who handled the federal monies. Surprisingly, superintendent Jim Archer conveyed a negative view of the Impact Aid program. He explained that the aid to each district is based on the numbers of students and the type of land and amount of acres. Apparently the amount for which the district qualified has been dropping steadily since 1975. Worse still, he added, the payments come quarterly and are often late. The moral of his complicated story was that only a clear-eyed superintendent could cut through the swamp of federal red tape.

Rather than press further, I said, "Many people that I have talked to here in town say that the Impact Aid is not sufficient. Do you receive enough Impact Aid to cover the loss in local property taxes?"

Those were apparently the magic words. Archer smiled and started giving a political speech, "I'm glad you have talked to other people. No, the Impact Aid is not enough." Then, like all good school bureaucrats, he drew me a pie chart showing a 25 percent shortfall in federal revenues. I asked him if he used local revenues to make up the shortfall, and he nodded yes. Having delivered his message, he had to run to a meeting. We smiled at each other, and he reassured me that we would talk again. I left feeling as if I had just dined on a cotton candy conversation.

It was hard to believe that the district had a 25 percent shortfall in federal monies, so I decided to interview other school administrators. The district's fiscal officer confirmed that they had a shortfall in federal aid, but he placed the amount around 10 percent. He also explained that anyone with at least one-fourth Indian blood who lived in town could be counted. Since there are 220 half-breeds and Mesquakis living in town, "breeds" are obviously a new source of revenue.

Then I finally hit paydirt, a school administrator who was not making a political speech. Mr. Z, a retired administrator, explained the politics of portraying Impact Aid to the public this way,

> I wouldn't say there was really a shortage of funds. The federal monies were sufficient, but you had to plan way ahead because of the quarterly payments and late payments. You'd try to explain this to people, but they didn't want to hear it. They always screamed that taxes were too high and the monies too little. Everyone can interpret it wrong, but we've never had a 2.5 mill tax — and well over 50 percent of the districts had it — because we had the money from the non-taxable students. We didn't explain it because they [Mesquakis] will say we're making money from the Native American students. Most people only want to hear what they want to hear. Like they say, a closed mouth doesn't gather much trouble. No group ever got irate.

In other words, superintendents and school boards told the taxpayers what they wanted to hear. In this case, whites want to hear that they do not benefit greatly from having Indian students. Most whites complain about the burden of "non-taxpaying Indians." Conversely, Mesquakis want to hear that the district is making lots of excess money off them. So the less school leaders say, the more maneuvering room they have.

The huge gap between white and Indian views of Impact Aid left me eager to document how much federal aid the district really receives. So I obtained a printout of the district's 1989–90 federal and state aid from the Iowa Department of Education. To estimate whether the district actually has a shortfall of impact aid for Mesquaki students one must have two key figures: (1) how much state and federal aid the district receives for each enrolled Mesquaki student: $4,292 ($2,403 of state aid and $1,884 of federal Impact Aid); and (2) how much the district spends yearly to educate each student enrolled: $3,125.

Clearly the district takes in more federal and state aid for each Mesquaki student ($4,292) than it spends ($3,125) to educate one STC student. It would appear that in 1990 each enrolled Mesquaki student generated an excess of $1,167. If you multiply $1,167 by the number of enrolled Mesquaki students, 250, in 1989–90 STC schools actually received $291,750 more in outside aid than it spent to educate for each Mesquaki student. So much for the superintendent's fancy pie graph with its 25 percent shortfall.

Moreover, the financial benefit of having Mesquaki students grows even more when one adds the 1989–90 federally funded programs for low-income and minority students. The district was eligible for the following federal and state grants because of their 250 low-income minority students: the PEP dropout program ($280,000), the Follow Through Program ($200,000), the Center for Student-Based Youth Services ($250,000), and Title V ($36,000). Many low-income whites also benefit from these programs.

In short, having Indian students has been a major financial plus for many years. Unfortunately, school leaders have pandered to racist attitudes about the financial burden of having Mesquaki students. Given the aforementioned figures, all the white complaining about the financial burden of Indians is ridiculous. What fair-minded whites should be irate about is how school administrators have deceived them on the Impact Aid issue.

The Right to Vote at Last

Another key educational issue that turned up was the disenfranchisement of Mesquakis in the local school board elections. If you look at the South Tama County School District plat, you will see this donut-like configuration. The hole in the middle of the district is the Mesquaki settlement. When the STC district was created in the 1960s, they simply left out the Mesquakis. Former administrators and school board members reasoned that, since the Mesquakis paid no property taxes, they had no right to vote. Mesquakis might rightly ask, what about all that impact aid that the federal government pays for us?

Unfortunately, whites do not consider Impact Aid a "tax." After many interviews, it was obvious that whites viewed themselves as dutiful "taxpayers" and Indians as "tax cheats." Once whites define themselves as morally superior taxpayers, they are apparently capable of denying Mesquakis their constitutional right to vote. A typical white response was, "I didn't know that Mesquakis can't vote in school board elections. I guess it's because they don't pay taxes."

One Mesquaki family has been fighting the voting rights battle for years. Tribal councilman Fred Seawolf, a longtime employee at the local paper mill, recounted how he tried to register as a candidate for the STC school board in the late 1950s. Fred was told that he was ineligible to run because he lived on the settlement. A number of years later, his daughter Jenny took up the cause. She wrote a paper on Mesquaki voting rights while studying for her MA in early childhood education. Then in 1990, Jenny, a tribal school kindergarden teacher, registered a complaint with the STC Title V coordinator, Don Johnson. Her complaint set in motion a chain of events that eventually overturned the STC school policy.

On hearing her complaint, Johnson, a veteran of the civil rights movement, was shocked that Mesquakis were still disenfranchised. He had experienced a very different situation while working on the Pine Ridge reservation. Fearing that the school district was violating the voting rights of Mesquakis, he began researching the voting status of other tribes attending white districts. Don discovered that most districts receiving Impact Aid had enfranchised the tribes attending their schools years ago. He presented these findings to Superintendent Jim Archer and urged him to take some action. The superintendent responded by ordering Don to stop his unauthorized research. Johnson was also stripped of his Title V and at-risk coordinator positions.

The superintendent's reprimand forced Johnson to strike back on several fronts. First, Don requested the Iowa State Teachers Association to review his actions, and they subsequently cleared him of any professional insubordination. Meanwhile, he quietly applied for positions in other districts and joined the SeaWolfs in their fight to enfranchise Mesquakis. The Seawolfs and their new white ally then enlisted the help of University of Iowa law professor Robert Clark, who specializes in Indian law. After several conferences, Clark sent a letter to the STC school board outlining the issue and requesting a meeting. Eventually, the Department of Education lawyers concurred that a change was needed, and the STC district quickly included the Mesquakis in the fall elections. What the school board did not do, however, was redraw the voting districts to assure Mesquaki representation. Although settlement residents can now vote, it is highly unlikely that a Mesquaki will ever sit on the STC school board.

A Mesquaki-White Alliance to Change Teacher Attitudes

Along with assisting in the voting rights campaign, Title V Coordinator Johnson also sent six STC teachers to a Native American training institute at Bemidji State College. Inspired by the institute, these delegates organized the first inter-racial educational reform group in STC's history. The group then raised money from federal grants and local contributions to run a week-long summer institute for other STC teachers. The Bemidji staff helped organize the institute, and a number of Mesquaki educators, writers, historians, and parents were invited to participate. To create an intensive residential experience, the institute was held on the idyllic campus of nearby Grinnell College.

Although local skeptics on both sides said it was too little, too late, the institute was an impressive mixture of idealism and realism. The first two days were dominated by Phil Baird, a bouncy, quick-witted Sioux, and a number of outside Native American speakers. Their presentations ranged from very touching personal stories to rather pedantic lectures about treaty rights and learning styles. What really made the institute special were the stories that Mesquakis told. These personal and revealing presentations put a human face on any stereotypes the participants may have had.

For example, Aaron Peacemaker, an alcohol and drug counselor, revealed his own troubled past to illustrate the kinds of problems of that Mesquaki youth face:

I wasn't ready for the town schools. At first I didn't want to stay. They locked the doors on me. It was a scary situation, and I ran away several times. I started drinking in high school; yet looking back, what were my parents doing? Nothing. They didn't want to look at it. I got encouragement from my father, who was an artist , so I went to Santa Fe. But I carried my drinking with me. Then I went to Minneapolis and had a good six years and started my family, but the drinking moved from weekends to all day — you know university students and a lot of cheap happy hours. Now I am a single parent, and my three boys and daughter live with me. It ruined my marriage. Now I have to cope with that. I've had to relearn how to be a parent. I was selfish and did the least I could. Now I know better what to do, but they are struggling, too. My older son has been in treatment twice, and he's struggling in school.

As I listened to Aaron, I could not imagine a proper middle class, college-educated white counselor being so open about his personal and family problems. Such a humble confession would not set well with the prominent, "respectable" people who run school boards. In white society you are taught to hide your personal failings. A mask of invincibility helps preserve your social status and professional credentials. Your money and degrees, not your personal experiences, give you authority. In contrast, Adrian was showing that he was human and had the same failings as his youthful clients. He was saying this is life. I do the best I can as a parent and counselor.

And then there was Rick Rock Island, a tribal councilman and machinist at John Deere Company, telling it like it is in the white school:

My parents weren't pushing education. It was something we had to do. It wasn't my priority. South Tama was a place I had to go to. I had my friends on the settlement. I was happy there. After you get older, I can see I could have done better. I didn't feel support by the staff to accelerate; maybe I couldn't have anyway. I didn't have no problems with school. I just didn't want to be there. I just wanted to play football. Soon I got out. I was happy. Now there's lots of support, and the tribal council's priority is to push kids to better themselves.

Rey Peacemaker, the commodity program administrator, agreed that many parents were not big on education, especially for girls: "As long as you clean the house and do dishes, it's ok." She went on to portray how she handles her daughters' education, "If they get Cs, it's like death now. I jump down their throat. I told the teacher I want to be aware. If they sneeze wrong, I want to know!" Other speakers admitted that their parents and many contemporary Mesquaki parents are less concerned and "pushy" than Rey. Nevertheless, these parents left little doubt that they were less permissive about their children's education than whites imagined.

The parents also responded to numerous questions from teachers about contacting parents and doing home visits. One white teacher said, "We felt like there is this veil, and we are afraid to go out there, afraid that the parents won't want to talk to us." It was obvious that a large gap existed between the teachers and settlement parents, but a good deal of reassuring discussion ensued. Participants were encouraged to contact parents by phone, relatives, or the social service people who work on the settlement.

Another major fear that teachers expressed was over how much Mesquaki history and culture they should teach. Several said they did not know where to find materials and felt inadequate to judge the accuracy of them. They wanted to know what heroes to teach, who the Mesquaki George Washington was, which legends were too sacred to teach, whether it was all right to display a medicine wheel on bulletin boards. One teacher summed up the mood when she said, "This class makes me feel like a child. I have so many misconceptions about your culture. I don't know where to start even when I want to teach about it. I want to do a good job, but I need help."

Mesquaki speakers encouraged the teachers to invite elders to speak, to let the kids write their own experiences, to consult with Jonas CutCow, the tribal historian. There was even talk about setting up some sort of Mesquaki committee that approved cultural materials to be used in the South Tama County schools. CutCow, who had given a well-received history talk, responded to the questions on teaching Mesquaki culture in the following way:

My job wasn't to teach the whole culture like our summer house for religion. I don't dare teach religious things, winter stories. So I try not to teach legends. I teach about how we survived in our history, about where we come from. There are things we've accomplished, like buying our land, how we got back to Iowa. I added a few stories about how we beat up the Sioux, how we were strong. I don't know how you Tama people see us, but we are a livin' culture. We're good, bad, greedy, giving, honest, dishonest. But we're Mesquakis. We live, and our culture is alive. We go through our ceremonies, praise our god, play politics. We have our Republicans and Democrats. *when like you. . .*

The stark contrast between the teachers' sincere but naive questions and Jonas's easy assurance both inspired and scared the participants. He gave them excellent advice. Show the tribe's accomplishments but forget the George-Washington-never-told-a-lie-stories. Mesquaki cultural heroes are always portrayed in a more realistic, less romantic way. Their heroes and gods are flawed, not some Hollywood creation. Unfortunately, such an approach requires far more knowledge than clichés about noble settlers and grateful Indians celebrating Thanksgiving joyously. His own history talk, although told in a gentle, humorous manner, underscored exploitation, land grabs, racism, and forced assimilation. His story of Mesquaki survival cannot be told without ruffling some white feathers.

Then Jonas told a story about his own son. He was warning teachers that Mesquaki kids are a strange, delicate blend of Indian and white culture. He wanted them to realize that they need to nurture Mesquaki kids:

My son wanted to go to the pool every day. I asked him why he wanted to jump in a little box with whites. He said "I like to." We never had a desire to mix, but Ned, he gets along. He mixes better. But mixin' and bein' accepted are two different things. He has had a good life around white people, but I'm afraid the whites will teach him to hate. It's like a dog. When I went to school we weren't afraid of whites. We'd sit in the back and say, "I don't know." It was easier to say I don't know. But our kids are more outspoken and like little puppies. They'll run up and get petted and be accepted, but later they might get kicked and not be accepted.

Other Mesquaki parents expressed the same fears. They too were quietly exhorting the teachers to protect their kids from nasty whites. For them, teaching about their culture and history is not some dry curriculum to be regurgitated on a test. When you send your puppies into a den of white lions, you hope and pray that the animal trainers will protect them.

Much more could be said about this historic institute, but I will close with a story that illustrates how hard changing racial attitude is. During one of the small group discussions I witnessed an incident that surely goes on every day in the STC schools. Unlike barroom battles, racism in schools is more subtle. Had I been in the classrooms daily, I would have seen similar incidents.

During our small group discussion the issue of involvement in extra-curricular activities came up. Shortly after we began, a teenage Mesquaki boy and his parents joined us. As we talked about attendance, a teacher asked the boy, "You are in band, aren't you?" He replied that he was during junior high.

Another teacher, who had been talking about the need to build trust, retorted in a joking tone, "Why aren't you in high school band? Did you quit?"

The boy started to say he had not quit, but the teacher answered her own question with another, "What's the matter, were you too lazy?" To my surprise, no one batted an eye at that comment, which left the boy scowling.

The conversation continued as if nothing insulting had been said, but the mother was provoked to interject, "He didn't quit." Her quiet protest went unnoticed, and the conversation moved to another topic. The parents and boy sat there in sullen silence. I sat there in amazement. Five days of cultural sensitivity training, and this teacher was still spouting lazy Indian jokes. Meanwhile, her colleagues just sat there without uttering a protest.

Then as if to add insult to injury, another teacher said to the boy, "You are a student, tell us what you think teachers should be doing to improve relationships." I sat there wondering how this wounded Mesquaki boy would handle her patronizing question.

He said softly, "You need to build trust." His quiet irony shook the heavens. He had turned their professed concern for Indians against them, and not one of them seemed to get it. I probably should have played action anthropologist and forced them to talk about the incident. I could have made them take responsibility for their insensitivity. But I bit my tongue and simply recorded the incident.

When we returned to the big open meeting room everyone was packing up to leave. A cluster of the most dedicated teachers were talking about trying to keep the momentum going. The night before, these same teachers that had told stories from the Lakota *Times* about treaty violations. They had eagerly shared tips on which resource books to buy. Today the mood had turned more somber. The institute was ending, and they were left wondering whether the teachers who needed it most had been touched. They confided that half of those attending "would probably just blow the institute off." Then someone confessed that he rarely challenged the racist comments of other teachers at school. Another added that a school code of conduct was needed to restrict such comments.

For all their brave talk, the air was thick with pathos. They knew and I knew — particularly after that small group discussion — that you cannot kill a dragon with a water pistol. Too many of their fellow teachers looked on skeptically, and their "leaders," the administrators, had made a pathetic token appearance at their institute. That evening I wrote the following fieldnotes:

The institute was great, but I feel as exhausted as the liberal whites do. It isn't the kind of tired that you get from plowing corn all day. It's the kind of tired you feel when gazing up at a mountain from its base. But these earnest young white teachers and I will get over it. The anguish we feel isn't like the anguish that Lone TB expresses in his story about Hardy's. As long as he lives, he can never go in there because he's sure they spit in Indian customers' food. Even something as simple as buying yourself a hamburger can be degrading. Being an Indian is a lot harder than being an anguished white liberal.

The institute left me feeling good about some white teachers, but a dozen follow-up interviews revealed that various participants were unmoved by the touching personal stories. Having taught multicultural issues for years, I know the limits of courses and institutes, but I still applaud the Mesquakis and whites who joined hands to do something.

Classroom Performance and the "Silent Indian"

Without observing lots of classrooms, it is hard to say what teaching techniques will or will not work with Mesquaki students. Many of the teachers at the institute left feeling a little short on practical advice. They asked a number of questions like the following one:

We see these kids excel, and suddenly they just turn around in high school. It leaves you standing there. What happened? You find yourself chasing shadows. Did I do it? Did the peer group do it? I don't understand what I need to do. I need some ways to reach these kids. Give me some things that will work.

The institute was long on good cultural material but short on teaching techniques and curriculum aids. Unfortunately, there are no magic bullets to make alienated, low-income minority kids care more about education. It is rarely a matter of techniques and educational gimmicks. It is mostly a matter of hope. Once kids lose hope in their future, reaching them is very difficult. The first step any white teacher must make is that of an anthropologist. The teacher must listen and figure out why their minority students act the way they do. What follows is what I heard about silent Indians in white classrooms.

When you ask white teachers how well Mesquaki students do academically, they give an interesting range of responses. In thirty interviews of teachers and administrators, most agreed that the majority of Mesquaki students are "at-risk" of dropping out. These students are also characterized as "underachievers." In educationese that means their grades are lower than their achievement tests scores. Underachievement is usually interpreted as a sign of low motivation. In addition, many white teachers think that Mesquakis are exceptionally talented in art and creative writing. Teachers who talk like this say that Indian cultures place an emphasis on storytelling and the aesthetic, so Mesquaki kids excel in creative, "right brain-type" activities.

Finally, the teachers reported a great deal of silent, non-participatory Mesquaki student behavior. This image of Mesquaki students as "silent Indians" is a common one in the anthropological literature. A number of educational anthropologists have documented that white teachers are quick to read the "silence" of Indian students as low motivation, limited English competence, and low cognitive ability (Dumont, 1972; Erickson and Mohatt, 1982; Philips, 1983). Consequently, white teachers tend to lower their expectations for Indian students and include them less in classroom activities. As white teachers lower their expectations for Indian students, a "self-fulfilling prophecy" kicks in. The less teachers expect, the more Indian youths withdraw. As in other studies, many of STC teachers read Mesquaki silence as a lack of ability, motivation, and/or self-esteem.

Anthropologists have generally avoided such psychological explanations of student failure. For example, Susan Philips (1983) portrays the silence that Warm Springs Indian youth express in white classrooms as a widely shared, traditional speech style passed from generation to generation. She says that these students tend to be silent in white classrooms because they learn a very collective, democratic style of communication. The "Indian speech style" is marked by little competition for adults' attention, talking out of turn, and drawing attention to oneself as a speaker. She goes on to describe how Indians use less nodding and gazing, less body and facial movement, and a lower voice tone—all of which teach the importance of stillness. Indian youth also use visual channels of communication more, thus become keen observers who use subtle, indirect cues. Since white teachers do not understand this Indian style of speech, miscommunication transpires, and Indian students feel less like participating in white classrooms.

Although most teachers, and Mesquakis themselves, describe Mesquakis as more quiet and nonparticipatory than white students, there are notable exceptions. It is important to note that most Mesquaki children are initially anything but silent and passive. A few minutes of observation in the Mesquaki tribal school will establish that Mesquakis in the early grades are neither passive nor particularly silent. They talk and play like any children. But town teachers reported that Mesquaki students become less participatory and more silent around the fifth or sixth grade. It would seem that the longer Mesquakis stay in school the more silent they become. By high school no more than a handful of Mesquaki students were verbally outgoing and college-bound. Teachers generally portrayed academically talented Mesquaki youth (10 percent) as more outgoing in classes and active in extracurricular activities.

Another necessary qualification is that Mesquaki students are more silent in classroom settings than they are in the hallways and on the playgrounds. White students, especially girls, remember sarcastic remarks and whistles from clusters of Mesquaki boys hanging out in the hallways. White athletes remember Mesquaki players talking back and making fun of them when no whites were around. Several white students exhorted me: "Don't make them out to be angels because they aren't! They like picking on whites, and they do!"

One white student, who actively supported a recent Mesquaki walkout, explained how white teachers respond to Mesquaki silence:

I heard there's a policy by teachers. If Native Americans don't want to answer, they can't keep asking the question. There must be a policy because they kinda act that way. Teachers let Native Americans stay in the back row and let them be. They give up and go on to others. They don't even ask them questions. If they do, the Native American kid just shrugs and says, "I don't know." They say that is how their culture is. They want to be left alone. The teachers need to try. It isn't fair to whites or Indians, I mean Native Americans. The deal is, lots of Mesquaki students don't really care. They don't work at school. They can't see any future in it.

This student went on to explain that many white students resent the nonparticipation of Mesquakis. They think white teachers are reluctant "to push Indians as hard as they do whites." They also think that Mesquaki kids take advantage of timid white teachers, who fear being labeled racists. For them, Mesquaki kids use the "silent Indian" thing as a ploy to get out of work. They get white teachers to accept their indifference towards school as a legitimate cultural difference. When I tried this explanation out on Mesquaki ex-students, a few laughed and admitted that there was some truth in that observation. But, as we shall see, silence means different things to different Mesquaki students.

Mesquakis Talk About Their Silence in White Classrooms

When I first started to explore this silent Indian image, I was skeptical about previous anthropological explanations. I tried out this image on Mesquaki elders and got a good dose of common sense logic. I asked Lee Kingfish, an old classmate and clan leader, why he and other Mesquakis were always so quiet in class. Lee answered my question with another question, "When you and other whites come out to the settlement, do you talk as much as you do in town?"

I sat there speechless, and Lee sensed he had an anthropologist in his muskrat trap. He said slyly, "Why not?"

I had to answer, "Well, it's a strange situation. Anyone with any sense would hold back to see how you should act."

That brought a big smile to his face, and Lee said it was the same with Mesquakis. He was just trying to say that Indians are people like everybody else. If you have any sense, a strange situation calls for less talking. My grandfather, a taciturn Iowa farmer, could not have said it better.

There is a basic truth in what Lee was saying, but other Mesquakis confirmed Susan Philip's thesis about an Indian speech style that emphasizes quiet observation and verbal reserve. There probably is a general speech style difference between whites and Indians. This difference in speech styles explains some of the Mesquaki reserve and silence, but it overlooks the feelings and motivations Mesquakis often expressed. Youth counselor Aaron Peacemaker gave a poignant, more psychological explanation of Indian silence in white classrooms:

When I look back on it, most of the Indian kids chose to sit in the back and were very quiet, but that is changing a little now. I didn't talk much because I wasn't sure if I had the right answer. I felt like the whites were looking at me and might laugh if I got it wrong.

As we talked, Aaron said he knew other Mesquaki kids who also had "self-esteem problems." Then he cited cases of other youth with whom he works who were bored with school and had many personal problems. For Aaron, silence in the classroom was either a self-esteem problem or a question of boredom and indifference. Both of these themes occurred again and again in discussions with former Mesquaki students.

One excellent example of the stories people told is that of the Bigtree children. They are the children of an old friend and star quarterback, Greg Bigtree. The three Bigtree children recalled how strange it was to transfer from an urban Iowa school to STC. After getting along well with whites, they were suddenly a minority and it was "us versus them. We were no-good Indians. The white children on the bus did not want to sit beside us because they said we stunk." The brothers, Jack and Jayson, recalled junior high days as marked with gang fights between Mesquakis and "the better off white kids who got all the praise and good grades." All three remembered teachers calling on rich white kids more, giving them little privileges, joking with them. They all had friends among whites who played sports or were farm kids, but "racial lines were hard to cross in the early 1980s. There wasn't much racial dating like today."

Academically, all three were A and B students in grade school but slipped down in high school. They all went to academically demanding Iowa State Unviersity where Sally finished a BA in art, Jack all but one semester in an engineering program, and Jayson two years. Finishing at STC High School was a very different matter, however. Sally stuck it out because she made friends, "Eventually the farm girls in sports became friends, but white boys who dated Indians got a lot of crap about their 'squaws'. Being part white, we also got it from Mesquakis, even though we were enrolled." Meanwhile, her brother Jack sat quietly in the back of class until his junior year. His silence was a mixture of feeling angry and very bored, so like many Mesquakis he opted to drop out and do a GED.

In contrast, Jayson was more openly rebellious and eventually got into trouble with the law. His story of quitting school and football during his senior year was told with a mixture of sadness, pride, and relief.

When I finally quit I went to school and turned in my books. Then I went to the football game that night. I was just standing there on the sidelines in my jersey watching. Several guys came up and asked me why I wasn't suited up. I didn't say anything because I had proven what I wanted to. I got good grades when I wanted to. I started on the football team. It wasn't a big a deal, so I just left.

So there was Jayson making his final statement. On returning to Tama he had been made to feel inferior. He had gotten himself into trouble with drinking and drugs. He probably had some self-esteem problems, but he also wanted to prove that he was as good as rich white kids in academics and sports and that succeeding in rinky-dink STC was no big deal. In Jayson's story he is standing silently and stoicly at the whiteman's football game. Then in one noble, heroic act he gives it all up and just walks away from his tormentors. Although teachers called the Bigtree brothers "dropouts," a better label for what happened to them and many other Mesquaki youth might be "pushouts."

Keith Basso's study of Apaches (1979) helps explain the silent retreat of Mesquaki youth like the Bigtree brothers. Using Apache stories and jokes, Basso demonstrates brilliantly that talk about "silent Indians" and "loud whitemen" is all about racial politics. In many Apache stories and jokes the whiteman is back-slapping, garrulous, nosey, and arrogant. He is a rude person who asks too many questions and never listens. The stories lampoon whites as talking rapidly in loud, demanding, high-pitched voices. In effect, the Apaches are symbolically reversing the whiteman's image of the inarticulate, unfeeling, dumb Indians with a more positive image. Apaches portray their silence as a reserved, noble, wise response to the foolish, noisy whiteman.

In other words, Mesquaki youth are part of a much larger verbal battle over cultural and racial images. Mesquaki students' silent retreat is sometimes a very self-assured political statement. As University of Iowa graduate Lance Firstley put it, "I sat there and said nothing because it was easier. I just wanted the whites to leave me alone." Lance, who now runs the tribal housing program, was a quiet, self-assured kid. He dealt with sometimes loud, blustering whitemen by just sitting there quietly. Both white and Mesquaki educators may be too quick to psychologize silence as a sign of low self-esteem.

To sum up, Mesquaki silence has roots in a somewhat different speech style and in a long history of racial and political resistance. For many Mesquaki youth, sitting silently in white classrooms is also a political statement about racism. On the other hand, Mesquaki youth are still unique individuals. Some may be shy or have self-esteem problems. Others may be indifferent or rebellious. The silence of Mesquaki students is a complex form of self-expression and is always a product of unique cultural forces and of unique personalities. Professional researchers must stop feeding teachers monolithic explanations that emphasize only "speech styles," or "low self-esteem," or "rebellion." Teachers must get to know Mesquaki students as unique individuals trapped in a complex historical situation.

Unfortunately, silent rebellion in the classroom does not lead most Mesquaki youth to the academic promised land. Too many Mesquaki students end up getting a GED. Others like Danna Rock Island transfer to boarding schools like Flandreau "to get away from all the racial stuff." The GED and boarding school alternatives may leave Mesquaki students less well prepared academically and with little motivation to go to college. The price for heroic retreat into silence is often lost future educational opportunities. Most Mesquaki students end up feeling like outsiders at the white schools. As in my era, few Mesquakis attend homecoming and prom dances and high school reunions. And as the events of 1992 reveal, racial tensions are alive and well in the STC schools.

Déja Vu, Walkout Two

Sometimes it seems as if events are staged for anthropological travelers. The day I got back into town, Mesquaki high school students were organizing another walkout. Their leader, Sonia Snowflake, bounced up and said, "Hey, you got here just in time for the walkout! Did somebody tell you what we were doin'?" I wanted to tell Sonia that I was omniscient, but I suppressed my sarcastic streak. Meanwhile, Tribal Council chairman Richard Moline, STC administrator Renee GreyEagle, and the ever-present Claude Windsong helped load about fifty Mesquaki and a few white students on school buses bound for the tribal center. Maybe fifty other white kids followed the buses in their cars.

Earlier that morning the counselors and their "conflict management team" of students had led several discussions. The summaries of these meetings covered Mesquaki grievances from name calling and teacher

prejudice to no Native American courses. They also recorded white grievances about Mesquaki fighting, cliquishness, and indifference to school
unity. Several teachers were hailing the group discussions as a real opportunity. Counselor Bob Heart said, "This has been building all year. It is
good that things finally came to a head. We needed to clear the air." High
school principal Jim Lemon put a less controversial face on it, "The
friction is limited to a very few. But we have some kids that cause the
problem on both sides" (DMR, May 16, 1992).

The newspapers claimed that a fight and suspension of three boys —
two Mesquaki and one white — sparked the walkout (Waterloo *Courier*,
May 17, 1992). According to many locals, that was a very simplistic account of why the walkout occurred. The fight was apparently preceded by
several unpublicized racial incidents. The most serious occurred at the
junior high school when a Mesquaki boy pushed a white boy down the
stairs and broke his arm, wrist, and elbow. One coach described the boy as
"a star quarterback, who had all-state potential, so it upset lots of folks a
bunch. There was a lot of talk about getting those damn Indians when it
happened. It really was a shame. Both kids were athletes you know."

According to one junior high teacher, there had been some name
calling and scuffling between the boys prior to the incident. What ap-
palled this teacher was how the administration handled the incident:

At first they told us it wasn't racial, so we downplayed it to our classes. We glossed
over a moment when we could have been talking about name-calling and prejudice. The older kids saw it as racial. Lots of parents put a racial interpretation on
it. It left me with egg on my face. It sends kids the wrong message. We were lucky it
didn't turn out a whole lot worse with lots of organized gang fights the way it was
during the AIM era. There was lots of violence. White kids who had Indian friends
no longer associated. It was a very stressful time.

The proverbial straw that broke the camel's back was the fight reported in
the Waterloo *Courier*. The local story goes that a popular Mesquaki athlete
was defending a much smaller Mesquaki boy from a well-known redneck.
This story had a familiar ring. In my era, star athlete and boxer Jay
WhiteHawk defended the smaller Ryan GreyEagle from a redneck bully.
Reflecting on the walkout a liberal-minded, Tama-born white teacher
confided that, "My own father is a bigot, but he doesn't go out of his way to
hurt Indians." I played football with her father, so her honesty was impressive. She described the attitude of local whites as follows:

Indifference is the biggest thing. The amount of whites who ignore the Native
American is astounding. This is not some kind of KKK thing. The kids get along
fairly well most of the time because they basically ignore each other. It's the same
with the townspeople. But how many really know anything about the Mesquakis
and their culture? This situation is like a pest. You live with it.

So, for this white teacher and others, "walkout two" was born of continuing white indifference to racism. The townspeople live with it like they live with high humidity and pesky mosquitos. Like the school administrators, people never really do much about irritating racial incidents. Many Mesquakis and whites doubted that the walkout would have a positive effect, but even the most hardened cynics were shocked that so many white kids went to the settlement to hear Mesquaki grievences. I wanted to read that as a sign of softening racial attitudes. The white kids in Mr. Zimmer's talented and gifted class cautioned me. Yes, some white kids were against racism and joined the meeting to change things, but other whites went to the settlement as a way to get out of school.

Another concerned white student gave the following perceptive account of the walkout and historic meeting at the settlement:

Sonia Snowflake called and asked me to sign a petition. She called a few white kids to get support and a few of us signed. Most of us went to the settlement in cars. People felt good that day. There was tension about the problems and trying to solve them and people brought up stuff that was said, incidents on both sides. More whites talked than Native Americans. It seems like they were scared to talk. It was usually the girls who talked, but a lot of the problems are with guys. This older guy who was pretty bitter gave a long talk like it was all the whites' fault. Then their head guy, Moline, said if things don't get better they'll go to Legrand, which is stupid if they don't do anything to improve things. The white speeches from the administrators didn't say anything—sorry it happened, not much we can do, we'll try to do something. They were kinda political speeches.

Her unvarnished view of the STC administrators was shared by several teachers and a number of Mesquakis. A few weeks later these same administrators were in action at a tribal council meeting to address tribal concerns. A whole string of Mesquakis came forward with complaints about no Mesquaki history and culture, discrimination in sports, insensitive teachers, students' racist remarks, unexcused absences for funerals, and lack of funding for summer school. After each passionate Mesquaki speech came pasty-faced nods and bland assurances. Every angry accusation was countered with talk about the need for better communication and a committee to study matters. No exchange of ideas ever occurred. The white administers had come to let the Indians rant and rave. If they avoided a shouting match, the storm would blow over and they could run the schools as before. Amanda Firstley summed up the theatrics and mood of the moment, "We've always had committees to talk, but it's gonna die down. It always does."

Sitting there watching the walkout and tribal council meetings, I was pleased to see some whites genuinely concerned about racial problems. But it all had a familiar ring. The Mesquakis told their stories and made their threats. The school administrators expressed their concern. The townsfolk wondered why the Indians were complaining again. It was a series of meetings to talk the problem to death. As the talking died out, this walkout left most Mesquakis with a new resolve. Unlike the 1975 walkout, the tribe were now united to remove their kids from STC. Most Mesquakis want the plan for a new K–12 bilingual/bicultural tribal school completed as quickly as possible.

"Missing-in-Action" in the Sports Scene

The other aspect of schooling that interested me was the sports scene. When I returned home, many townspeople claimed that Mesquaki participation in town sports had declined dramatically. The upsurge of Mesquakis on the new women's volleyball, basketball, softball, and track teams belies such talk, however. Given this influx of female Mesquaki athletes, is such local talk a sexist discourse that privileges male participation? Has Mesquaki sports participation really declined, or simply changed its general character?

To historically reconstruct Mesquaki sports participation, I reviewed high school annuals from 1946 to 1990. The annuals did corroborate local talk about declining Mesquaki sports participation. From 1947 to 1960 the football squad never had fewer than six Mesquakis. In sharp contrast, no more than four Mesquaki players were ever pictured on the football squads from 1960 through the 1980s. The same general pattern of decline can also be seen in other major male sports such as basketball, baseball, and track and field. Since the tribe has doubled in population during the post-World War II era, the decline is even greater than the raw numbers suggest. So why the decline in Mesquaki males who participate in high school sports?

The "Golden Era" of Mesquaki Sports

At least a partial answer lies in what historian Ralph Samuels (1981) calls the "popular memory" of the local sports scene. By the 1950s Mesquaki participation in football reached mythical proportions. Prior to World War II most Mesquakis went to out-of-state, all-Indian secondary boarding schools. After the war Mesquaki males began participating on the Tama High School football and basketball teams. The first sign of their ascendancy was a front-page story that ran a picture entitled "One little, two little, three little Indians" (TNH, October, 1947). Although a crude attempt at humor, the article does portray Milo Buffalo, Richard Papakee, and "Jeep" Youngbear as the "heart and soul of this year's conference champs."

This new post-war trend of Indians playing for the town team peaked in the mid-1950s. In 1955 virtually every Mesquaki male enrolled in the high school was out for football (12 of 18 on a 55 player squad). Indeed, Indian athletes were so active that Coach Richard Bunting decided to field an all-Mesquaki team. The all-Mesquaki team, which used a no-huddle offense and called signals in Mesquaki, actually played only one quarter against the town of Montezuma. Nevertheless, the spectacle of real Indians playing the Montezuma Braves garnered considerable press coverage and a kind of folkloric immortality.

There is some truth in the image of unrebellious Mesquaki youth who were beginning to assimilate into American society. Various anthropologists from the University of Chicago portrayed Mesquaki teenagers as beginning to be interested in American popular music and Hollywood movies (Polgar, 1960; Brunel, ND). The cliques identified by these anthropologists exhibited little of the rebellious teen culture idealized in James Dean movies. These youth were very much under the control of their parents. The girls had strict curfew hours, and dating tended to be in groups. These teenagers had no personal transportation and came to town either in the family car or, more frequently, in rented taxis. Their main recreation was attending Saturday movies, summer softball league, and high school sports events. Although teenage drinking and pregnancies existed, they were still not major social problems. So where does school sports participation fit into this profile of non-rebellious, assimilating Mesquaki youth of the 1950s?

Fellow white classmates from this era generally remember Mesquaki youth as conforming, clean-cut types who were eager to play white sports. As for white males, playing sports was one way that a young man proved his manhood. The Mesquaki commitment to this ideal was considerable. In that era few Mesquaki families had cars and there was no school bus, so after practice many Mesquaki footballers ran the three miles home. The sight of a group of Indian athletes running home was a spectacular expression of their physicality. For white kids like me, this greatly added to their mystique as "natural athletes." In retrospect, such a view of Indian athletes was also partially shaped by romantic images in the popular press.

The Indian as a Natural Athlete

In the 1920s, the Tama *News-Herald* carried several stories about how the Mesquakis helped find the bodies of people who had drowned in the swift Iowa River. They were extolled as fearless, strong swimmers and "natural athletes." In another editorial they were characterized as exceptional runners who were able to travel great distances with little rest. While growing up, I heard people say that Mesquakis were exceptional swimmers and long-distance runners. As I mentioned earlier, the image of white frontiersmen with the physical skills of Indians was a staple of American popular pulp novels and movies. Given these popular culture images, whites created a nature-culture dichotomy. Indians were strong, cunning, and closer to nature than the "cultured" whiteman. Indians were "natural men," hence "natural athletes."

Many whites remember the earlier golden era of Mesquaki sports and "natural Indian athletes" with nostalgia. Many townspeople rhetorically evoke the all-Indian team as a sign of how much Indian sports participation has declined. In this myth Mesquaki youth happily joined white youth on the battlefield of high school sports and harmony prevailed between the races. Whites search for reasons why so few Mesquaki males now play on their teams. Some attribute the decline to a string of losing teams, the size of the school, and the "softness" of all modern youth. Others speculate that the tribe encourage their children to boycott town teams. During the turbulent civil rights era, white talk about "natural Indian athletes" became much more negative. The two images that emerged in the civil rights era are the wildly romantic "super-Indian" and the decidedly negative "hell-raising Indian."

The Whiteman's "Super-Indian" Athlete

In my era the ideal of a good, positive Indian was Billy Warrior. His father, Ron, was one of the only Mesquakis to have been an officer in the Boosters Club. He was a state champion half-miler and star halfback who "escaped the settlement way of life" by marrying a white and becoming a businessman. Today, Billy rarely visits the settlement. When I asked the company secretary for Billy, she replied, "Oh! you want to talk to Chief." When Billy answered, "Hello, this is Chief speaking," I was a little let down.

We eventually did talk, but Billy had little interest in reminiscing about being an Indian sports star, or in recounting his success in the white world. I did, however, come across several interviews of Billy in the Fox Project fieldnotes. At the time, he was apparently quite determined to get away from settlement life. To my surprise, he also distrusted his white friends more than we realized. Billy claimed that two whites, whom I remember as his buddies, intentionally clipped to nullify several of his touchdown runs. Even the most successful, white-oriented Mesquaki sports star of my era, the class president and king of the prom, deeply distrusted his "white friends."

In the current era, Steve Moline—a two-year football letterman and the first Mesquaki to be accepted into the United States Military Academy at West Point—is the whiteman's idea of a good Indian. Steve, the unclaimed son of a local white businessman, was brought up by his Mesquaki grandmother on the settlement. His acceptance to West Point received considerable play in the Des Moines *Register* (June 26, 1988). The headline rang out, "Indian Cadet's Hope Conquers Jealousy." The story portrays Steve as having "ambition born of oppression and poverty." It goes on to recount the "crushing poverty" that Steve learned to hate as he vowed, "My goal has always been to leave. I have seen what happens out here; how people live. I don't want it. I want something better." In the article, white businessman Don Richards affirmed how remarkable Steve's accomplishment was, "He didn't go the Indian way, and for that he has been somewhat rejected."

A year later the *Register* did a follow-up story about "Iowa Mesquaki Beats West Point's Rigors" (July 3, 1989). The article still portrayed Steve as the object of resentment among fellow Mesquakis because "he shunned the Indian way and vowed never to return to the oppressive conditions of the settlement with its lack of homes with running water and unemployment around 70 percent." Both articles played up Steve as a role model for rejecting stagnant settlement life. Contrary to these articles, the only thing that Mesquakis resented about Steve's success was how he let whites make him into a symbol of the assimilated Indian. Many Mesquakis saw Steve as a confused half-breed and political pawn in an attack on Mesquaki culture.

The Whiteman's "Hell-Raising" Indian Athlete

In sharp contrast to these "super-Indians," most modern-day Indian athletes are portrayed as indulging in a self-destructive cycle of drinking and dropping out. Local whites agree that this cycle usually begins in junior high. The most popular white tale of Indian hell-raising recounts how Mesquaki youth invariably "squander their claims checks." A little background on the claims award is necessary to understand this tale. In the 1970s the tribe received $7 million in reparations for lands taken during the early 1800s. Approximately half of this money went into the tribal operations fund, and the other half was allotted equally to every tribal member. For each present-day Mesquaki youth who turns eighteen, his or her original share, plus interest, has grown to approximately $23,000.

The oft-told tale of profligate Indian youth wasting their claims money goes as follows: After receiving a claims check, the Indian youth drops out of school, buys and wrecks an uninsured car, loans his or her friends money freely, and drinks up the little money she or he has left. This story is usually told with a great deal of concern and solemnity. As one white teacher said,

It is such a waste of resources. White parents would make these kids invest in a college education or business. But it just seems like these kids go buck wild when they get the money. So many let their grades go and drop out. It just ruins them.

Many whites also referred to the weekly DWI arrests published in the paper as proof that most Indian youths have a drinking problem. The sheriff and assistant county attorney say they prosecute a higher percentage of Mesquakis than they do whites. Most Mesquakis explain that difference as racial bias. They say Indians are systematically targeted more than white drinkers. I lacked the time and resources to do a systematic survey of youthful alcohol and drug use, so I am not sure if Mesquaki youth are significantly more abusive than white youth. When I went to school in the 1950s, most white students drank every weekend. That was the major form of recreation, and according to white youth, it still is. Moreover, the school counselors report that many white youths have drinking problems.

Nevertheless, local whites continue to talk about youthful alcohol abuse as if it is strictly an Indian problem. What I found interesting in this talk was the underlying racial and cultural assumptions of whites. Whites often assume that — given their superior work ethic and sensible notions of play and recreation — they can drink yet not lose control of their bodies. In the white view, Indians are unable to be controlled "social drinkers" like whites. Indians allegedly use alcohol to escape, rather than to moderate the competitive demands of work and sports. Consequently, Indians who drink are invariably unable to stay on the job, on the team, or on an upwardly mobile track to college.

I heard this line of argument often, but "super-Indian" Steve Moline really drove the point home. When I asked Steve if there was any difference in racial drinking, he said, "Everybody drinks around here, but Indians drink to get drunk, and whites drink to be social and have fun." He went on to give the standard white account of uncontrollable Indian drinking. When I asked him if his white genes were stronger than his Indian genes, he laughed and said he had learned the "white way to drink." He went on to describe how whites were more educated and sensible about drinking. As I was leaving he joked, "Don't let any drunk Indians run into you on the road." These racial beliefs about alcohol and the work ethic of Indian athletes are apparent in the following tales told about the Indian athletes of the 1980s.

Some Tales of "Hell-Raising" Indian Athletes

White coaches generally perceive Mesquaki athletes as less reliable than white youth because they are more likely to be late or absent from practice. Another white coach explained that they are unreliable because they lack consistency. "It's a real roller coaster with Indians. One game they will play great, and the next they don't feel like playing, so they get pounded." This leads coaches to have lower expectations, and, as several Mesquaki players put it, "You have to prove to the coaches that you aren't like other Indians." Despite a high dropout rate, some male Mesquaki athletes did stick with high school sports and achieved considerable success. Unfortunately, even the most successful Indian athletes became grist for the white rumor mill. The following two cases will illustrate how little slack whites cut Indian athletes, even the exceptional ones. They tend to look for reasons why these supposedly "natural athletes" fail to live up to their potential.

Perhaps the most recent spectacular case of "Indian failure" was Tyson James, a state wrestling champion as a sophomore, runner-up as a junior, and dropout as a senior. At the beginning of his senior year Tyson received his claims check and began to drink and skip practices. Eventually he transferred to a Cedar Rapids school but was declared ineligible. Since he disappeared from the high school wrestling scene as a senior, recruiters from various universities stopped coming around. The general consensus among local sports fans was that Tyson "let it all go to his head." Like other Indian youth, Tyson got caught up in the rite of consuming his claims checks.

Apparently his wrestling coach tried to help Tyson. Mr. and Mrs. James faulted neither the coach nor white racism for the demise of their son. What they did resent was the way some whites, in particular the coach's wife, "turned on our son." Before the drinking spree, she wrote Tyson a note about a journal entry by one of her students. It was an essay on the person they most admired and wanted to model their lives on. This first note extolled Tyson by saying, "This 7th grade boy has watched you from afar. You are his hero."

After his disastrous senior season, on January 24, 1991 she apparently wrote a letter to another student and wrestler. A friend of the family gave that letter to the James family; it said:

I remember a journal entry that Will wrote about the person he most admired. He described a wrestler known to most in the state, a kid who'd fought his way to the top despite numerous obstacles along the way. Unfortunately, Tyson won't get "admired" any longer. It's easy to blame it all on alcohol, though that was a contributing factor. People say he got "too much, too fast" with his state championship in 1989. His name became a legend, prematurely I'm afraid. The pressure, the power, the money. It's tough to say. My husband and I have sadly watched this once hero begin his downward spiral, hoping he'd wake up before it was too late. I'm sharing this with you so you can explain the facts to Walker. His hero let so many people down, yet he's incapable of seeing his problems and/or correcting them now. Best of luck to you, Wade. This is one lesson I'm sure you won't need to learn!

The James family complained to her school district and eventually received an apology letter (May 21, 1991), but the damage was already done. It was an old and familiar story for Mesquakis. White people are your friends when you are on top, but when an Indian "role model" stumbles, whites feel betrayed and turn on them. Tyson said that Mesquakis were never as vocal in their praise of him has whites, nor did they reject him when he lost control of himself his senior year. Most understood all too well that the only person he really hurt was himself. For Mesquakis he was just a boy who won some wrestling matches for a time. Mesquakis play to win, but athletics is something to be enjoyed, a recreational pursuit, not some life-or-death character test. No one accused Tyson of letting down his race, and certainly not the whiteman's school and town.

After hearing this story, I asked Tyson if he still wanted to be a Division I wrestler. He seemed anxious to redeem himself, so I suggested walking on at my alma mater, UNI. The UNI minority counselor and coach acted enthusiastic about Tyson, but since he was a non-scholarship student no concessions were made on his low grades. He was told to finish a year or two at a junior college then transfer to UNI. So there it was, another promising Indian athlete lost in the shuffle. Conventional white wisdom has it that star Indian athletes like Tyson will break your heart. So whites ask, why go out on a limb for them if they do not show up for the big game? The answer is simple. They are human beings just like white kids.

Another notable case in the late 1970s was that of Don Kingfish, one of the best basketball players in South Tama County history. Unlike Tyson, Don never drank away his big chance for a college scholarship. His story is more typical of the cultural barriers that Indian athletes generally face. Don was a finely sculptured six-feet-two-inch athlete who "could do Dr. J-like dunks from the free throw line." As a sophomore he high-jumped six-foot-four inches with absolutely no training. Nearly everyone interviewed said he was a sure Division I athlete, but he apparently received little press coverage. According to one coach, the basketball coach never really "showcased Don" in his controlled-style offense.

Nevertheless, Kingfish got a scholarship to Wartburg, a small, all-white, church-affiliated Iowa college. Unfortunately, Don stayed only one week because he felt homesick and out of place. He ended up starring for Haskell Junior College and was recruited by two Division 1-AA schools, the University of Texas at San Antonio and Hardin Simmons. But Don had injured his knee and was facing an operation and rehabilitation. Rather than go to far-off Texas, he returned home. When I asked several white sports fans what ever happened to Don Kingfish, they explained that he "did not really have the drive and competitive desire to play in college." They were quick to label him either "too lazy" or "too laid-back to develop his natural ability."

There were other successful Mesquaki players whom coaches considered at least good Division II or III small college prospects. Most of these youth started out in white colleges but had difficulty adjusting and were homesick. Several also reported being "sucked into all the partying at college." Five of the six ended up transferring to an all-Indian junior college and playing a successful season or two. Then they returned home to marry and take up a variety of jobs. Although they were never white college sports stars, most finished technical degrees and now help run the new tribal enterprises.

I also tracked down what happened to the successful Indian athletes of my era — the golden era in Mesquaki sports. Cris GreyEagle, a state champion miler, had a scholarship at UNI, but his family was too poor to send him to college. Jay WhiteHawk, a fleet halfback, got married and moved to Chicago to find work and box. Billy Warrior, the state champion half-miler, and Marion Moon, a fine baseball player, went to the University of Iowa instead of playing sports at a smaller college. The University of Chicago scholarship program sent an excellent group of athletes to Simpson College. They played their respective sports until the scholarship money ran out. Eventually one, Al GreyEagle, graduated and became a highly successful basketball coach in Wyoming.

Each Mesquaki athlete from these two eras has a somewhat different story, but most experienced painful cultural isolation in Iowa's predominantly white colleges. Others simply ran out of money or were not mature enough to handle the relative freedom, partying, and stricter academics in college. In the end, most opted to go to all-Indian junior colleges rather than small and medium-sized Iowa colleges. Since whites place little value on going to an all-Indian school, they continue telling the ungenerous tale of Indian athletes as "failures."

Small towns and small tribes rarely produce Division I athletes, so Tyson and Don were the most dramatic examples of exceptional prospects who never "made it big" in white universities. Too many whites used these cases rhetorically to indict "the settlement way of life" that allegedly breeds self-destructiveness and a poor work ethic. Meanwhile, Mesquakis counter these white tales about failed Indian athletes with discrimination stories about the white Booster Club.

The Booster Club and White Privilege in Sports

Nearly all Mesquakis contend that the white Booster Club puts enormous pressure on coaches to play their sons and daughters. They frequently cited the example of Cal Clay, a Hawaiian football and basketball coach, who was fired because he was "too sympathetic" to Mesquaki players. Cal was hesitant to blame his demise on racist sentiments, but, he said, most Mesquaki kids felt there was discrimination. Many played sports in junior high then dropped out by the ninth or tenth grade. I think academics eliminated many of them. They'd say that the teachers didn't like them. I am not sure how much discrimination was really going on. I did see a real difference in the culture. The Mesquaki kids would miss practices for wakes, adoptions, and their own tournaments. Long hair was also an issue. White kids complained that Don had long hair. They also complained about Indian kids coming to practice and games late. They operated on Indian time. When they get around to it, they will do it, but most whites can't stand this difference. They get impatient and start yelling and cussing at these kids. That is a sure way to turn them off. They are taught not to cuss and yell at each other like whites. Only the uncles are supposed to discipline kids. For example, we had one case of an Indian girl slapping this white girl. Right away the principal wants to kick this girl out, but the parents demanded a conference. Fifty people were there, and it got settled peacefully. It was just a little spat between two kids, but the principal overreacted.

On his success at keeping Mesquaki players out for sports, he described the extra effort needed to recruit and retain Indian players:

During the summers the tribe hired me for summer school programs, and I worked with the parents committee and the people who really pushed their kids to succeed. We also hired some of the high school kids as aides. You have to convince some parents that the town coaches will give their kids a chance. You also have to get the kids into summer recreation programs. Very few kids participated in the summer baseball and swimming programs, or worked out. They are brought up to be physical, they dance a lot, run in five K races, but overall I'd say they have become less active. Too many parents who are working or drinking leave their kids alone in front of the TV. If you really want to help these kids, you have to break through the suspicions and show them you really care and will give them a chance.

Apparently Coach Clay, whose Mesquaki nickname was "mukader" (black man), must have done something right. When he left town, Mesquaki friends had a feast for him at the powwow grounds. As coach told the story, he was moved to tears:

I never knew how close I was to them. So many people were there. They gave us money, shawls, blankets, beaded work, shirts, all kinds of stuff. And people were coming up and hugging us. I was good friends with lots of whites too, but the Mesquakis have a special place in my heart. I told them that I would come back someday.

On the other hand, Coach Clay's memories of the Booster Club were not so fond. He stopped short of naming specific incidents of coaches being pressured to play whites and said the following:

The Booster Club was the worst group. I didn't get to know them very well. They didn't understand about sweats, wakes, and funerals. The teachers were more culturally aware. Some tried to make things right. The exceptional Indian athlete got taken care of, but they did not make the same effort with the average Indian kid, so they dropped out.

It was difficult to verify Booster Club lobbying without a more direct, extensive study of the sports scene. During interviews, several coaches flatly denied any Booster Club influence in local sports. Nevertheless, four other coaches recounted negative experiences with Booster Club and/or prominent citizens. Unfortunately, no coach wanted to be quoted for fear of upsetting these people. I also collected many stories from Mesquaki athletes. One that nicely illustrates Mesquaki attitudes was about a basketball player named Curtis Skywalker.

In the early 1980s several Mesquakis were starters on the sophomore team. Mesquaki sports fans had high hopes that this group would play on the STC varsity team. By their senior year, however, only Skywalker, a point guard with a good outside shot, was starting. Although only five-feet nine inches tall, Curtis was averaging twenty points a game and had hopes of playing in junior college. As his senior season wore on, he came in conflict with his coach. Curtis was chastised for his lack of dedication and for missing practices. From his perspective

Coach started riding me in practice. He was always criticizing me. Then he started saying that there are other players who are more hungry and can replace you. At the time me and my parents heard that the Booster Club didn't like Indians playing, that they eventually split us up. Lon and Ray tried to stick it out, but they ended up riding the bench. Then we heard that this son of a big shot in the Boosters was going to be brought up from sophomores to replace me. He was a good player, but so was I. The difference was I was supposedly this dumb, wild Indian, I guess, and he was this rich white guy. No, Coach was a good guy. He wasn't really prejudiced. It was those other guys, the Boosters that made him get rid of me. My dad heard them talking at the games.

The coach involved refused to discuss this incident, but two fellow coaches offered their accounts. One described it as a clash between two different cultures:

Mr. X was this straight-laced type guy who ran a very slow, pattern-style offense. Curtis was a decent ball player, but he liked the run-and-gun style like most Indians do. The more he tried to discipline the Mesquaki kids like whites, the more they rebelled. It was more of what you would call cultural conflict that outright discrimination. Mr. X just turned most of these kids off, and of course the white players were complaining that coach was "too soft" on the Indian kids about missing practices and showing up late. Sometimes the Mesquaki's easygoing attitude puts the coach in a tough position with whites. You can't have a double standard. On the other hand, if you want to keep the Indian kids there, you have to recognize these differences. And I don't doubt if there was some pressure to play this guy's kid. He was good, and his old man is vocal and prominent.

I am not sure whether Curtis really lost his starting position because of Booster Club pressure, but such things do happen in small-town sports scenes. I saw similar incidents in South Texas during the football season that I chronicled (Foley, 1988; 1990). In that case the "outsiders" were Mexicanos and the prominent whites definitely put pressure on the coaches to play their kids. The coaches and school administrators, who were mostly ex-coaches, hung out at the country club and hobnobed with the Chamber of Commerce and Booster Club types. If the Mexicano kids were exceptional, they played no matter what, but if a white and Mexicano kid were more or less equal, the white kid from a prominent family played more. Racial and class biases worked hand-in-hand against working-class Mexicano kids.

Moreover, many studies of small American towns have documented how prominent families control local affairs and treat outsiders (Lingeman, 1980; Vidich and Bensman, 1968). In my hometown, the people who lived in nice houses on "the hill" looked down on the people who lived in modest houses in "smoky row" near the railroad tracks and creosote plants. Now that the railroad track and the creosote plant are gone, "smoky row" is called "Third and Fourth Street." The label has changed, but the class bias is the same. People still look down on "Third-Streeters."

On moving from the farm to town, I ran headlong into these class prejudices. As an outsider with no social credentials, I was picked on, challenged to fight, and ganged up on in football practice. As a junior, I found myself playing behind the doctor's son in football and battling senior Bill Carter for the fifth spot on the basketball team. I started the first three games, but a few weeks into the season Coach Levi took me aside and explained why he must bench me. He lauded my progress but confessed that the seniors and our star point guard, Greg Willis, preferred Carter. What coach left out in his speech to me was that these guys were buddies. They were the prominent whites who lived on the "hill" and ran the school, and I was a newly arrived farm kid, a social nobody.

That was my first lesson on how social class differences work in small town sports. And these things apparently never quite die. At a recent class reunion, I met "Willie" again, and we talked a little about his induction into the Iowa Basketball Hall of Fame. Being an all-Big Eight player at Iowa State University, he was probably the best basketball player Tama High ever produced. After recounting his accomplishments, we reminisced on the season when Tama High won twenty-seven games and almost made it to the state finals. To my surprise, he asked me, "Were you on that squad?" Thirty-seven years later, and I am still an outsider! I felt like protesting his memory lapse, but high school reunions are not the place to be churlish.

My experience illustrates nicely what _all_ outsiders are up against in small towns like Tama. Being white, I eventually gained social acceptance, but only the "super Indians" like Billy Warrior and Steve Moline ever gain the social acceptance that I did. Most Mesquaki youth face far greater cultural barriers than I did, and as several coaches said, "The average Mesquaki athlete kinda gets lost in the shuffle." After listening to many coaches and players, I have no doubt that sports help maintain the racial and class privilege of whites. Any white or coach who thinks Mesquaki kids have an equal opportunity to play high school sports is naive about how class and race works in American society.

There were, of course, some hopeful exceptions in the current sports scene. The women's volleyball and basketball teams have recruited a number of excellent Mesquaki players. These teams seemed more open, and Mesquaki girls were somewhat more optimistic about their chances in sports. Nevertheless, the Mesquaki community tells similar discrimination stories about girls' sports. Female Indian athletes also hear the same racial slurs and war whoops when they play. A common Mesquaki story about female sports is that whites get nervous when too many good Indian players are stars. An oft-cited example was the Kingfish sisters who were basketball and vollyball stars in the early 1980s. Like brother Don, they eventually played for Haskell Junior College.

A similar story was floating around about the 1992 sophomore girls' basketball team. They were predominantly Mesquaki, and rumor had it that whites were moved up from the freshman team "to give the sophomore team more racial balance." The coach explained the situation as non-racial, an effort "to get consistency and add more depth by replacing two ineligible and one injured Mesquaki player." Since moving white players up caused considerable friction, few Mesquakis believed this explanation. The other rumor was that the star player, Terri Warrior, was not given a chance to play on the varsity team. Terri reported feeling so much pressure that she asked to be left with her Mesquaki teammates on the sophomore team.

Summing Up: The Decline of White Sports as a Rite of Passage

The whole sports scene has changed a great deal since the so-called golden era. Mesquaki youth of the 1990s must contend with many new social and psychological pressures. Thomas Hill's (1974; ND) discussion of adult Indian alcohol use as a "hell-raising" phase or lifestyle is useful here. This hell-raising phase that Hill describes among adult urban Indians seems to begin for many Mesquakis during adolescence. According to tribal elders, many Mesquaki youth do get caught up in drinking sprees. Such hell-raising is best understood, however, as a brief phase in life, as part of a conflict-filled adolescent rite of passage to adulthood. Various studies of working class adolescents suggest similar patterns in other racial groups (Eckert, 1989; MacLeod, 1987; Willis, 1981; Leemon, 1972).

One unique cultural event that marks the rebellion of Mesquaki youth is sharing claims money with friends. Contrary to the white stories about wasted claims checks, these events are not entirely self-destructive. In Mesquaki culture, the conspicuous consumption of this money among friends and family is a little like an Indian "give away" or "potlatch." The worst thing one could do is hoard the money for personal use. The point is to share your good fortune with others, who will in turn will be obligated to share with you later. These adolescent potlatches, which are clear expressions of cultural and racial solidarity, seem to be supplanting white sports as a rite of passage to manhood.

Most of today's tribal leaders reported going through this hell-raising stage before marrying and settling into jobs. Most Mesquaki males now valorize themselves and their culture through rebellion against white sports and society. Unfortunately, that rebellion may involve some self-destructive drinking and hell-raising. The white school sports scene has become a racial border that many Mesquaki youth simply refuse to cross. Authoritarian coaches, strict practices, white racist comments, and riding the bench discourage most Mesquaki athletes. In addition, there is always the suspicion that rich whites rig the sports scene for their kids. Moreover, Mesquaki youth of the 1990s now have many alternatives to the white sports scene. They have cars, a little money, more job prospects, and better organized all-Indian recreational leagues and traveling teams. It would seem that the "golden era" of dedicated Mesquaki athletes running home after practice is gone forever.

Chapter 4
White and Indian Portraits of Mesquaki Culture

Over the years many outsiders have come to the settlement to portray the Mesquaki. Everyone comes searching for the remnants of "authentic" Mesquaki culture. Journalists often write sensational articles about the religious custom of eating dogs. Anthropologists describe the character and values of Mesquakis. Folklorists long to collect the sacred winter stories. What follows is a selective overview of how outsiders have portrayed Mesquaki culture. It also includes what Mesquakis have written about themselves since World War II.

The hardest thing any anthropologist does is portray a different culture. I often tell students in my graduate seminar this story to motivate them to write more sensitive accounts of other cultures. It goes like this.

Long, long ago, when I went to graduate school, my professors were cocksure about writing cultural portraits. They lived in scientific castles with laboratories and loyal "hunch-backed" graduate students. Some students thought our professors were ancient wise men who wrote with quill pens. Others thought they were ordinary modern men who wrote with whirling, flashing computers. Whether by low-tech or high-tech, their studies were served to us on a platter engraved "a true picture of the natives."

Then I became a professor and began professing the same thing. For years I delivered papers at anthropological meetings with a knowing face. But one day a band of outlaws called postmodernists rode into anthropological town. To everyone's surprise, they began criticizing the books being written. "You misrepresent the people you study!" they cried. "You pretend to know more than you do! Down with Positivism. Long live Nietsche! Long live skepticism!" Soon everyone was shouting such things. Feminists, phenomenologists, Marxists, hermeneuticists, ethnic scholars, one and all, were clamoring for change. Down with science! Up with poetry!

Some practicing anthropologists sensed that their scientific gig was ending, so they began trying to write poetry and anthropological novels. These new ways were strange, but the postmodern converts were determined. They longed to express their feelings in a personal voice. They even formed their own journals so others would know that they were truly different. There were many important-sounding names for this new approach. Some called it a post-positivist revolt, others the return to humanistic anthropology.

Then the wily old architects of the castles began inviting these postmodern rebels to dine at their long table. Soon the graduate students at my university began talking with great assurance about "texts" and "tropes" and "dialogic moments" and "rhetorical devices." No one wanted to wear the immortal cape of Count Dracula any more. No one wanted to suck the natives dry and write bloodless scientific portrayals. No one wanted to make knowledge claims that would live forever. So the immortal count and a few loyal hunchbacks retreated deep into the scientific castle. They presently lie in their coffins waiting for the bright postmodern sun to set.

Meanwhile, the new postmodern converts shout "free at last!" Their leaders proclaim that one can only "write" not "discover" other cultures. They talk of being "translators" and "mediators" of "polyphonic voices." They envision an anthropological fiber-optic cable that lets a thousand voices speak. The rebellion will be complete when the natives speak for themselves and write their own texts. And an anthropologist who still dares speak for the natives must first be cleansed. She or he must trade Dracula's cape for a hair shirt and be self-critical and "reflexive," and suffer "epistemological doubt."

So here I am, fresh from the academic wars over "writing cultures." I have replaced my blood-sucking cape with a new hair shirt. I have beat my breasts until they long to be ethical. My epistemological crisis has come and gone. Maybe now I am ready to "write Mesquaki culture" and to let Mesquakis "write themselves." But these noisy postmodernists left no instructions for building a better text. How am I supposed to write differently from the scientific hunchbacks? For lack of a roadmap, these are some voices I heard — the common voices of the streets, the voices of journalists and academics, and finally the voices of Mesquaki. Listen to this cacophony of voices claiming to portray Mesquaki culture, and you will understand how difficult it is to write about another culture.

Here Comes the German Journalist

My first encounter with Mesquaki portrait painters was a German film crew. They were shooting a TV special on the American heartland. The middle-aged woman in charge had been a foreign exchange student in the tall corn state. She was back on the settlement on a sentimental journey. She wanted to recapture the whirling feathers and tom toms of her youth. Her five-minute Mesquaki segment would give this heartland tour some color and pageantry. She admitted that Germans were quite fascinated with all Native Americans.

One scholar has chronicled how German hobbyists reinvent themselves as Indians (Taylor, 1988). They get together in carnival-like events that include "cowboy" activities such as roping, whip-handling, and square dancing and "Indian" activities such as archery and knife and tomahawk throwing. Dressed in their finest beaded buckskins, these groups pitch teepees and sing and dance for three days. Hobbyists stage these events throughout Europe, and the Plains Indian style of the Sioux dominates everywhere.

Iowans should be familiar with whites "playing Indian" because of buckskinner or mountain men rendezvous. These Iowa groups are quite craft-oriented, so many members become proficient in bead, quill, and feather work and in costume making. Like other hobbyists, they are always interested in having real Indians help them learn to sing and dance more authentically (Powers, 1988). One Mesquaki, Jonas CutCow, has camped out with these groups many times. They make him feel like a celebrity because he is a "real Indian." As Jonas puts it, "You meet lots of girls at the rendezvous."

At any rate, this nostalgic German lady ran around the settlement interviewing people. She said the tribal chairman was so wise and serene you could barely hear him. A Mesquaki laughed and said, "Yeah, he talks so low nobody knows what he is saying!" She found one of her prime interviewees a little too fast-moving, "I do not understand why, if he is a world-renowned poet, he does not want to be interviewed?" Ted Pipestar had given her a courteous smile, but he beat a hasty retreat. As he was leaving he pointed at me and said with a wink, "Talk to that guy. He is an anthropologist. He's writing a book. He can tell you what you need to know." Right, talk to the anthropologist lurking there. He probably knows enough to fill this TV segment. I respectfully declined and urged her to corner Ted, the wily trickster-poet.

She ended her whirlwind shoot by interviewing Fred Peacemaker. Fred had a housepainting business for years, and he was the tribal planner for a time. He is also an artist who owned a store that sold Indian art and crafts. Fred makes a real effort to be an ambassador of good will and host many foreign visitors interested in Mesquaki culture. To give her piece more ethnic bang, the reporter interviewed Fred at the King Tower truck stop, which has the town's only neon sign of an Indian Chief in war bonnet. The place also sells a few Indian trinkets and postcards. Quite unexpectedly, Fred brought a bag full of Indian artifacts made by a German hobbyist friend. I watched them talk about German-made Indian artifacts under Tama's finest neon Indian warbonnet! Surely some German intellectual will revel in the irony of German hobbyist art showing up on a real American Indian settlement. This TV show incident inspired me to collect as many white written and oral stories about Mesquakis as possible.

The Train Track Story

Before reviewing selected journalistic writings, I must illustrate how the local press perpetuates a white storytelling tradition about Indians. Whenever I asked whites to talk about Mesquakis, they invariably mentioned what I now call the train track story. The story has become a major white folktale that each new generation learns. Tama whitemen who want to portray the Mesquakis as a doomed, backward, immoral culture recite the tragic train track story.

The typical story begins with an Indian who comes to town to get drunk. Then in the early morning hours he or she decides to walk home to the settlement. Instead of taking the road, the drunk Indian follows the railroad tracks that run directly back to the settlement. Some say it is because the track bed is warmer and less icy than the roads. Others say it is a shorter route. Everyone agrees that it is the more dangerous route. Invariably the drunken Indian cannot make the two miles home without sitting or lying down to rest. So the poor thing curls up on the warm track bed and goes to sleep, just not knowing any better. Since it is pitch black, the poor train engineer can never see much. The sleeping Indian is no more than a dark blob on the track bed. The engineer cannot tell whether the blob is a log or a dog. And since the train is going full steam through the settlement it just rolls over the Indian. End of story. End of one more drunk, lazy, dumb Indian.

What shocked me about the newspaper accounts of these deaths was the amount of gory detail. Perhaps the following gore helps plant this tale deep in the psyche of the ordinary whiteman (TNH, 1961):

The head had been cut off at the neck and was found about 20 feet from the rest of the body. The right arm was cut off at the shoulder. The rest of the body, stripped of all clothing, was badly broken and bruised. His loafer type shoes were found along the track. One can of beer, unopened, was found near the body. Three more cans of beer, also unopened, were found further west down the track.

Or in another incident (TNH, 1962):

The head had been cut off at about the middle of the back of the head to under the chin. The face was not mutilated and was recognizable. A peculiarity of the mutilated corpse was that the tongue of the victim was still attached to the neck, it was not in the mouth of the severed head. A six-pack of beer, with five full cans still in the cardboard carton, was found near the body. The sixth can was never found.

Stories from the early 1940s to the late 1960s chronicle a dozen other track deaths. Another story (TNH, August 10, 1961) describes how both legs, the left arm, jaw, and skill were fractured on contact, and how the unrecognizable body was dragged for a mile, thus scattering severed feet, hands, and arms along the train bed. Then the final piece of vital detail, "when the train stopped at Savannah, Il., a leg was found wedged under the train." One way to explain this white fascination with body mutilation is that it allows the storytellers to imagine themselves gazing down on the crushed body of the poor Indian. Perhaps the more spectacular and public the story of these body mutilations, the more powerful the white observer feels.

If ever a story cried out for symbolic analysis, it is the train track story. What better symbol of the whiteman and progress than the railroad train. What better symbol for the treacherous path of assimilation than being run over by the "white" train. There were undoubtedly good economic and engineering reasons for ramming a train track through the heart of the settlement. It had to follow the flat Iowa river bed that winds through hilly Tama County. At the time probably no one worried about invading the Mesquakis' little sanctuary. On the contrary, some whites undoubtedly advised the Mesquaki that having a railroad was a good thing, a sign of progress. Every little grease spot of an Iowa town had a railroad station.

But the railroad has always functioned differently on the settlement. The train passes through the settlement, but it never stops. The settlement never had a railroad station for sending off passengers and products. So if the railroad was not an agent of commerce, what was it? Local whites have made the settlement train a story rich in cultural meaning. For whites the train that passes through the settlement is an avenging angel. It brings death to those Mesquakis who disregard the power of white commerce, white technology, the white way of life. These stories always emphasize the link between alcohol and the mutilated body. Rather than pay the price of hard work and rectitude, the Mesquaki takes the easy road to life — the shortcut home — and thus perishes beneath the white wheels of progress. The lazy, morally dissolute Indian who casually walks the righteous white tracks is destroyed.

For whites this story apparently represents some kind of universal truth about the Indian. This one tragic story is a key metaphor for all the white disappointments and hopes for "their Indian." So every white who tells this story, no matter how ignorant and illiterate, imagines himself waxing poetically about a truth that eludes the poor Indian. The story surely fills a deep need in many local whites to portray Mesquaki culture negatively.

In sharp contrast, Mesquakis undermine the white train track story with their own version. Their strongest counterstory has the white policeman putting the allegedly drunken Indians on the tracks to die. This story has several variations, but they generally boil down to corrupt, vengeful cops murdering innocent Mesquakis. Sometimes the Mesquaki has been arrested and badly beaten up in jail. To avoid discovery, the authorities must put the body on the tracks so the body mutilation from the train will cover up the police brutality. In another version of the story, a white gang dumps the beaten Mesquaki body on the tracks to avoid prosecution.

Finally, there are versions of the story without white foul play. In these stories the train tracks claim the hard-of-hearing or near blind. There is also a major variant that emphasizes the possibility of suicide. More than a few relatives speculate that the person killed may have wanted to die. Feeling tipsy, a person can lie on the tracks without any guilt about suicide. But giving in to the whiteman's train sends chills through the surviving relatives. If it really was suicide, the person's spirit may be doomed to remain in a tortured state of limbo. This unthinkable possibility quells excessive speculation about suicide. Nevertheless, people are left wondering, and such stories reaffirm how hard it is to be an Indian.

Some of the Mesquaki counterstories may contain denials of the loved one's drinking problems, but the aggressive, condescending tone of this story invariably compels Mesquakis to tell strong counter-stories about white racism and policy brutality. As important as this battle between local storytellers is, the most prominent site of cultural misrepresentations seems to be in the writings of journalists and academics.

The Dreaded Des Moines *Register* and Other Journalistic Accounts

Iowa newspapers represent Mesquaki culture in a variety of positive and negative ways. I was unable to do an exhaustive survey of the major newspapers, but I did collect hundreds of *Register* articles from the Des Moines public library, the Fox Project files, the Iowa City Historical Society Files, and Jonas CutCow's personal files. The *Register* has a file on Mesquakis, but they were unwilling to let Jonas and me copy it. The articles I collected tend to cluster around key controversial events like the tribal school fight or annual events like the powwow. On other occasions, some reporter will do a feature story or series of articles on the settlement. These more in-depth pieces were the most interesting because they involved more fieldwork. They represent journalists' best attempts at portraying Mesquaki culture and politics.

Both whites and Mesquakis complain about the coverage of "Iowa's

Figure 1. From Des Moines *Register*, December 29, 1968. The original caption read, "Mesquakie Indian children in the settlement near Tama, whose eyes reflect the plight and despair of their parents." Original photo by William Kesler.

Paper," the *Register*. Many whites think the *Register* is a "bleeding heart liberal" view of the Mesquakis. Since the 1950s, the *Register* has pilloried Tama in much the same manner as the Civil Rights Commission Report did (1981). Local white authorities received considerable "bad press" over earlier law and order, prohibition, tribal school, and school walkout controversies. They claim that *Register* reporters get most of their information from angry Mesquaki activists; consequently, the town is portrayed as a hostile, redneck place. Unfortunately, critical portrayals of white racism do not automatically lead to insightful portrayals of Mesquaki culture.

Many Mesquakis complain that the *Register* portrays the settlement like any low-income minority community. Too often, these liberal, white, middle class reporters write stirring, sentimental accounts about the Indian's noble struggle against poverty. A lovely example of this type of story is shown in Figure 1 and the caption that oozed: "Mesquaki Indian children in the settlement near Tama, whose eyes reflect the plight and despair of their parents." To the reporter these nameless, faceless children were just poor Indian kids playing outside their run-down home, grist for the obtrusive, paternalistic gaze of his Nikon F camera. But to Jonas CutCow the picture had an entirely different meaning. When he and I found this photo in State Historical Society files he said, somewhat surprised, "Hey, that's my niece and nephew on their grandma's porch!" He and I laughed because Lonnie looked puzzled over what that serious, funny looking white guy was doing. She and Lance are now University of Iowa graduates who run social services programs, so their "despair" must not have been too debilitating. Apparently this photo served the reporter's purpose to portray Mesquakis as living in a despairing "culture of poverty." Historian Michael Katz (1989) calls this the "poverty discourse" perspective. This way of talking about low-income minority communities dies hard. Many journalists and academics still use a poverty discourse to describe the Mesquakis.

Part one of Amy Davis's 1992 feature story gives a dramatic portrait of an ex-drug dealer trying to escape the vicious cycle of poverty through Golden Gloves boxing (Waterloo *Courier*, May 3, 1992). His heroic, pull-yourself-up-by-the-bootstrap story is juxtaposed to the University of Minnesota's study of adolescent alcohol and drug abuse and suicide. The boxer's dramatic story hooks the reader, and the Native American adolescent study is the authoritative scientific voice that confirms drugs, crime, and suicide on the settlement. Then the boxer and a friend testify that they have seen lots of self-destructive behavior and broken-down families on the settlement. So a circle of truth has been drawn. The scientific survey and two Mesquaki youth agree, the settlement is a culture of poverty and despair.

To Davis's credit, she does try to balance her noble-Indian-struggling-against-poverty story. In part two (Waterloo *Courier*, May 3, 1992) she says,

Normal people live here with average lifestyles. Some are happy, some are bored, some work two jobs, others are unemployed. Some are alcoholics; some are raising illegitimate children; others have violent streaks.

The second part of her article also features two Mesquakis as successful role models. Unfortunately, the blend of poverty stereotypes and scientific studies in part one overwhelms part two. In the end this well-intentioned journalist has written a typical liberal middle class story of poverty that is a sentimental tear-jerker. This type story probably sells papers to the mainstream, but it is a very one-dimensional view of Mesquaki culture.

In sharp contrast, Sherri Ricciardi's feature stories in the early 1970s (DMR, 5/5/1973, 8/6/1973) generally avoid using a culture of poverty perspective. Her three-part feature story seeks to persuade mainstreamers that the "sixties rebellion" was an expression of cultural pride, not a mindless, lawless revolt. Ricciardi puts a nice face on AIM with vignettes of Mesquakis wanting to preserve their traditional religion. A story of one man's return to the settlement after years in the city is used to illustrate the Mesquakis' love for homeland and culture. The article also gives glowing portraits of painters, dancers, finger weavers, and bead and ribbon workers. Overall, one gets a rather positive view of the Mesquakis as a reviving culture.

Unfortunately, the assumption that Mesquaki culture needs outsiders like AIM to reawaken it is a very misleading idea. A strong core of traditional religious leaders have always promoted the old ways. They hardly need urban Sioux Russell Means and Chippewa Dennis Banks to reinspire pride in their traditions. As Vine Deloria (1985) explains so well, AIM is best understood as "ethnic Indians" fighting racism and demanding basic civil rights. They were the young warriors who pushed "traditional Indians" to be more assertive and political. This is a distinction that escapes Ricciardi, so her portrayal of AIM is largely a projection of her liberal, sympathetic, civil rights views. She seems to have no real knowledge of what was going on at the settlement at the time. This is decent, non-stereotypic journalism, but rather poor historical and cultural analysis.

Another major journalistic piece done in the early 1970s was by John Zielinski entitled *Mesquakie and Proud of It* (1976). The Iowa Arts Council financed the initial phase of this study, which is sold today in the Casino's gift shop. Several current Mesquaki leaders called the book "too romantic, a joke." Others liked the pictures and said it was "OK, not offensive, but it doesn't really say much about life on the settlement." To the extent that one can understand a people through photographs alone, the book contains some marvelously intimate and touching family-of-man type photos. As for most "coffee table books," the photos dominate, but it has more historical and cultural material than this type of book usually does. The author stitches together the addresses of ancient chiefs and old historical documents with his own short narratives on Mesquaki history and culture.

The historical section is reasonably accurate and chronicles the Mesquakis' valiant survival against the French and their heroic return to Iowa. Unfortunately, it ends with the same stereotypic portrayal of how Mesquaki culture changes that journalist Riccardi used:

The younger people no longer feel it is necessary to hide their Indianness in the outside world. Even some of the older Indians have adopted some of the white man's methods. I talked to one religious leader who would gladly use a tape recorder to preserve some of the most sacred songs and stories that the oldest people know. The only problem is that these old people regard the tape recorder as sort of a device of the devil and prefer to go to their graves with the memories rather than pass them on in such a non-traditional way. (1976, 52)

Once again, a white outsider imagines that the youth are leading the way against superstitious elders. What this author overlooks is that Smithsonian anthropologist Truman Michelson collected thousands of pages of lore and many recordings from 1910 to 1930. The tribal elders have been speaking into the "devil's device" quite freely for many years. Mesquaki traditionalists have never been so unwilling to selectively borrow white cultural practices as most whites imagine.

Zielinski's sections on Mesquaki culture are also very problematic. They lament the loss of traditional cultural practices such as weaving cattail reed mats, butchering buffalo, and building bark canoes. He concludes that cooking practices have changed little because Mesquakis still grow Indian corn, dry squash, and make maple syrup. Forget all the junk food and burgers that Mesquakis eat. Some of the old ways are still visible, so he highlights them like precious nuggets of "real culture." He goes on to list a few curing herbs still used.

The cultural section of Zielinski's work ends with Michelson's description of the chants and wailing songs of a religious ceremony. Taken out of context, it is hard to see how this would make any sense to whites. It ends up being an exotic fragment that is supposed to prove that Mesquakis still practice their ancient religion. He concludes with a voyeuristic, unsubstantiated observation that "reading between the lines of what I have been told about their religious ceremonies, I would say that the above material comes close to the way the ceremonies actually are today" (1976, 74).

Here again is the white outsider trying to find traditional Mesquaki culture in essential material cultural objects and practices like reed mats, curing herbs, and ancient religious ceremonies. The logic of this approach goes like this: If these people have some obvious traditional traits and objects, surely they are still Indian. Modern Mesquaki culture is too complex a synthesis of the old and new to be captured in a simplistic inventory of traditional objects and practices.

Nevertheless, Zielinski pushes his search for ancient Indian traits further still by quoting a long speech by Youngbear, the son of Chief Pushetonequa. Youngbear's 1928 speech to a group of Des Moines teachers is supposed to illustrate that Mesquaki children still learn different cultural values. The speech is a example of Mesquaki cultural ideals: stealing is evil, kindness is good, food is for the needy, the old people are sacred, never lie, and follow the great spirit. But, like all lists of moral precepts, this is a list waiting to be broken. Mesquakis are no more able to live up to this list than Christian whites are to the Ten Commandments. Presenting this list as authentic Mesquaki culture is like presenting the Ten Commandments as authentic American culture. This idealistic view of Mesquaki culture reverses the temperance view of Indians as hopeless sinners and drunks. Unfortunately it substitutes an equally ridiculous view of Indians as innocent and morally superior.

When Mesquakis scoff at this book as "too romantic," they are simply demanding a more realistic, multi-dimensional portrait. They are sick of being portrayed as either incarnate evil and savegry or as noble and virtuous. Unlike many Christian friends, they have no illusions about being good because they spout moral precepts or attend church regularly. As one clan elder put it,

Walking the right path is hard. You have to choose the right path yourself. Being an Indian is a lot harder than being a whiteman. There isn't anybody to forgive you like a priest, if you mess up. And when you mess up, that stays with you forever. You can't get out of what you did wrong so easy.

In some ways this is a harsh, yet realistic view of life and morality. Someone with this view knows that Indians, like all human beings, are capable both of great kindness and virtue and of viciousness and evil.

But in defense of Zielinski's and Riccardici's romanticism, they were caught up in the sixties era. It was fashionable to counter racism with positive portraits of minority cultures. Zielinski's heart is in the right place, but his replacing highly negative culture of poverty portraits with romantic portraits of the old ways is scarcely an improvement.

Anthropological, Literary, and Art History Portrayals of Mesquaki Culture

Lest I be accused of picking on non-anthropologists, we anthropologists have written both pessimistic cultural breakdown and romantic revival portrayals of the Mesquakis. As the French scholar Michel Foucault (1972) reminds us, different historical epochs are marked with different "discursive regimes" that influence how all writers portray reality. We are always parroting some conventional wisdom of the popular press and scientific establishment of the times. Stepping outside the dominant discourses of our times is exceedingly difficult. The University of Chicago's Mesquaki study (Gearing et al., 1970; Gearing, 1970) is an excellent example of this dilemma.

On the one hand, these action anthropologists portrayed the settlement as a badly factionalized, "structurally paralyzed," leaderless community. Their rather negative portrayal of cultural breakdown on the settlement was, however, more critical of white society that most journalistic accounts. They blamed the BIA's policy of forced assimilation for undermining the modern Mesquaki political system. They also emphasized how local white racism further demoralized the Mesquakis. On the other hand, they ultimately presented a highly romantic portrayal of Mesquaki culture in a technical ethnography (Gearing, 1970) and in a series of newspaper articles (Gearing, 1953). These publications were meant to counter white attitudes that cultural assimilation of Mesquakis was inevitable. They wanted to show that despite the breakdown of leadership and the political system, traditional Mesquaki culture was alive and well. Unfortunately, like many crusading liberal journalists, these anthropologists slipped into the noble-savage image of Indians. Because popular press materials are more accessible than academic writing, they better illustrate this tendency to romanticize Mesquaki culture and character.

During the winter of 1953 Fred Gearing wrote sixteen articles in the Tama *News Herald* (Fox Project fieldnotes, Box 4). These articles apparently caused a stir on the settlement. Tribal Chairman Ed Davenport and the so-called progressive Youngbear faction thought action anthropologists were allies of the protraditionalist or Oldbear faction (Gearing et. al, 1960). The project fieldnotes show that antagonism developed between Davenport and some of the students, particularly Gearing. So when this young graduate student tried to portray Mesquaki culture to whites, a distrusting tribal council was ready to pounce on him.

One of the most remarkable things about the articles is their narrative style. Gearing writes in the first person plural "we" rather than the first person singular, "I." This has the effect of making him a Mesquaki, or at the very least, an honorary member of the group. He also uses an un-academic style which tries to simulate a Mesquaki oral storytelling style. For example, at times he uses animal stories to make his point. His series of articles begins with the following justification:

> It's a funny thing about America; most people find differences a little hard to take for some reason. Communities that are different generally have a pretty rough row to hoe. That is another reason why we are writing these articles. We'll be talking a lot about differences. How we are different and how we are not, and why. And why being different isn't necessarily a bad thing. We're going to be around here forever, so it'd be a good thing if we could get some of those things straightened out. (Fox Project fieldnotes, Box 4)

A common theme in many of the articles is that Mesquaki culture will not disappear but will change very gradually. Mesquakis will adopt some white ways like warm houses, cars, education, and new skills to earn a living, but will never abandon their spiritual, religious views. Nor will they ever run after money to such an extent that they stockpile wealth and lose their generosity towards each other.

Perhaps the central cultural image of all the essays is the gener-ous, communally-oriented, nonaggressive, noncompetitive Indian. The fourth essay, "Why we'd just as soon not farm much," lays out the idea that Mesquakis view their land as a "place of safety, a refuge, a permanent home," not as "something from which to earn a living" like the white-man. Gearing goes on:

> We keep the land in one piece, owned by the tribe, and any of us can build a home here and find room for a garden or get a few acres to farm if he wants. But no one can sell the land and the land will always be here for everyone. We like our land just as it is. The trees are good, the river is good and the hills are good. OUR LAND WAS NOT BOUGHT TO BE USED. It was bought just to be there for us, always. (Fox Project fieldnotes, Box 4)

The image one gets is that no one squabbles over or uses settlement land as a productive resource. Land is there to be used by all as they see fit. Given the Mesquakis high-minded spiritual and communal view of land, its use is decided as easily as water flows down hills. In real life there are, of course, titanic struggles over who farms what, who lives where, who cuts down what tree, and who gets what piece of land. This essay presents a very idyllic view of how present-day Mesquakis use their lands.

The fifth essay, "How our poverty isn't really grinding," extends this image of the nonmaterialistic, nonentrepreneurial Mesquaki through a discussion of their views on money and houses:

> Out here no one spends a lot of money on things he really doesn't need like some people do, just to "Keep up with the Joneses." If a Mesquaki tried that everyone

would be angry with him for trying to be a "big shot" better than others. So we don't build houses bigger than we need, or fancier; our houses are just places to sleep. We think generosity is very important; it is one of the marks of a truly good man. So a Mesquaki always is doing things for his relatives and friends. If someone dies, we always help out the family. If a man is temporarily out of a job we help him out. (Fox Project fieldnotes, Box 4)

The tenth essay, "What the powwow really is," continues this portrayal of Mesquakis all working together harmoniously to celebrate their culture. "Even if we didn't make a cent there would still be a powwow." The powwow is a joyful homecoming, but this portrayal is a little too harmonious and happy. Organizing the powwow is always a huge, conflictful ordeal. Money is always short, and many people who volunteer to help never show up. And nearly every year there is controversy over missing money from last year's powwow committee. Somehow things always get done, and to the pleasure of everyone, a powwow always happens, but it is never all gentle, smiling harmony.

Another narrative tactic Gearing uses to convey this image is by telling stories with animal characters. Essay twelve, "Nature stories," tells the story of the gentle, honest, noble bear who eventually has to box the ears of the gossipy, rude, deceitful rabbit. In the end the rabbit loses his beautiful looks to pay for his meanness to the bear. In essay three, "A story that is sometimes told," an adventurous hunter, Mantoka, trades a blind old man his eyes for the blind man's hut and beautifully painted magic bag full of buffalo meat and venison. After a time the greedy young hunter falls in the river and becomes cold and miserable until the old man trades back his eyes. Ultimately, both find out that they cannot be the other and that what is good for one man is not necessarily good for the other.

Finally, the image of the harmonious, generous Mesquaki is taken to even greater extremes in essay fifteen, "How our ethics are different and should never change." Gearing waxes on in the following way:

We have ethics, for instance, that are not just like the whiteman's. It would not be progress to change those. YOU NEVER SEE TWO MESQUAKIES ARGUING VIOLENTLY WITH ONE ANOTHER OR CALLING EACH OTHER NAMES. Another thing about our ethics that most people don't know about is that WE DO NOT LIKE OUR PEOPLE TO PUSH THEMSELVES FORWARD, TO BE "BIG SHOTS," even if they do it for the benefit of the tribe. White people sometimes think this kind of behavior shows a "lack of ambition." That is not so. If you disagree with another man you must tell him in a round-about way or tell his sister so that she can tell him. Another thing, OUR PEOPLE DO NOT LIKE A PERSON THAT TALKS TOO MUCH. There is no such thing as "small talk" among us. We do not feel uncomfortable if we sit with each other in silence for long periods. These are the ways which make it possible for us to live together in harmony. (Fox Project fieldnotes, Box 4)

Caught him !
Stereotyping !

It is true that Mesquakis are circumspect and careful about publicly insulting each other. They can also be quite taciturn. And they dislike braggarts. Mesquakis do tend to communicate in a quiet, circumspect way. They are not as showy, loud, and aggressive as many of my urban white friends are. One would never mistake them for the emotional, fast-talking, urban Italian and Jewish characters of TV and cinema.

On the other hand, the sharp tongue of Jenny EagleFeather and the quick wit of Jerimiah Jangles does not fit easily into action anthropologists' "modal personality" portraits. The problem with these kinds of global portrayals of an entire culture is they leave out more than they describe. Where is all the face-to-face arguing that goes on in council meetings, homes, sports events, and so forth? Where is all the gossiping, joking, and horsing around that Mesquakis do? In the end such sweeping portrayals make Mesquakis seem a bit like silent, stoic cigar-store Indians.

Perhaps these liberal-minded anthropologists wanted to counter racism so badly that they exaggerated Mesquaki virtues. Their desire to replace negative images with positive images comes through in many essays. Essay fourteen, "Wardship. What it is and isn't," attacks negative white stereotypes about the special federal privileges that Indians supposedly get:

Yes we pay taxes. Yes we are subject to federal and state laws. No we don't get a monthly government hand out. Yes the government has a treaty obligation to protect our land and to provide educational and health services. (Fox Project fieldnotes, Box 4)

Three other essays on the tribal school counter local white views of the need to assimilate the Mesquakis. Finally, essay thirteen, "Why it is necessary to keep most of our traditional ways to progress," even critiques the newly elected tribal council. This essay must have been the final straw for Tribal Chairman Davenport. It sounds like a plea for returning to the hereditary chieftainship.

When Gearing and I talked, he wondered aloud what people thought of his book. Many Mesquakis remembered Gearing and other students fondly, but few had read the book. Fewer still volunteered their opinions of *Face of the Fox* (1970). Several white teachers searching for information on Mesquakis found it dry and difficult to read. Old-time white leaders remembered the newspaper series as stories about animals and the school battle. Hearing these vague recollections and seeing the disappointment on Gearing's face shook my confidence a little. I could imagine my own efforts disappearing in a great void of indifference.

Another academic portrayal of Mesquaki culture that Mesquakis liked, or at least found amusing, is Fredrick McTaggart's *Wolf That I Am* (1976). McTaggart would probably object to the idea that he ever intended a "scientific" study of culture. His aim — to collect some winter stories, thus verifying the survival of Mesquaki core culture — was far more modest than those of other anthropologists who came to the settlement. McTaggart was actually a doctoral student in English; so doing a study of Native American folklore was a marginal, undervalued activity in his department. Nevertheless he did find two sympathetic faculty members, so he set off on his great adventure to record sacred Mesquaki winter stories.

His book is a beautifully written account of how the Mesquakis politely but firmly refused to share their winter stories. Previous investigators — Mesquaki anthropologist William Jones (1907) and Smithsonian anthropologist Truman Michelson (1910–1930) — had already recorded many winter stories. Consequently, McTaggart wanted to find out whether Mesquakis still told these stories, and if so, whether they still told them in the same way. He admits there was no original thesis being tested, no discovery of new texts expected. What his project boiled down to was a fascination with "Indian literature." Like recent literary scholars (Krupat, 1989), he wanted to show that Native American oral traditions were sophisticated forms of storytelling or "literature." In addition, he was also fascinated with Indians as a source of personal wisdom and self-knowledge. So McTaggart's adventure is part formal academic project and part personal quest for knowledge.

I found Mesquakis' views of McTaggart's book particularly intriguing. Several agreed that, "It is a good book, but it doesn't say very much new about Mesquakis." Claude Windsong used the book to lecture me on the ethics of studying Mesquakis. For Claude, McTaggart was a sensitive white who showed respect for Mesquaki religious beliefs. He did not get his story, but, unlike other greedy white researchers, he was gracious in defeat. McTaggart ended up writing a self-parody of his futile efforts to "study the Mesquaki." He portrayed himself as the foolish, relentless wolf. The wolf did not know the difference between green-corn-dumplings and dung. Yet he still tried to feed off the clever, elusive Mesquaki. In effect, McTaggart has written a story not unlike a classic Indian "trickster tale" (Vizenor, 1990). In his trickster tale the wise and wily Mesquakis outwit the greedy, stupid academic looking for his pot of cultural gold.

To understand the moral implications of this tale, one has to remember that journalists and academics have replaced the white pony soldiers. Whites took most of the land; now they are after this strange thing called "authentic culture" or "ancient wisdom." Now they come searching for genuine cultural artifacts and for juicy, exotic stories. The white intruders have traded in their Gatling guns and repeater rifles for cameras and tape recorders, but they still come looking for what they do not have. Still relentless. Still attacking. Still greedy. But McTaggart is one white who had his tape recorder silenced, and the Mesquakis let him live to tell his trickster tale and honor them. Historian Jonas CutCow may not list this among Mesquaki military victories, but it is a victory in the war with white portrait-makers.

Some observers of American culture argue that we desperately need positive portraits of Indian cultures. Now that we have destroyed many Indian cultures, liberal-minded whites feel what Rosaldo (1989) aptly calls "imperialist nostalgia." We are a little like the huge, ignorant one-eyed cyclops of Greek mythology. We have begun to wonder a little about what we have crushed. Maybe the Indians were not so bad. Maybe we can learn something from them. Maybe we should send in the journalistic and academic scavengers to salvage what is left.

My only beef with McTaggart is that he sounds a little too breathless and romantic about Indians. His scholarly quest thwarted, the personal quest for spiritual understanding comes to the fore. Especially in the dissertation, he is very effusive about how the Mesquakis taught him to be more gentle, wise, and human. Such a claim may well be true, but this white literary trope is wearing a little thin. Literary, bohemian, counter-culture types and anthropologists have long used "Indian spirituality" to criticize white civilization as morally corrupt and to extoll their experiences with Indians as spiritual growth (Berkhofer, 1978).

Finally, art historians Gaylord Torrence and Robert Hobbs (1989) have produced what has become the standard reference on Mesquaki art. Their book presents stunning color photos of 110 pieces of traditional Mesquaki wood carvings, sculpture, rush mats, bead work, bags, sashes, and ribbon applique from far-flung collections. These pieces were assembled from over fifty private and museum collections as a first-ever Mesquaki art exhibition at the University of Iowa museum. The show attracted record crowds that included nearly 300 Mesquakis on opening day.

One of the most interesting aspects of this project was what Torrence, a Drake University professor, did to assure tribal cooperation. First, he had a group of six religious elders determine whether any pieces could not be displayed for religious reasons. They also advised how to display the objects. In addition, the religious leaders smoked and purified the pieces before they were displayed. Finally, to assure the maximum tribal access to the exhibit and opening-day symposium, money was raised from private donors and the Iowa Arts Council to sponsor the buses, feast, and speakers. These donors also provided the funds to distribute Torrence's and Hobbs's book to every family on the settlement.

Most of the elders who worked on the exhibition praised the project for involving them and for giving whites a positive image of traditional Mesquaki arts. Most Mesquakis I talked to seemed proud of the exhibit and the publication. Nevertheless, a few of the younger artists like Ted

Pipestar were critical of the exhibit (DMR, January 29, 1989). Ted wanted the exhibit organizers to use some of the grant money to support the work of contemporary Mesquaki artists. Moreover, as in the case of all outside programs and grants entering the settlement, there was speculation about how much money the exhibitors raised and whether the organizers profited in any way. Given the history of race relations, such suspicions are probably inevitable, even when the outsiders work with tribal elders extensively. In retrospect, the symposium might have included a public financial statement of the grants received and expenses incurred for producing the exhibit, symposium, feast, and publication.

Gaylord Torrence's portrait of Mesquaki culture places a strong emphasis on the relationship of their art forms to religious beliefs. Native American art is hardly my forte, but his essay seems to provide an excellent historical overview of all the various Mesquaki art forms. The essay places the forms within the larger historical context and distinguishes between those art forms that may have been uniquely Mesquaki and those that were shared with neighboring woodland and plains tribes. The essay also hints at how twentieth-century pan-Indian styles have become popular and concludes with the judgment that "the great age of Mesquaki art ended with the nineteenth century."

Robert Hobbs's essay elaborates the importance of outside white and twentieth-century, pan-Indian influences on Mesquaki art. He seeks to portray nineteenth-century Mesquaki artists as innovative in their use of designs from nearby Scandinavian immigrants. In a highly speculative piece, Hobbs claims that the embroidered skirts from the west coast of Norway were probably the inspiration for the curvilinear beadwork designs of Mesquakis. He also sees the influence of Scandinavian sweater and sock designs on Mesquaki bags, and of Scandinavian horseheads on Mesquaki wood carvings. Finally, Hobbs argues that late nineteenth-century Mesquaki clothing may have used the beadwork designs on Victorian dresses and the ribbon work on European folk clothes as a springboard for design. In the end, this portrayal of two cultures in contact and a few similar designs inadvertently reads like an assimilationist tract. Despite his efforts to portray "cultural borrowing" as a creative, innovative act, Mesquakis generally read Hobbs as saying they were mere copycats of dominant white art forms.

Early Mesquaki Writers and Cultural Portrait-Makers

Many other whites have written about the Mesquakis, but there is also a long tradition of Mesquakis telling their own story. Krupat (1989) argues that autobiographical accounts of what anthropologists call "life histories" were common from the late nineteenth century on. Initially prominent Indian leaders told their stories to white journalists and anthropologists. Since the post-World War II era, Indians have begun writing their own autobiographies without white academics. One can more or less see these general trends on the Mesquaki settlement.

The earliest Mesquaki to tell his story was Alfred Kiyana. Smithsonian scholars are just beginning to translate and interpret the vast legacy he left (Goddard, 1990). Kiyana wrote approximately 20,000 pages of stories and lore in the Mesquaki syllabary for Truman Michelson. In addition, there are the writings of William Jones, the only Mesquaki anthropologist to date. Jones, an Oklahoma Mesquaki-Sac, collected and translated a number of winter tales (1907). These two writers are well known to a handful of Algonquin scholars, but they never portrayed Mesquaki culture to the general public.

George Youngbear was really the first popular presenter of Mesquaki culture and history. The grandson of Chief Pushetonequa, he was an early graduate of Haskell Institute and quickly became an interpreter for the tribal council in the 1920s. From the 1930s on he was a council member for twenty-four years and the chairman for sixteen years. The Toledo *Chronicle* (March 7, 1929) introduced George as the new editor of Mesquaki Indian news, and he proceeded to write a column for ten years. These columns give some insight into how George portrayed life on the settlement.

Being what whites called a "progressive" and a Christian, George took it on himself to emphasize how rapidly Mesquakis were adopting white ways. One of the most consistent themes in the columns was how the Mesquakis were rapidly taking to farming. George promotes that image in the following article (Toledo *Chronicle*, March 28, 1935):

There is much rejoicing in every Mesquaki home for a good spring, and the Indian farmer is swamped with hundreds of requests for information about horses, seeds, wells, cows and gardens. This shows that Mesquakis are definitely planning to do some real farming.

He also emphasized frequently the importance of handiwork sales and the Mesquakis' devotion to running souvenir stands on the old Lincoln Highway. "Practically every household makes handiwork during the winter months" (Toledo *Chronicle*, Oct 10, 1935). He constantly reassured white readers that the Mesquakis were becoming more business-minded and marketing their unique cultural heritage. The articles on the powwow also stressed how important the agricultural and homemaking exhibits were for promoting the whiteman's ways.

There were many columns portraying Mesquakis celebrating major white holidays. One column (Toledo *Chronicle*, January 2, 1930), entitled

"Indians Appreciate the Christmas Spirit," reassures the readers that "our good white friends have come to us, and all the time we have known them to be our true, humble, understanding friends." He continues with an enthusiastic description of the toys, candy, games and dolls given to the Indian children and concludes that "More than ever the Mesquaki has taken truly the spirit of Christmas just like his white brother." Other columns show the Mesquaki celebrating Thanksgiving Day enthusiastically (Toledo *Chronicle*, December 1, 1938): "The Mesquakis have always been appreciative of things they enjoy to their great spirit and observe sacred Thanksgiving ceremonies. The story of the pilgrims joining their red brothers in praise of the great spirit is well-known by the Mesquakis."

Another frequent theme was the beauty and bountifulness of the settlement. There were reports on maple syrup gathering, trapping, and hunting. George was careful to explain that the syrup was primarly for religious and family use and not for sale. At other times he laments the lack of game in the streams and woods. The overall image is that the Mesquakis still live close to nature and hunt and fish in the old ways.

At times his columns invited whites to come out and enjoy the natural beauty of the settlement. He asks them "to be careful of the young trees and not carry away too many hickory and walnuts, or hit the woods with a rifle and plenty of ammo" (Toledo *Chronicle*, October 10, 1935). In "Ceremonials Begin Sacred Rites on McIntosh Hill" (Toledo *Chronicle*, April 28, 1938), he explains a little about the sacred ceremonies and invites whites to observe them:

So many of our white friends have made inquiries regarding the beautiful Mesquaki sacred ceremonies and their desire to be with their Mesquaki friends. This year of good rain and good prospects for a good crop the Mesquakis to their great spirit, the creator of all things, and the white friends of the Mesquaki are welcome.

In other columns he addresses the touchy issue of whites attending ceremonies. Youngbear usually tries to reassure whites by saying that outsiders can attend Drum Society ceremonies and adoptions. He never directly invites whites — come one, come all — but he does not discourage them either, especially if they attend with Mesquaki friends. He says that whites often find the ancient ceremonies beautiful and impressive. Judging from Youngbear's columns, the tribe were generally more open to having white visitors at adoptions, wakes, and burials than they are today.

Given this attitude, George Youngbear often led tours and school field trips through the settlement. A local teacher remembers the tour and the costume he wore. She said, "George was always in full regalia during the tours," which meant he wore a Sioux warbonnet, a beaded, fringed elk jacket, a porcupine quill bag, and a blanket draped over his arm. During this trip her class visited the McIntosh Hill burial grounds. There George showed them a special circle where many different medicinal plants grew and Mesquakis communed with nature. He said the woods were a place to go when someone wanted to think about his or her problems. He contrasted the serene, quiet Indian to the whites, who were more like noisy, jumpy magpies. He also took them to his house to see his teepee and the handicrafts for sale. During the tour he talked about the Mesquakis' return to Iowa, the history of the powwow grounds, wickiups, and the old Indian sanitarium. By the late 1960s the tribal council outlawed these tours because they disturbed the sacred burial grounds.

Another of George's major activities was giving speeches on Mesquaki history and culture to various church, civic, and educational groups. I was unable to find any tapes of these speeches but did find six newspaper accounts. Since George did hundreds of these presentations, this is an exceedingly small sample. As in the newspaper columns, he was always trying to convey the image that the Mesquakis were open to white ways and progressing rapidly. Everyone went to schools, could read and write English, lived in frame houses, paid taxes, fought in the war, and worked like whites (Ottumwa *Courier*, July 17, 1946). This message was interspersed with historical stories of the return to Iowa, the Black Hawk Wars, how the Mesquakis were misnamed the Fox, and why they were the red earth people.

His talks were also much more autobiographical than the columns. He liked to portray how he was part of the ancient culture as a boy. He frequently painted images of himself sitting in the long house or wigwam before an open fire listening to the elders (TNH, September 30, 1943). The image of his "full regalia" and his accompanying drummers and singers must have given his oral presentations the aura of ancient culture that his written columns lacked. He liked to talk about how every Indian boy aspires to become a warrior and sit in council. How the Mesquaki symbol system uses trees, vines, flowers, and animals while the Sioux use geometric designs. Clearly these presentations were an entertaining mixture of the personal with historical and cultural vignettes.

A Pageant Celebrating White History

The other type of cultural presentation George Youngbear became involved in was county fairs. Perhaps the highlight of his career was Tama County's gala eighty-fifth anniversary celebration. For several days George ran an "Indian village" on the courthouse square. The wickiups displayed arts and craft exhibits, and every afternoon his group performed "ceremonial dances." The celebration also had a papoose show, agricultural and homemaking exhibits, and a grand historical pageant entitled "Iowa Beautiful Land" (Toledo *Chronicle,* July 14, 1938).

This historical pageant, which involved George Youngbear and fifty other Mesquakis, is worth describing in detail. I cannot imagine contemporary Mesquaki leaders, especially those touched by AIM, coming to town and participating in such an event. The pageant, held at the football field, was so popular that it attracted seven thousand people (Toledo *Chronicle,* August 5, 1938). The article says that "the Indians, who are natural born actors, were the main attraction." They appeared in many of the major scenes and enactments.

The pageant, called a great "romance of the prairies" starts with Marquette and Joliet smoking the peace pipe to the accompaniment of tom-toms. As the explorers and Indians depart, the band plays "Waters of Minnetonkoa." Scene two is the burning of Fort Madison. The whites are only building a trading center, but the Indians say they are frightening the game, building arms to fight, and plotting to take their lands. Lots of fighting ensues, and the whites heroically defend the fort. Then during the war of 1812 and after a "barbarous siege of seven days, the soldiers burn the fort rather than leave it for the Indians." Shades of the Alamo story that Texans love to tell!

In episode three, entitled "Iowa," the story of the return of the Indians from Kansas and the rise of Iowa as a progressive state is reenacted. Banished to Kansas, the homesick Mesquakis yearn for their beloved Iowa River and Tama County. The generous white settlers and wise Iowa governor let the Indians return if they promise to live in peace. Early pioneer life is then portrayed in colorful detail. This part portrays horse thievery, notorious outlaws, Indians peacefully bartering with pioneers, the first train, and the coming of new industry. Finally, the pageant ends in a flourish of patriotism and pride in the land and Iowa. The St. Patrick's Church priest and forty young men and women plant a cross, build an altar, and say thanks for the bounty and blessings of the rich fertile Iowa land. Meanwhile their Indian neighbors look on approvingly.

The pageant never bothers to say what happened to the Mesquakis. One is left feeling that they must have been happy to assimilate into this white paradise called Iowa. George Youngbear and Ed Davenport, who ran an all-Indian marching band, had reorganized the Mesquaki political system into a white-style, elected government in 1937. A year later these Mesquaki tribal council leaders were willing to put up an "Indian village" on the Tama County square, play street band concerts, have their children judged in papoose contests, and play subservient parts in the county historical pageant. Little wonder the merchants of this era long for the good old days. Tribal political leaders like Youngbear and Davenport were quite accommodating to them.

Yet, in fairness, George Youngbear was hardly the subservient assimila-tionist that some Oldbear traditionalists claimed. True, he had his lapses when he guided tours through the burial grounds, extolled adopting white ways, and helped stage a white version of Mesquaki history. Never-theless, the Fox Project fieldnotes show him expressing more critical atti-tudes than he usually expressed in his diplomatic columns and speeches. Although no AIM radical, he always challenged overt white racism, and he fought the BIA school closing vigorously. Moreover, his speeches in-cluded touching stories about racial fears, like the time he convinced a boy at camp not to fear Indians (DMR, March 29, 1961). He took the boy into the woods and told him that a whirlpool of leaves was the wind dancing the way all nature dances. He explained that when the Indian moves his arm in dancing he is imitating birds in flight, or butterflies. In his own gentle, accommodating way, George Youngbear consistently fought for Mesquaki civil rights

The Cartoonist, Letter-to-the-Editor Writer Extraordinaire

Perhaps the loudest and funniest Mesquaki voice in the popular press of the 1970s was that of Ernest TrueTongue. When I finally caught Ernest at his apartment near the tribal center, he saw me through the screen door. I had never seen him, so I asked, "Is Ernest TrueTongue here?"

He responded in a matter-of-fact tone, "No, he took off for Chicago last night. He went to see the Tyson fight."

"Oh, I'm sorry to bother you. Will you leave him a message that Doug Foley came by. I'm an anthropologist from the University of Texas? I wanted to talk to him."

"What do you want from him? People say he's an old windbag who doesn't know anything. Nobody ever listens to him."

At the time I though this was a self-deprecating comment. But after hearing several Mesquakis actually call him an "old windbag," and an "obstructionist" (of progress), I realized Ernest was just being honest about what some of his people say. For some he is a highly respected religious elder. For others he is an old faker who glorifies Indian ways yet partakes in modern things like everyone else: "If that guy is so big on the old ways, maybe he'll give me his new trailer. I could use his color T.V., too."

When I visited Ernest I had no idea what he believed or what his people thought of him. His letters-to-the-editor intrigued me, so I re-sponded, "Well, uh, I came across lots of his letters when I was going through the old newspapers, and somebody told me he published a book of jokes and drawings. I just wanted to talk to him about his writings."

That seemed to satisfy him, so he said smiling, "Sit down, sit down. I'm Ernest. What do you want to talk about?"

As we began to talk he pulled out the Zielinski book and said it was a "goody-goody book that showed everything nice." He was goading me into saying that I would write about the real stuff. So he quickly launched into a stinging criticism of the council for pushing gaming so hard. In response I said, "Now I can see why some people consider you a gadfly or troublemaker. You definitely speak your mind." He bristled at my using the troublemaker label, and said that he speaks the facts, not opinions.

For several years he wrote long, passionate, rambling letters to the Tama *News Herald* on tribal politics. These letters were probably the first open, frank commentary on Mesquaki politics ever published. The issue that launched his letters-to-the editor career was trees. In the early 1970s the tribal council sold a stand of walnut trees near the river to white loggers. Ernest — back from a hectic life of powwowing and working construction and factory jobs in Chicago and Los Angeles — was just settling down into Mesquaki ceremonial life. He was shocked that the council would cut down sacred trees. They were acting like whitemen by putting money over spiritual matters.

Another fascinating aspect of his letters was that he called whites "pilgrims" and Indians "savages." Several whites and Mesquakis scoffed at these terms and said they were neither funny nor made any sense. When I asked Ernest to define these terms, he explained that the idea came from his favorite authors, Mark Twain and Will Rogers. According to Ernest, Twain once joked that whites think they are less savage than the rest of the savages. Rogers also said that whites make war and call it progress. Playing off these thoughts, Ernest often ended his letters with a story about "civilized whites" doing savage things to "savage Indians," or "savage Indians" taking up uncivilized "civilized" white practices. Apparently his ironic play with these labels escaped many local readers.

Ernest's monthly *News Herald* letters usually lambasted the council for poor record-keeping, lack of public disclosures on claims monies, corruption in assigning new houses, improper audits, and incompetence in installing the new water line. BIA policies were also a frequent target. Some whites also have a difficult time understanding this commentary. Some mistake him for an AIM radical. Others think his message is the same as that of white journalists — that Mesquaki politics are corrupt and inefficient. What white readers miss is that Ernest speaks as an Oldbear traditionalist. He wants to abolish the elected, white-style tribal council and return to a divinely ordained hereditary monarchy. For Ernest, the Mesquaki political troubles began when the so-called Youngbear faction convinced the tribe to adopt an elected government in 1937. His letters-to-the-editor keep alive a very old Mesquaki political controversy.

The Case of the Missing Mesquaki Treaty

What is also unclear in Ernest's letters is how his commentary fuels a conspiracy theory of Mesquaki politics. One of the most fantastic stories I heard circulating on the settlement is about a missing treaty that would compensate the tribe for bad treaties signed in the early 1800s. According to traditionalists, the Sac chiefs who represented the Mesquakis in 1804, 1832, and 1840 gave away Mesquaki lands too easily and cheaply. The story goes that these false chiefs made bad treaties that the government and history books say are the Mesquaki treaties.

Ernest and other traditionalists firmly believe that the real hereditary Mesquaki chiefs signed a wise and favorable treaty with the federal government. Unfortunately, the federal government keeps this treaty hidden because it would cost a fortune to honor it. So when Ed Davenport's "progressive" tribal council joined the Sacs in a land claims case in the 1950s, the federal government was delighted. The government only had to pay the Mesquakis a pittance (seven million dollars) of what they had promised in the real Mesquaki treaty. For Oldbear traditionalists, the hidden treaty proves the wisdom of the hereditary chief. It is also a tale of tribal redemption that holds out the promise of justice and fair compensation — if only the missing treaty would appear and be honored.

All this is known to Ernest and other traditionalists by oral tradition. It was also reaffirmed in 1948 when Bertha Waseskuk of the Oldbear faction apparently found an old treaty in Washington, D.C. Others believe that the Mesquaki copy of the treaty has passed from heir to heir in the Oldbear family. If this is so, why have the Oldbears never stepped forward with this treaty and pressed their claims in the courts? The answer to this question is where the secret treaty story gets very murky. Some say that Bertha and a white lawyer put the treaty in a safety deposit box in a Des Moines bank. Others say that another well-known traditionalist has hidden the treaty in a Waterloo bank. Most say that the government would never honor the treaty anyway. It is said that one of the president's assistants trembled when presented with the treaty. Only great chiefs and presidents are supposed to handle it.

When Ernest criticizes his tribal government in white newspapers, he speaks a very old Mesquaki political discourse. This type of political criticism has very little to do with white reformist talk about graft and corruption. A much deeper moral principle is being addressed. Mesquakis expect whites to lie to them and hide a treaty that would cost whites money. But for any Mesquaki to hide the treaty from the tribe is a profound breach in the sacred pact the red earth people have with their creator; consequently, this moralistic political discourse about the missing sacred treaty continues to cause considerable ill-feeling among tribal members.

Some people tell the story of the missing Mesquaki treaty to indict whoever they believe is hiding the document. I have no idea how true the secret treaty story is, but the survival of this tale illustrates the continuing political discontent that Oldbear traditionalists express.

In short, Ernest is definitely not giving whites a "goody-goody" view of Mesquaki politics. He is expressing a no-holds-barred, religious critique of Mesquaki politicians who have drifted from their divine origins. He and others who wield this discourse seek to renew and revitalize the divine force of Mesquaki culture. Probably none of this makes much sense to the average white because our politics and political figures are so thoroughly secular. Earlier white political figures like Puritan fundamentalist Cotton Mather denounced the secular politicians and government of his times in a manner similar to that of Ernest. But unlike white fundamentalists like Mather or Pat Robertson, Ernest has a sense of humor and a greater tolerance of religious diversity.

The tolerant, funny side of Ernest comes out in his book of drawings and cartoons entitled *Larry Andy People Fun Book* (1986). This delightful collection is his gentle, ironic commentary on coping with the contradictions of being a modern Indian. Mesquakis are constantly confronted with stereotypic popular culture images of Indians. Ernest's commentaries and cartoons are his way of dealing with these contradictions and images. As he says, "You need a good sense of humor to survive as an Indian." Two of my favorites are shown in Figures 2 and 3 on the next two pages, and should convey some of his perspective.

The Mesquaki National Literary Treasure

"A national treasure" is how UNI professor of Native American literature Robert Gish describes Ted Pipestar. But the average Tama white and Mesquaki are not always sure what to make of Ted's writings. Several whites told me, "It's too deep for me. I don't know what the hell he is trying to say." The commentaries of my old schoolmates, whom I considered literate and intelligent enough to understand Ted's books, confused me. Was this white denial of a strong, critical Indian voice? Or was it just mental laziness to read serious poetry and prose? For whatever reason, not all white and Mesquakis readers shared the enthusiasm of Douglas Glover (Los Angeles *Times*, April 12, 1992). His glowing review of Ted's autobiographical novel (1992) characterizes him as follows:

He is a dancer at the world's rim, a fan dancer, for he conceals as much as he reveals of himself and his people. As an Indian who sets himself up as an author in the white sense, Pipestar is freighted with a terrible dual responsibility: to satisfy his readers that he is being truthful and informative, and to satisfy his personal

"Towards the ending of the smoke signal, it says there is forest burning."

Everybody has sign languages and signals that can be sent via a distance using lights, mirrors, etc., this without sounds. So was the Indian able to send sign signals or messages in certain ways, one of them I hear was by puffs of smoke, using fire and a blanket. A few years ago in Chicago, some Indians were trying to do a demonstration of Indian smoke signaling and their blanket caught on fire. I don't know. (TrueTongue, 1986)

Figure 2. From Ernest TrueTongue, *Larry Andy People Funny Book*. Used by permission.

---

and tribal need for secrecy. This process of becoming a writer fascinates Edgar [Ted], who sees himself wrapped in a paper cocoon, changing, altering, saving himself from the usual fates of a reservation Indian. Learning to translate between worlds redeems him, though with redemption comes alienation and survivor's guilt, since he must separate himself from the normal communal life of his people.

I tend to agree with Glover's appraisal of Ted as a fan dancer living at the world's rim. In fashionable anthropological jargon, he lives in a "cultural borderland" and goes back and forth from Dylan and the Doors to the Mesquaki creation story, from the sixties drug culture to the joys and indignities of being an "Indian." He calls his latest book a collage of

"It says here, WARNING: The Surgeon General has determined that smoking this is dangerous to your health."

Smoking is, I reckon, dangerous to one's health, but I do know it is getting to be one expensive habit. I don't indulge, I would rather buy some cheese and crackers and bologna and have a meal, than blow smoke in the air. Am not making fun of no one, more power to those who smoke. Indian tobacco is considered sacred by most tribes in the States. I respect. (TrueTongue, 1986)

Figure 3. From Ernest TrueTongue, *Larry Andy People Funny Book*. Used by permission.

experiences. Indeed it is, and the book leaves in its wake the postmodern "narrative experiments" in my field. Unlike our little forays into other cultures, his "fieldwork" spans forty years, involves real matters of the heart, and is written in blood.

As I write these glowing words of praise, I am reminded of my conversation with Ted about postmodernism. After his new book came out, he asked me why a literary critic called his writing "postmodern." Because I am a professor, he probably figured that such esoteric jargon was my forte. As I babbled a few inanities about "a revolt against old forms and assumptions," my ears rang with pedantry. Here I was giving a useless academic definition to a guy who actually does what literary critics only theorize. So I stopped my little lecture abruptly and said, "Look, Ted, nobody really knows what it means, and if you knew, it surely wouldn't make you a better writer." Being only vaguely interested, he registered no protest and, mercifully, the conversation moved on.

What follows is a brief vignette of this gifted writer — some of his remembrances, how he portrays his people, and a few local reactions to his book. Hopefully, this portrait conveys how hard it is to be an artist in a cultural borderland. Being an anthropologist, I label Ted an "organic intellectual" (Gramsci, 1971), that is, a homegrown, self-made intellectual who owes more to his tribal roots than to the culture of white academia. After getting his first essay in seventh grade ruthlessly red-penciled, "This is a poem, not an essay on a day in your life!" Ted vowed to master English and become a writer. This self-acclaimed underachiever "found school boring," however. He finally got some encouragement to write in Luther College's summer Upward Bound program for minorities. The poems he wrote in the program won him a scholarship to prestigious Pomona College near Los Angeles.

After considerable campus high-jinks (Pipestar, 1992), he entered the snake pits of constructive criticism called creative writing programs, first at Pomona and later at the University of Iowa. Since then he has been in and out of white universities and heard enough "crude racist jokes" and seen enough fights over copying machine privileges to prefer catfishing in the Iowa River. But "academic gigs pay pretty good," so he has done semester teaching stints at various state universities. Despite his formal education — or perhaps to spite formal education — Ted has become a writer's writer. He is well known and highly regarded in the field of Native American Literature (Gish, Des Moines *Register*, March 1, 1992). In short, he is a self-made writer who portrays a strange cultural borderland that few whites understand.

If he were a white, he would surely be Iowa's great Horatio Alger story and new literary hero. But he is not Robert Waller, the former UNI business school dean who wrote *The Bridges of Madison County* and became a talk show celebrity. Although Doonsberry cartoonist Gary Trudeau has never seen the life-sized photo of Waller hanging in the business school, he has Waller and his trashy love story pegged. In stark contrast, Ted Pipestar lives in a little trailer and is mislabeled a "Native American writer." Unlike Waller, Ted will only break into the mainstream when some liberal like Robert Redford makes a movie of his book, or when university literary critics decide that Native American literature is simply good literature. Like most minority writers (Saldivar, 1990), he is up against the literary preferences of the mainstream mass media and the literary conventions of English departments. If he were a white like W. P.

Kinsella, who also writes about Indians, the University of Iowa's renowned writers' workshop would have featured him long ago.

Like his people, Ted comes and goes in the white world and takes from it what interests him. In return, he gives whites many poetry readings and drum performances. He exhibits his wood carvings and the works of other friends and family in museums. He writes an occasional journalistic essay and has even done a radio talk show. Ted is tirelessly out there representing his people and fielding questions about whether his people still live in teepees and eat deer meat. He also occasionally does battle with the white editors and art collectors and patrons who claim to be promoting Native American arts (DMR, January 29, 1989). To the state bigwigs in Iowa arts, this national literary treasure can be prickly and contentious.

And what about his life on the settlement? Do most Mesquakis consider him a national literary treasure? Or, to use my stilted academic phrase, an organic intellectual? I did no systematic scientific survey, so my portrayal is plucked from bits and pieces of opinion. My impression is that Mesquakis are generally proud of Ted's accomplishments in the white world, but as one traditionalist said, "It is fine that he publishes books that the whiteman likes, but when he becomes more involved in our ceremonies, he will become someone important here."

This is not to say that Ted is uninvolved in settlement life. He has taught creative writing at the tribal school. He has helped write grants and has tried, without much tribal council support, to develop a museum and artists' workshop. His idea is to give other practicing Mesquaki artists a permanent place to produce, exhibit, and sell their works. He has a particular passion for promoting all Mesquaki arts, from traditional to contemporary forms. His efforts to raise money from foundations and corporations would probably merit a good citizen's award in white society. He does not, however, participate in the clan ceremonies and is critical of some religious leaders for not living up to a higher moral standard.

Since Mesquaki society places little importance on individuals excelling in the arts, there is considerable gossip about Ted getting grants to feed himself; about Ted writing books that use tribal lore to make money; about Ted organizing museum exhibits to promote himself. Whatever pride the tribe has about his accomplishments seems laced with envy about his books, his drum group, and his workshop-museum plan. What such criticism overlooks is the tribal recognition that his writing and conferences generate, the performance fees he shares with others, and the personal money he spends taking Mesquaki students to plays, museums, and science fairs.

And what about his status in the local white community? What does

"Why Cheer," his pseudonym for my hometown, think of Ted Pipestar? A number of liberal-minded local teachers hold Ted in awe. The English teacher was hesitant to give an opinion about the literary merits of his poetry. She was almost reverential. The elementary school teacher who watched him teach children says, "He is wonderful with kids. So patient, and they really look up to him." The high school counselors extolled his impact as a role model for Native Americans. They all feared that their Iowa Arts Council writer-in-residence would become too famous to have time for them. Whether they understood his poetry or not, most whites were respectful of anyone who is literate and published. Nevertheless, a few complained that he probably only got it published because he was an Indian, "You know, more of that affirmative action stuff." Lots of varied opinion, generally favorable, with less envy and jealousy than in the Mesquaki community.

In short, being an artist on the Mesquaki settlement can sometimes be a lonely, unforgiving pursuit. Listening to local comments on his new novel was a sobering experience. I thought the local reviews of his book often missed the point of such a novel. From my perspective a terrific book has finally broken with the earlier culture of poverty and noble savage portrayals. But as we shall see in the following comments, his new novel is too realistic for readers brought up on highly negative and overly romantic views of Indians.

A Modern Portrayal of Mesquaki Culture and Race Relations

Unlike earlier Mesquaki voices, Ted Pipestar has already produced a body of writings that deserves a careful reading. One day soon doctoral students in literature will be picking his literary bones. They will write detailed textual commentaries that will make my remarks seem cursory. Worse still, I have fast-forwarded through his dense, rich poetry to focus on his autobiographical novel. For an insider's view of the settlement and its white neighbors, his new novel is a must.

One thing that threw many local readers is the narrative form of Ted's novel. In some places it looks like prose with marked characters and dialogue. But often Ted narrates in a free verse form of prose-poetry. Unfortunately, some readers could not get beyond the poetic-looking format. Instead of relaxing and reading it as a series of short stories with vivid characters and events, some were "scared of all that deep symbolism stuff." Perhaps some Tamaites were taught that poetry is not what normal, red-blooded Americans read. Getting too near poetry makes ordinary folks break out in hives. That stuff is for sissies and snobs, not men and women of action.

Or maybe Ted's anger and surrealistic imagination is what made some readers anxious. This is no "goody-goody" portrayal of life on the settlement and relations between the races. In the novel, Edgar, the young artist, grows up under the loving wing of his wise grandmother, but outside her haven he experiences strange things and people. His comic portrayals of run-ins with local rednecks and half-breed "hyenas" are angry and satirical. Youthful excitement, boredom, exuberant camaraderie, desperate aimlessness, wild hormonal rushes, and anger are all rolled up in one torrent of words and images. For whites steeped in the classics, it is Dante's *Divine Comedy* Indian-style. A cultural borderland with more than a few potholes in the road, but a road to be traveled and searched for meaning.

Take for example the story of Claude Youthman, who is sent to the pen for throwing cantaloupes at state officials. Claude drops out of school and stays away from the ceremonies in an attic reading about Hollywood heroes Audie Murphy and Liz Taylor. Born an oily-haired, fish-lipped hunchback, he goes off to prison with his shriveled aboriginal self in a Kinney shoe box. There he studies cathedral structures, and a priest gives him an art book; so he masters pointillism and paints the Gray Indian Series, 365 days of color in prison light without humanity. Bingo! *Life* magazine gives him a few minutes of fame. An article entitled "From Cantaloupes to Cathedrals" chronicles his noble climb from prisoner to prison artist.

Eventually, Claude gets out of the pen and returns to the poverty and apathy of the settlement. This makes him want to fight the Mesquaki establishment. At first the tribal council and the people accept him — until he likens tribal politics to a party of children bursting balloons. Claude portrays envious, falsely-elected leaders as busily popping each other's balloons without knowing why. Eventually he loses his new-found political zeal and becomes a disillusioned art instructor at the tribal school. Unfortunately, Weeping Willow tribal school is a snake pit of gossip and stupidity that gobbles up its most professional Mesquaki teachers. Ted goes on to give a savage portrayal of unprofessionalism and wagging tongues at the health clinic as well.

And then there is the character called Ted Facepaint. Ted is Edgar's cultural mirror. He shows Edgar where he has been and why he must reaffirm his Indian heritage. Ted is a street-wise high school buddy of many a drinking, fighting, girl-chasing adventures in the town of Why Cheer. He also goes off to California and helps Edgar taste the fruits of the sixties — ethnic militants, drug-tripping, and a little existential philosophizing. But when the will to stay runs out, the budding poet Edgar flies home on a poetry gig. This leaves Ted to hitchhike alone on a hellish trip through the desert.

Ted survives the desert by doing in a pathetic old white guy. The white guy wants to die, so Ted obliges, bashes him with a Pepsi bottle, and takes his left-over pork chop and a few bucks. Later a state highway patrolman peels Ted off the baking desert sand and drives him to the bus stop. He buys a pair of cut-offs, thongs, and a Hawaiian shirt and drifts back to dreary Why Cheer. He ends up being assaulted by three half-breed Indians in Halloween masks and lands on an emergency room table. The masked destroyers have busted Ted's arm and punctured his ribs with a sharpened screwdriver. A long-live-George-Bush-spouting, racist doctor patches him up with the help of Gita, a shapely Danish nurse. Ted then wanders back to the good care of medicine woman Rose Grassleggings and begins finding his way. Ted's story ends with his dreaming about a spotted eagle who is testing his mending wing and flying away.

Although Ted's redemption from his directionless life is just a dream, another major character's redemption is real. Junior Pipestar, a second-generation Ontario, and his family were exiled to the Iowa heartland in 1916. The Pipestar family was driven from their village when Junior's grandfather had an affair with the daughter of a notorious medicine man. In a rage the angry medicine man uses witchcraft to kill off everyone except the Pipestars, who escape to Claer, Iowa. Junior lives on a farm in Claer and frequents the Black Eagle Child settlement. He joins in on the wild, youthful adventures of Edgar and Ted, but eventually a feeling compels him to hitchhike to his real home. There he does an apprenticeship with a medicine man and "detoxes" himself of longings for cokes, burgers, TV switches, cars, alcohol, and the tanned bodies of white girls. As prophesied, he returns to learn the ancient ways so he can pass them on to others.

As Glover's review so eloquently puts it, Edgar's writing saves him. He never quite descends to the cultural wasteland of his major characters. Although Edgar is constantly tasting the white world, its ways are as unsatisfying as the pathetic dinners he has with his professor benefactor and dull wife. Writing is his momentary salvation, but he longs for something less fleeting and less white. The cocoon of paper that sometimes engulfs him seems more a trap than a source of regeneration. Consequently, Edgar is greatly influenced by the old stories of his grandmother and by unknown spiritual forces. One gets the feeling that the frightening spirit-lights will inexorably lead the author back to the ancient ceremonies.

Ted Pipestar's anguished yet loving Mesquaki-based portrayal of modern Indian life has no precedent. This is not George Youngbear in a Sioux warbonnet talking about Indians adopting modern white ways. Nor is it anthropologist Fred Gearing talking about the gentle, circumspect, noble traditional Indian. Ted portrays life on this cultural borderland as like walking on a tightrope without a net. Some Mesquakis descend into incest, drunkenness, and despair. Others go off into the white world and get degrees. They return to battle envy and despair and help the settlement stagger on. Others find redemption in the old ways. His Mesquakis are full of the contradictions and complexities that make them flawed and human. His poetry (Pipestar, 1980; 1990) contains similar themes, but tends to be more cryptic and lyrical. Ted celebrates the people, animals, and trees around him more than he does in his first novel.

Perhaps it is the biting humor and the flights of surrealism, but some local readers were just not comfortable with Indians portrayed realistically. One young professional couple from a rural, church-oriented background claimed to be sympathetic to Indian issues, but they were offended by the sharp language, drinking, and violence of some characters. "I was disappointed that he used vulgar language." These readers also found the scene of a school board member sucking-off a half-breed hyena very offensive. They exclaimed, "Some people who don't like Indians will read these things and say,' I told you so!' It leaves a bad impression of them and the settlement." These whites wanted a more dignified portrayal of the Mesquakis and said,

It will be great if he mellows out with age and writes something like Black Elk Speaks. His bitterness worries me. It must be his way of express ing his frustration with life.

In contrast, several of the liberal whites applauded the realism, but still had their doubts. The following person expresses this perspective particularly well:

There is that feeling, we need you for groceries and cigarettes, but we don't wanna mess with you. We are outsiders. That feeling comes across strongly, and I wonder how we will ever get the races together. Too many whites feel that way too. I guess Ted is a man with very traditional values forced to live in the whiteman's society. He is this bridge between the two and does not like it. I worry, too, that the criticism of the tribal council and the portrayals of drinking and drugs will feed whites' stereotypes, and that is scary. Whites are pretty ignorant and unappreciative of Indians. I'm not so sure if this book will help.

Other liberal whites agreed with this assessment. They too feared that a grittier, less romantic view of Indians would not improve the tribe's public image.

Surprisingly, some Mesquaki readers tended to agree. One said, "He shows too much of the drinking and hell-raising out here. He doesn't show any ordinary families and much of normal everyday life. It might reconfirm too many white stereotypes of Indians." In a similar vein, another person worried that "he dwells too much on mysticism and superstitions and peyote. You know, sensational stuff that makes good movies."

Finally, another Mesquaki added, "He doesn't give away any tribal secrets, really, but he is a window to the outside world. What he says will have a big influence on how whites see us."

On the other hand, Mesquakis generally liked the criticisms of racism and the tribal bureaucrats that run the school and health center. Several people said, "He tells it like it is. That is pretty much how I have experienced these things." Nevertheless, some disagreed, and as one person said, "He leaves out what we are trying to do — the positive developments like gaming — and he is too critical of the school and health center. We are doing the best we can."

Despite misgivings about Ted's biting realism and vivid language, everyone, white and Mesquaki alike, agrees that Ted is a "Helluva writer. Says things very strong. Has a way with words. Makes you think." As I said before, being a national literary treasure in a cultural borderland can be a thankless calling.

A Note on Other Realistic Mesquaki Voices

I must close with a brief comment on the writings and public presentations of tribal historian Jonas CutCow, the traditionalist and half-breed guest of the Mesquakis. Jonas is also a new, less accommodating, more realistic Mesquaki voice. He has given many oral history presentations around the state like the one I described in the previous chapter. Unlike Christian assimilationist George Youngbear, Jonas champions the survival of Mesquaki religious and cultural traditions. He always tries to emphasize the strength and perdurance of Mesquaki culture. Having come of age in the turbulent 1970s, he also highlights Mesquaki political resistance and educational self-determination more than George Youngbear did.

As we shall see in the next chapter, Jonas portrays Mesquaki culture more dynamically than white outsiders who are searching for fixed "authentic" cultural objects and traits. He believes that Mesquaki culture changes slowly yet stays the same through the efforts of both "progressives" and "traditionalists." Since the whiteman's arrival, Mesquaki culture has become an ever-changing, complex fusion of Indian and white cultural practices. To break with the earlier static portrayals of Mesquaki culture and politics, we must turn to such matters.

Chapter 5
Borderland Ceremonies and Border-Crossers

A number of American ethnics have begun writing about life in what they call "the cultural borderland" (Anzaldua, 1987; Vizenor, 1990; Hooks, 1992). Anzaldua writes that whenever two or more cultures and races occupy the same territory a psychological, sexual, and spiritual borderland is present. She says,

I am a border woman. I grew up between two cultures. It's not a comfortable territory to live in, this place of contradictions. Hatred, anger and exploitation are the prominent features of this landscape. (1987, preface)

Anthropologists have also begun evoking the cultural borderland metaphor (Rosaldo, 1989; Clifford, 1988). Their definitions of the borderland are never very precise, but it generally refers to a psychological space at the conjuncture of two cultures. A cultural borderland is a contradictory historical situation in which complex cultural identities are produced (Clifford, 1994).

A cultural borderland is also a political space in which ethnic groups actively fuse and blend their culture with the mainstream culture. Eugene Roosen's studies (1989) highlight the cultural struggle that ethnic groups wage between adapting to the dominant society, yet preserving old ways. He calls this creative process of fusion between two cultures "ethnogenesis." From this perspective Mesquaki culture is a highly dynamic, unfixed set of forms and everyday practices being constantly invented and reinvented.

A more traditional, fixed notion of culture would focus on the loss of tradition as a deadly, irreversible process of cultural assimilation. That is how earlier anthropologists talked about Native American cultures. That is how many contemporary Mesquaki traditionalists talk about their culture. They sound the same alarm that traditionalists in the 1940s sounded to earlier anthropologists. They lament collapsing family unity, fewer people at the ceremonies, the gradual decline of spoken Mesquaki. They fear that someday the elders will be unable to conduct the ceremonies in Mesquaki. If that comes to pass, the clan ceremonies will surely disappear and soon the culture will die. Do these lamentations on the imminent death of Mesquaki culture mean that assimilation has finally succeeded?

This is where a dynamic, less fixed notion of culture helps present a more accurate representation of the changes in Mesquaki culture. Although traditionalists often sound pessimistic, they also emphasizes the perdurance of Mesquaki traditions (Claude Windsong, 1978). One young "traditionalist," Jonas CutCow, had a very interesting notion of how his culture was changing as it perdured:

Our culture is a living thing. We don't do the ceremonies exactly the way they were done a hundred or two hundred years ago. We may be doing some things different. Some people who don't come to the ceremonies might say we do it wrong, but we do the best we can. We are trying to keep alive what the creator gave us. I was taught that the tribe has always had conservatives and progressives. We have always had to decide how much of the whiteman's ways we will use. Sometimes we don't bend fast enough, and we hurt ourselves. Others times maybe we give up our old ways too fast, and that hurts us too. The ones who want us to be more modern drag us along, and the ones who are more traditional save what we have. And we are still here.

Jonas is describing Roosen's ethnogenesis concept in lay language. An ethnic group preserves and renews its culture through this life and death struggle with the dominant culture. Traditionalists lament the passing of old practices with a discourse of decline. Conversely, tribal progressives extoll the adoption of new practices with a discourse of renewal. The discursive battle between these two groups actually creates a healthy tension in Mesquaki culture. From that tension and dialogue springs an ever shifting cultural consensus. The tribe is always working out what mainstream educational, political, economic, technical, and artistic forms to borrow.

The result is a rich, dynamic culture rather than a dying, dysfunctional culture. The tribe's creative adoption of mainstream cultural elements remains rooted in ceremonies for worshipping, naming, adopting, mourning, and burial. To capture the complex mix of tradition and innovation, I would like to present a few vignettes of both traditional and modern ceremonies. Having portrayed old and new ceremonies, the chapter ends with a few sketches of mixed-bloods and whites who cross the racial border.

The Anthropological Search for
Traditional Mesquaki Culture

The stubborn survival of Mesquaki religious ceremonies has long fascinated anthropologists. Even action anthropologists, who were dedicated
to helping the Mesquakis change, had a strong impulse, as do most anthropologists, to document ancient cultural traditions. When Sol Tax
studied Mesquaki kinship in the early 1930s, he encountered resentment
against the only anthropologist who ever recorded clan ceremonies, Truman Michelson. In his work for the Smithsonian, Michelson began visiting the settlement on and off from 1910 to 1927. A Boasian-style anthropologist, he collected a vast corpus of native texts on religion and folklore.
His ethnographic portrayals of the bundle pack ceremonies recorded a
number of sacred chants and prayers in great detail. These texts would
satisfy any puerile white curiosity about how puppies are sacrificed and
consumed. Fortunately for the Mesquakis, these revealing texts, although
available in the local libraries, are too technical and tedious to interest
most non-specialists.

The main aspect of Michelson's work that apparently became controversial was his role in the purchase of two sacred bundle packs. According
to Ives Goddard, a Smithsonian anthropologist working on the Michelson papers, one of the packs purchased was a Sac war bundle. There was
little protest over the sale of this bundle, since it was not Mesquaki and
had lost its power. It ended up in a New York museum. The other bundle,
which ended up in the Museum of Natural History in Chicago, was apparently purchased from a youth who had no right to sell it. The purchase of
this pack drew considerable protest from the settlement. In a letter to the
Indian agent, Michelson explains that he merely acted as an intermedi-
ary, not as a purchasing agent. Apparently the packs were taken to a local
harness shop where Mesquakis often pawned their family heirlooms. On
receiving fifty dollars, the owner, Joseph Svacina, sent each museum its
pack.

Whatever Michelson's precise role, the residue of these unfortunate
events greeted Tax when he arrived on the settlement in 1932. As a result,
his student anthropologists arrived on the settlement with explicit instructions to avoid studying these ceremonies. Despite these admoni-
tions, the issue continually pops up in the students' fieldnotes. The initial
group of six students were invited to observe Drum Society and Peyote
ceremonies, but a lingering desire remained to see a sacred clan ceremony. One of the students, Lynn Rich, writes about Peter Morgan inviting them to the Wolf Clan dance as an exciting breakthrough. Instead of
going to the ceremony directly, the young anthropologists decided that

they must bring something. Her description of them frantically trying to find a store open that sold chicken is almost comical. In desperation, they finally bought the chicken from a local restaurant and showed up late for the ceremony.

Her companions, Lloyd Fallers and Walter Miller, report that Wilson Roberts greeted them outside the long house. When the students asked him about going in, Roberts said he did not know whether they should go in. Fallers continues,

Feeling uncomfortable, we wandered to the summer house entrance. Another old man met us and said we should wait outside, the dancing would begin in a little while. (Fox Project fieldnotes, Box 2)

So at first the young anthropologists dutifully sat on the ground near the entrance. They strained to see what was going on inside. Fallers reports that after a time Peattie went to the summer house entrance and beckoned for Wolffson to come in. The others followed, and like an anthropological hunting party, they slipped into the long house and quietly seated themselves on the platform opposite the musicians. The notes describe the sequence of dances, prayers, singing, and eating in some detail. One of the participants waxed enthusiastic: that the long house was

dark and filled with Indians sitting silent and praying, the ceremony was exciting to me. It gave most of us, I think, a quite different idea of the importance of Indian rituals to the Fox. The costumes were in perfect repair. Not a feather out of place and the colors brilliant. (Fox Project fieldnotes, Box 2)

The notes convey an intense feeling of exhilaration and discovery. At last the young anthropologists had hit cultural paydirt. They had seen a real Mesquaki ceremony and could pronounce the culture alive and well. But relentless data-gathering has its price. Despite their enthusiasm, they worried about the cost of seeing an authentic religious ritual. One of the students wondered why they were not fed like the others, "We weren't offered any food. There are several explanations for this: (1) unfriendliness, (2) we did not dance, (3) we brought food, thus became hosts."

This reflection leaves out the most obvious explanation. The old man told them to wait outside. But some invisible anthropological spirit clouded their senses and pulled them into the long house. To the Mesquakis they were uninvited guests, so they ignored them and conducted their ceremony. Apparently this was the students' first and last observation of a clan ceremony. Nevertheless, other field diaries express a continuing longing to see these ceremonies. Another student's diary conveys this feeling particularly well:

Lacking the moral fortitude to watch through the open slat door, we sat whispering in the car. Finally, I stealthily start around the west end of the summer house. I found thirty pair of eyes directed at me, and I walked on as if I lived there for years. I went over to Bessie YB who was cleaning a chicken and talked a while, then walked back towards the other end of the house and Lon Longknife said hello, so I signalled the boys in the car to come over. Jay WhiteHawk asked if we had been invited and said some ceremonies are for everybody and some like this one are private. Had anyone else been watching from the outside, we'd have joined them, but we felt too conspicuously alone, so we left. (Fox Project Fieldnotes, Box 2)

Rebuffed, these student anthropologists had the sense to stop lurking outside the long house like puppies waiting to be fed. They knew that Mesquakis rarely invite outsiders to their clan ceremonies. Mesquakis do, however, let white friends attend their adoptions, wakes, and burials. During fieldwork I never hovered outside the ceremonial center like some anthropological wolf in heat. But, I must confess, I too felt the same anthropological siren call of the sacred ceremonies. After a winter and three summers of fieldwork, I became very curious about all Mesquaki ceremonies. So when invited to an adoption, a wake, and a burial, I went to pay my respects and to learn.

My First Wake Among Mesquaki Storytellers

What I discovered is that dying keeps Mesquaki culture alive. People had told me, "A Mesquaki may go off and live a whole life as a whiteman, but if you grew up here, you come back here to die." Never was this more true than in the case of Clyde GreyEagle. Only weeks after we talked about his return after years among whites, he passed away. He told me many stories about his twenty years in the service, and stories about living and being a sheet metal worker for Lockheed Corporation and an ammunitions inspector for the U.S. Army. Clyde found life in California a struggle. After many years away, he began forgetting his Mesquaki, and he said,

I came to be like whites. I felt like I was both, though. I kept thinking about my people. You never forget that. You live like they live, but I like people here better. When I came back I didn't know my own ceremonies. You learn them in your twenties and thirties, but I was gone then. Now I am learning them and it is hard, but I have picked up my Mesquaki again. That year I lived with Leon sure helped me learn lots of the things I lost.

He was distressed that so few kids still spoke Mesquaki, but said it was good to be living Mesquaki again. He had missed going to ceremonies with old friends and relatives. A number of other retired Mesquakis I interviewed expressed similar feelings. Those who never left the settlement say that Mesquakis living among whites always return. One man put it this way, "We may leave, but growing up Indian makes you want to die Indian." That was Clyde. He came home to reaffirm his Indian heritage before heading West.

Many cultures still hold wakes for their dead, but few take place in an earthen-floored long house that is eighty feet by thirty feet and holds two to three hundred people. The sides of the long house were lined with wide platforms suspended from poles. All the activity took place around a fire pit with huge cooking kettles hanging from log poles. The fire was what Mesquakis called a "real fire," a fire started with flint. The smell of burning wood and tobacco smoke flavored the air. People were sitting quietly on the platforms eating, talking, joking, and listening when there was a prayer. The mood was neither formal and somber nor jovial. There was an air of the everyday and ordinary. Maybe my anthropological imagination took over, but the simplicity of the moment made everything seem exceptional. The wake had the stain and smell of a time long past.

I walked to the front of the long house where the family was sitting near the body. Clyde was dressed in traditional clothes, but I was too nervous to note the details. After giving his widow something to help with expenses, I quickly retreated to the side of Leon GreyEagle, his uncle. This was the third time in a little over a year that someone close to Leon had died. The year before his sister passed away. During the winter his youngest son Art died under mysterious circumstances. Now his nephew Clyde, whom he was helping return to the faith, was gone. I was hoping to lighten Leon's burden a little.

Leon reminisced about his plans for Clyde, who had been his helper during ceremonies. After telling a few stories about Clyde, another nephew, the jovial, rotund Dickie Black, came by serving food. The mood shifted as Leon started recalling stories about chaperoning a tribal school trip to Yellowstone National Park. On seeing Old Faithful spout, Leon told his young nephew that the geyser always spouted by the clock. This was so because the whitemen had built a series of tunnels under the geyser. In the tunnels were these guys running around pulling gears and running pumps to make the geyser spout on time. As he retold the story, Dickie laughed and said, "It sounds just as good now as it did when I bought it back then."

After a couple more good leg-pullers, Leon introduced me to Dickie as a professor who was writing a book. He added that I had just returned from interviewing another "high-hat type professor" in Des Moines. He told Dickie the guy was probably too busy to see me and asked how I got him to talk. In the spirit of the moment, I retorted, "I just asked him, what's up, Doc?" I had almost sneaked one by Leon, but he regained his balance quickly and said,

You see how this guy is, Dickie. He'll say anything to get someone to talk to him! But I told him the other day I knew where professors came from. I asked him if he thought the stork brought them like regular people. He said sure, but I straightened him out. I told him the way I heard it was that a buzzard flies up on this fence post and squats there. Pretty soon he drops a little something on the top of the post and flies off. Then the sun starts heating up what he dropped, and all of the sudden it hatches a professor!

The story turned Dickie into a giggling, jiggling bowl of jelly, and our laughter only abated when someone told Leon he had to go get some shut-eye. Dickie went about serving food, and Leon said, somewhat pensively, "It is getting hard to keep going all night." His eyes moistened as he continued, "It used to be easy when I was younger."

Watching him control his tears recalled our conversation on how a Mesquaki grieved for a lost loved one. He had explained that Mesquakis are not supposed to cry and show their feelings. Such a show of emotion might throw everyone into fits of despair and sobbing. If you were going to show pain and grief, the only way was to go off in the woods alone.

As Leon became more pensive, he recalled a story about Clyde and his plans to move back to the old family place where they used to catch rabbits. The old place was full of good memories:

Our old house was heated by wood. After hunting, I'd walk towards that place, and you could hear the snow crackling under your feet, and I could see the columns of smoke going straight up into the sky. The air was so heavy that it just shot up into the sky.

As his pain turned into poetry, he reflected on the passing of his son. He harnessed his sorrow with a story about Art helping him collect maple syrup for ceremonies. He continued, "Art was beginning to show us who he was." Leon meant that after much personal turbulence, Art was beginning to settle down and search for his spiritual roots. In Mesquaki society, a father watches from afar as the uncles guide and instruct their boys. Fathers who keep the faith hope their sons will join the ceremonies. They take them to the ceremonies during the early years, but Mesquakis rarely proselytize their young adults. Young men and women are on their own to find the spiritual path they will walk. Just when Art was beginning to find his direction, his life was over. For all his pain, Leon remembered Art without a trace of maudlin sentimentality. He passed over the treasured moments lightly and returned to a world of buzzard-hatched professors and little men who make the geysers spout on time.

When I got home around five in the morning, I wrote down what I remembered of Leon's stories. For me, the way he acted is what being a Mesquaki is all about. Here was a man who had lost more than words could express. Yet, only his stories could save him. So Leon's people came to the wake with their pockets, hearts, and ears open. I could portray many other little details about wakes, but the important point is that they are a stage for sharing grief. If you watch closely, you can almost see the stories sew up the scars.

The sun was already up when I finished my notes on the wake, so I napped a few hours and went back around lunch time. A bleary-eyed Leon was still there talking to people. While we ate chicken and dumplings, he told me that flowers were never used because you cannot eat them. He also approved of my jeans because "Indians don't wear fancy clothes to funerals." When someone dies, everyone must pitch in and help. Someone makes the simple pine box for the burial. Someone else carves the wooden bowl and spoon for the trip West. Others pitch in to cook and serve the food, act as pallbearers, do whatever is needed. It was an impressive display of communal spirit, a time when political rivals and personal enemies put aside their differences.

In mid-afternoon they took the body to the cemetery for the burial ceremony. Everyone drove cars to the general vicinity of the burial site, but only the funeral car climbed the hill. Everyone else walked, and I followed a stream of people up a winding path through the woods and wildflowers. Near the top of the hill the woods were dotted with mounds of logs covering old grave sites. There were no grave markers with names and dates. No tidy rows of plots laid out in a grid. No lawn mowers mowing back nature. The effect of log piles scattered among huge oak and maple trees was awesome. This quiet, hidden place in the woods announced the survival of ancient cultural practices.

A crowd of at least 200 people were listening to a prayer in Mesquaki. After the prayer they formed a line and passed by the body near the new grave site. Since I had no sacred tobacco to put in the casket, I was unsure whether to join the line. Tribal elder Jessie Firstley chided me as he would a balky child to keep moving. The white in front of me had no tobacco, so she made the sign of the cross. I bowed and nodded awkwardly as I passed the body. Several of the relatives were going in different directions into the woods. They probably wanted to express their grief alone. The rest of the crowd stood in a silent vigil. Suddenly the tap, tap of a hammer was nailing the pine coffin shut, and I heard a rustle. They must have lowered the coffin into the grave. Then I heard the sound of rain falling on a roof top. They must be shoveling dirt on the pine box. The moment the raining sound came, people began leaving. As in the past a clan runner had summoned everyone, and the falling earth signaled the ceremony's end. Leon passed by me and said softly, "We gotta go down now."

The Day an Eagle Soared Above the Adoption

Another major ceremony that marks death in Mesquaki culture is the adoption of a living person to replace the deceased. When I first heard Margie Mason-GreyEagle trying to explain an adoption at our high school reunion, I realized how little whites knew about Mesquakis. Even though journalists have written about adoptions (DMR, August 1, 1954; DMR, July 7, 1966), most whites think that an adoption is a legalistic process to obtain a child. White society has no cultural ceremony to "symbolically replace" a deceased person with a living one. Like a wake and burial ceremony, an adoption helps the family share their pain and loss. But more important, the ceremony sets the deceased's spirit free to go West.

The adoption I attended was being held in the Bear Clan long house behind Henry Blackhat Sr.'s. Rather than just showing up, I went by the Jameses' to accompany the family. I imagined that walking in with their son Art, a six-foot-four, three-hundred-and-fifty pound giant, might make me less conspicuous. As we walked in, I felt like a white rabbit scurrying along in Art's giant shadow. An anthropological ghost whispered to me that the Mesquakis were joking, "Hey, Foley got himself a pretty good body guard to sneak into the adoption, Ayeeh! Anybody got a bow and arrow? Let's scare him a little. Ayeeh!" To my relief no one said anything. When religious leader Lee Kingfish greeted me warmly, I relaxed into the moment. Later Leon GreyEagle made an effort to explain what was going on, and Beatrice James made sure I was well fed.

The cook house near the ceremonial center was buzzing with activity. The helpers were laying two long (one-hundred-foot) lines of plastic tarp and carpet on the ground near the long house. A colorful table cloth, bowls and spoons, and various dishes of dumplings and ribs, corn and meat, Indian squash, Indian "oatmeal" (ground corn and brown sugar skillet fried), fry bread, pie, and cake adorned the tarp. The feast was set for at least three or four hundred people.

In the long house, the adoptee Gloria Bigtree was being dressed in moccasins, a beaded headband, and a dress with ribbon appliqué provided by the adopting family. Then a short ceremony took place inside the long house. Henry Blackhat Sr. reaffirmed this as a time to end grief and become happy again, a time for the adopted families to be like relatives and visit and help each other. A small wooden bowl of food was poured on the ground next to the fire to remember departed family relatives. The adoptee then walked clockwise around the long house four times and offered a prayer and tobacco. As she left the long house she gave eight pieces of wood to her eight attendants, thus inviting them to take part in the adoption dance. She then faced west and sat silently near a wood-pole structure filled with bolts of cloth and blankets.

The moment she sat down, the guests came to the place settings on the ground and began eating and chatting quietly. A separate table with chairs was provided for elders who had difficulty sitting on the ground. The clan hosting the adoption did not eat while feeding the guests. During the feast, a group of singers sang to the accompaniment of drums and rattles. Henry Blackhat Sr. gave the prayers and explained the meaning of the celebration.

Once everyone had eaten, the eight who had received the sticks joined the adoptee, and a circle of dancers formed in front of the gifts. Gloria led her attendants, and soon others joined in a spirited round of dancing. When the dances finished, gifts were distributed to the attendants, and they and the adoptee sat in a circle to play Indian dice. The mood of the dancing carried into the game as people joked and laughed. When the dancing and games ended, gifts were also given to the group of singers. Then Gloria left with a small tin of food, neither speaking nor looking back. The unconsumed food was set out on a table for those who wanted to take some home.

As people began leaving, Beatrice came over to bid me good-bye. She seemed pleased about the day. I told her I was glad she had invited me. We talked a little about her son Tyson's decision to try college. She was hopeful that UNI would accept him, then she said quite unexpectedly, "Did you see the eagle flying overhead earlier?" Being engrossed in events on the ground, I had not noticed what really mattered. Beatrice knew that the spirit of her mother was free to go West.

After the eagle story questions about detail seemed trivial, but Beatrice explained that adoptions must take place within four years after a death, and that most are held during the summer. The adopted family then hold a "return" or feast for the family adopting them. This more private ceremony between the two families further cements their bond. Finally, on the day of the adoption feast all the food prepared must be consumed before sundown. As I left I thought to myself, what a poetic way to celebrate dying.

This brief account of wakes, funerals, and adoptions has left out many details. The main point is to convey the continuing richness of cultural practices that whites think have vanished. Year in and year out, this sharing of food, gifts, stories, and prayers brings the tribe together. No matter how many Mesquakis have drifted away from the clan ceremonies, everyone comes to these tribal events. Members of the Drum Society and the few Peyotists and Christians on the settlement are usually there. Each time someone dies the tribe renews itself.

Although drawn to the traditional ceremonies, I was more interested in the modern ceremonies such as the annual powwow and the ceremonies to honor school achievement, a family member, and the land purchase. The following vignettes of secular ceremonies illustrate how Mesquakis blend elements of white culture into these modern ceremonies. The powwow in particular turned out to be a fascinating mirror of changing race relations.

The Mother of All Invented Ceremonies: The Powwow

Many local whites think of the annual powwow as a touristic, commercial event created solely for whites. Historically, outside observers have seen many different things in the Mesquaki powwow. It has been equated with Thanksgiving Day (Owens, 1904); a barrier to progress and industry (Rebok, 1900); a sign of progress and managerial skill (Hynek, TNH, 1925); a touristic "gold-mine" for the local merchants (TNH, February 1, 1962); and a successful modern ceremony based on traditional clans (Gearing et al., 1960; Gearing, 1970). Outsiders gazing upon the powwow seem to have found a kaleidoscope of different meanings. But what does the powwow mean to Mesquakis?

In an unpublished paper, Jonas CutCow (ND) says that people are taught that "the tribe should enjoy each other's company, to visit other people's camps, to put aside arguments and animosities." Many families erect tents and wickiups and camp out at the powwow grounds. Old friends and family return home and reunite with those who remained on the settlement. A powwow is four days of eating, dancing, singing, and socializing. It is a reaffirmation of Mesquaki culture. As a social event, the powwow is vaguely reminiscent of a white homecoming celebration. But the whiteman's football game and class reunion has been replaced with an invented Indian entertainment spectacle.

As old friends and relatives socialize, several hundred tribal members give dance performances in a large arena shaded by trees. The colorful costumes, thundering drums, and whirling dancers create a unique spectacle for thousands of outsiders. This commercial operation requires security guards, ticket-takers, car parking attendants, announcers, and all manner of groundskeepers. Various families also set up eating places and booths to sell Indian handicrafts alongside the booths of the professional vendors. These itinerant vendors travel the powwow circuit selling Native American art, jewelry, drums, rattles, clothing, blankets, and trinkets. One or two of the local Mesquaki artists also set up stands to sell their original drawings and paintings.

Mesquakis generally pride themselves in preserving many traditional dances, but point out that none come from their sacred clan ceremonies. Powwows are recreational, social events that celebrate Indianness. Doing social or secular dances and songs does not make them any less authentic culturally, but these secular celebrations have little to do with traditional religious rituals. The powwow dances generally celebrate harvests, battles, and the ways of animals. Some dances are Mesquaki. Some are borrowed from other tribes. The songs are sung in both Mesquaki and non-Mesquaki style. The dance costumes, often cloth and acrylic rather than buckskin, use Mesquaki woodland patterns and beadwork as well as plains Indian styles. To date, no scholar has analyzed the aesthetics of the powwow, but Torrence and Hobbs (1989) provide some commentary on pan-Indian art forms, and Phillips (1991) analyzes costume styles. It suffices to say that the modern Mesquaki powwow is an interesting mix of Mesquaki and non-Mesquaki cultural forms.

What fascinated me about the powwow was how this spectacle adopted and eventually abandoned white forms of popular entertainment. From its inception the tribe has cooperated with and tussled against local whites. Prominent whites like editor John Hynek propagated the view that local whites like Joseph Svacina created the modern powwow (TNH, August 29, 1924):

Mr. Svacina was instrumental in persuading the Sac and Fox tribes of the reservation in 1915 to start their annual powwow, which had developed into a stellar attraction. Nine years ago the grateful "redskins" conferred upon him the title, "Wa-bi-ke-ti-wah," meaning White Eagle. At his home and his shop the Tama man has hundreds of articles of Indian workmanship that have been presented to him by his friends on the reservation.

The article and others (TNH, August 24, 1933; Toledo *Chronicle*, June 20, 1935) make Svacina into a folk hero who kept the powwow "authentic, primitive, and uncommercialized." Hynek also claims that Svacina was so beloved the Mesquakis gave him an Indian name and many gifts. Mesquakis were grateful for Svacina's assistance, and they did give him an Indian name. But, being the local pawn broker, he could not have acquired his collection of Mesquaki heirlooms solely as "gifts."

Nor did Svacina or any other white invent the powwow. According to Jonas CutCow, the modern Mesquaki powwow evolved from the green corn dance to celebrate the harvest (CutCow, ND). On the urging of his son and others, Chief Pushetonequa established a policy of charging whites who wanted to see the harvest celebration. From 1902 to 1913 the ancient harvest celebration evolved into an affair called field days. This proto-powwow celebration lasted a week and had games and contests not practiced in the harvest celebration.

Around 1913 Svacina and several other white businessmen became active in the field day celebrations. They urged Chief Pushetonequa to appoint a permanent powwow committee and institute better business

practices. From 1915 to 1925 Svacina and Edgar Harlin of the Iowa Historical Society were quite involved in running the powwow. Svacina handled business matters, and Harlin organized an educational program of
speakers on the history and culture of the Mesquaki. They were also
instrumental in getting Mesquakis to put on powwows in other towns
during the early 1920s.

When Chief Pushetonequa died in 1919, the role of the white benefactors began to change. As in the case of Rebok's vocational school, the
Oldbear traditionalists were critical of the Youngbear faction's collaboration with whites. Soon after Pushetonequa's death, they sued the new
powwow committee and its white advisors for mishandling the profits
(Marshalltown *Times-Republican*, September 29, 1920). No record remains of what whites thought about being ousted from powwow management, but Editor Hynek lamented that the Mesquakis were taking up
white ways so fast that authentic powwows might soon end. He worried
that the powwow would degenerate into a carnival under all-Indian management. For Hynek, creating authenticity was setting up an Indian village of Sioux-style tepees on the east side of the Iowa river. This replica of
a village was to provide the perfect tourist's photo — the sun setting on
Indian tepees (TNH, July 29, August 26, 1926).

During the early years, powwows were a strange mixture of Wild West
show entertainment and educational lectures. While the whiteman Harlin gave lectures on Mesquaki history and culture, carnival-like activities
such as ferris wheels and merry-go-rounds entertained people. The program also included many competitive games between Indians and whites
such as a tug-of-war, a wrestling match, a boxing match, various foot races,
a horse race, a baseball game, a greased pig chase, and an Indian on pony
versus a Ford car contest. Dances were interspersed between the racial
competitions, as were flute solos, Indian love songs, bow and arrow shooting, lacrosse exhibitions, and tunes from the famous all-Mesquaki marching band.

Early powwow programs were occasionally topped off with some grand
finale that made quite a statement about race relations. In 1921 the finale
was entitled "Sham battle between Indians and Stage Coach." The battle included the capture, scalping, and burning at the stake of a white
maiden, and a victory scalp dance. The program closed with the audience and performers singing "America" and "Home Sweet Home" to
the accompaniment of the Mesquaki band. Apparently everyone singing
patriotic songs symbolically incorporated the Indian into civilization's
home sweet home.

A second major form of white popular entertainment that influenced
the early powwows was the county fair. The powwows of the 1920s began
introducing agricultural and homemaking exhibits. These county fair-

type activities become even more prominent in the 1930s and 1940s. Using the powwow to highlight Mesquaki farming and homemaking was clearly related to the BIA assimilation policy. By 1929, the Indian Agency and a number of local civic leaders commissioned a study of the settlement (Toledo *Chronicle*, March 31, 1929). The study urged the Indian service to purchase more farmland, increase agricultural training for males and gardening, canning, and homemaking training for women. To this end, prizes were given for the best corn seeds, canned preserves, and livestock. The local white doctors also gave blue ribbons for those "papooses" judged the healthiest.

The powwows of this era also included entertainment associated with county fairs. CutCow's study of powwows labels the 1930s "the era of pageants." In 1932 a cast of forty Mesquakis celebrated the Black Hawk war. In 1938 the pageant celebrated the early modes of transportation (Toledo *Chronicle*, August 6, 1938). Although the paper fails to elaborate on the pageant, the article says "The usual atmosphere of a community fair will prevail." It goes on to enumerate the attractive exhibits: the genuine Indian village, the council display of relics and family heirlooms, various agricultural exhibits, and girls' 4-H and woman's club homemaking exhibits. In 1939 the powwow staged a Hiawatha pageant and several Indian courtship and marriage episodes. They also put up a portable dance floor and hired white bands to play music for modern dancing.

The powwow's evolution away from Wild West show and county fair style activities was gradual. By the 1930s, the Wild West show elements had been completely replaced with county fair activities. By the 1940s, county fair activities were also declining. Agricultural and homemaking exhibits and baby contests became less and less prominent. Experiments with white dance bands and drum and bugle corps were abandoned (CutCow, ND). The only inter-racial contests left were a baseball game and an occasional boxing match. After World War II more emphasis was placed on the dancing, and several returning war veterans depicted their war experiences through honor dances. Various Indian games like lacrosse, the squaws game, and the moccasin game continued to lend the event a flavor of ancient Indian practices.

During the 1950s and 1960s local white merchants reappeared as more active promoters of the powwow. The same merchants' association that had tried to pass a city ordinance against selling Indians liquor was ever keen on making Indians a tourist attraction. The Tama Chamber of Commerce donated a hundred dollars for advertising and a billboard yearly. They also tried to organize their own "Frontier Days" weekend with a parade, and some merchants dressed in old costumes. Finally, the merchants and government agents began urging the tribe to move the powwow from the Iowa River site to higher ground near the new highway.

The merchants even tried to take over an action anthropology program to capitalize on the tribe's touristic potential. In 1956, Sol Tax sent Robert Rietz to the settlement to initiate a small handicraft program called Tama Craft. Artist Charlie Pushetonequa's drawings were silk-screened on ceramic tiles and greeting cards and sold locally and through mail order. After some initial success, the project declined when Rietz left in 1959. Orders went unfilled and workers went unpaid. In response, car dealer Robert Blythe headed a group of merchants who urged Tax to convince the tribe to accept their management skill and capital. A letter to Tax outlines a scheme to produce handicrafts on a much larger scale in a factory setting. Former project director Rietz replied wisely that it was up to Mesquakis to decide the matter. He urged the Tama merchants to approach the tribal council directly (Fox Project fieldnotes, Box 127).

Three years later the local merchants were still pushing the idea of an Indian souvenir factory (TNH, Februrary 1, 1962). They met with Governor Sam Erbe, the state tourism committee, and several Mesquakis to plan "Indian tourism." Having failed to enforce a unconstitutional 1960 ordinance against Indian drinking, they now wanted the tribe to help them mine what the Governor called "the gold mine you have here in the Indians." During the meeting they called for paving the settlement's gravel road, moving the powwow to high grounds, and putting tepees on the highway for dispensing information and selling souvenirs.

Nothing came of these schemes, but the powwow continued to add permanent bleachers and grow during the 1960s (CutCow, ND). During this era powwow programs focused primarily on singing and dancing and abandoned most of the county fair-style exhibits and entertainments. Even handicraft demonstrations on making fry bread, reed mats, yarn belts, and ribbon appliqué declined, as did exhibition Indian games and displays of family heirlooms.

The final transformation of the powwow took place in the turbulent 1970s. The flood of 1972 brought out an impressive show of neighborliness from whites. Many helped the tribe relocate their powwow on the Bolen farm adjacent to the settlement. But the following summer barroom fights and AIM protests ended any racial cooperation to stage the powwow. In response, Mesquakis began emphasizing more emphatically than ever that the powwow was an authentic expression of traditional language and culture, not some phony show for tourists. Some printed publicity even portrayed the powwow as a "quasi-religious" ceremony. Any hint of white Wild West show or county fair was now unthinkable.

In the wake of a Civil Rights Commission investigation, the emphasis on reinventing culturally authenticity was expressed even more boldly (TNH, July 31, 1980):

The Mesquaki powwow is one of the few all-Indian run and still authentic. It has a genuineness that others have lost. Mesquakis like to be friendly and hospitable, but this is not an occasion held solely to please outsiders. It is a time which white people may learn to understand, respect, therefore treat Indian people with dignity. It is an opportunity to see the Indian realistically and to hear him speak in his native tongue and to grasp a bit of the Indian's concept of life.

Another related development during the 1970s was the creation of a multi-cultural tourist attraction called the Double D PowWow-Rodeo parade and weekend (TNH, August 10, 1985). Rodeo promoter Duane Duncan approached the Chamber of Commerce about creating a joint event. Duncan apparently also "visited with some Indians and they thought it was OK" (Cedar Rapids *Gazette*, August 8, 1991). The Chamber of Commerce president remembers telling Duncan that he thought the event was a "natural." What most Iowans mean by a "natural" is the *Gazette*'s portrayal of a "Big weekend for Cowboys and Indians." The article ends by asking rhetorically if there is peace between today's cowboys and Indians, and Duncan responds, "I hear people say that."

Ninety years later and some newspapers are still playing up the old Wild West image! But now there is peace on the prairies of Iowa. The present Chamber of Commerce may long to revive the good old frontier/ powwow days, but rodeo participants dominate the parade. The powwow princess and a few young dancers and veterans have begun participating in the parade again. Nevertheless, most Mesquakis watch rather than participate in the parade. Settlement residents grumble that the whites are just trying to make money off their powwow.

Gone are the days when the merchants in cowboy suits and Mesquakis "in feathers and Indian costumes" whooped it up on horseback (TNH, June 18, 1925). On that occasion they "ambushed" a train full of Cedar Rapids merchants who were arriving to promote their rodeo. The latest attempt to recreate a Wild West event seems just as anachronistic as the 1925 attempt. Modern Mesquakis are simply too politicized to participate in such a cliche. After ninety years of experimentation, the Mesquakis have created a powwow that tries to entertain and educate whites a little about their culture. The event never gives too deep a view of Mesquaki life, but it is always a good tribal homecoming. Mesquakis stage the event to enjoy themselves, not to make money or promote tourism.

Over the years whites have tried with varying degrees of success to help stage the powwow and to gain a few tourist dollars. The best of whites came out when they pitched in and helped relocate the flooded out powwow of 1972. The worst of whites came out when they tried to make Tama Craft into a white-run factory. Perhaps the time has come for the Chamber of Commerce to sponsor a parade that parodies Wild West shows. Lampooning the local cowboy-Indian tourist spectacle the way Robert Altman did in his Buffalo Bill movie might lighten a few local hearts. It would also garner more national press coverage and tourist dollars than the "straight" powwow-rodeo parade does. Earnest young anthropologists would surely come and write about the event as a new postmodern form of racial consciousness.

Invented Educational and Familial Ceremonies

Mesquakis also put on other less well-known secular ceremonies that blend the two cultures. For example, their education committee organizes an annual powwow to honor high school and college graduates. As always, a large feast—part pot luck and part catered—was served to a crowd of several hundred people. The graduates were seated at the center table during the eating. Then the tables were cleared from the gym floor, and the graduates and their families led an honor dance. Everyone joined in a huge dance circle that ringed the gym floor.

After the dance a series of parlor games began. First a group of little kids ran a pop-the-balloon race. After several hilarious attempts to sit on the balloons, the crowd was ready for the graduates and their parents. Working as a team, each had to put on a t-shirt, bib, and diapers and carry a rubber toy to the chair, then undress. A partner had to dress and run the opposite direction. This madcap race in ridiculous costumes eventually shifted to a game of musical chairs. The prize for both winners and losers was a candy sucker. When the games finished the social dancing resumed.

The dancing got everyone involved with a choose-your-partner dance. No one was in costume, and the couples danced around and around the circle to the beat of the drums. After the dancing, gifts were distributed to each of the graduates. They all received a lovely painted mirror, a diploma, and an eagle feather. Having collected many stories about the schools, I could not help but wonder if the feather was for bravery in battle.

Usually these events do not single out any one graduate, but the announcer made a point of saying that Mike GreyEagle was the first Mesquaki to graduate from Philips Exeter. The guy next to me said with obvious pride, "That is where the Kennedys went to school." Poor Mike looked uncomfortable in his East Coast suit and tie. He was the only one dressed formally, and it exaggerated his shyness. His aunt Rene WhiteSky, not one to stand on ceremony, finally grabbed Mike and danced a smile out of him. The graduates were generally restless, but the adults were enjoying watching, chatting, quietly clapping, and being together as families. The pace was very slow, informal, and low key. The celebration, like most Mesquaki celebrations, went on for hours, but no one seemed restless or ready to leave.

This event reminded me of another all-day powwow held yearly for all school children. This powwow honored Mesquaki children and taught them a spirit of cooperation. For example, during an honor dance for contest winners, the powwow prince and princess danced around the center drum. As they danced, the audience joined in, shook their hands, gave them a dollar, and returned to the chain of dancers. Afterward, the chosen dancers placed their money back on the drum. Meanwhile the announcer praised the people for giving, and the winners for giving back to the drums in the Mesquaki way. It was an interesting mix of rewarding individual achievement, but within a tradition of sharing individual victories with the group.

Another dance that conveyed cooperative values was a Kiowa spear and shield dance. Two eight-year-olds in full regalia danced around and around each other until one had to "kill" the other. It was obvious that neither boy wanted to kill or be killed, and their hesitation and timidity brought laughter from the crowd. Finally one boy nudged the other to the ground. The moment the drums stopped, the victor picked up the vanquished and hugged him. The crowd clapped with great approval as the boys ran off arm-in-arm.

That evening the gym was packed with at least five hundred people, and kids were running everywhere with an abandon not permitted at traditional ceremonies. Outside, teenagers were pretty much doing what all teenagers do. They were celebrating new-found hormones by hanging out in packs teasing, flirting, and sneaking smokes. The whole scene was a little reminiscent of our family Fourth of July picnics, only on a much larger scale.

The evening dancing included door prizes such as Tupperware and a raffle that gave away a VCR, blanket, TV, and various smaller prizes. The crowd had great fun teasing each of the winners. Four local drum groups, one in each corner of the gym, accompanied the evening dancing. The dancing ranged from couple circle dancing to contest dancing for the youth. The dance prizes were fairly substantial — first, $75; second, $50; third, $35. This time there was no sharing of the prize money with the drum, but the victors showed little or no emotion about winning. The tone was polite reserve, which took the individualistic, competitive edge off the dancing.

I was struck by the strange blend of the old and the new at these two education powwows. I sat perched on a strange cultural borderland where cultures fuse. Having never seen such ceremonies, the white parlor games, door prizes, raffles, and individual awards took me by surprise.

The whiteman's ideal of individual achievement was there, but it was expressed within the context of family and tribal tradition. Parental and community pride in the children's educational accomplishments was obvious. Given the huge turnout and the sharing of time, food, and prize money, it was an impressive display of community solidarity.

Another secular celebration that combined the new with the old was a family "give-away" or powwow to honor Kurt Kingfish. The Kingfishes are generally considered a prominent traditional, pure-blood family. Kurt was an influential elder who spent many years as chairman of the tribal council. Family powwows to honor elders are common, but are usually held on the family's land. Apparently this was the first powwow sponsored by a family held in the gym. Several people said that putting on a large public give-away ceremony was more Sioux than Mesquaki.

The ceremony started with a potluck dinner of fry bread and various stew dishes. The gym was packed with at least four hundred people, and eight drum groups, several from Wisconsin and Minnesota, were on hand. After the feast the Kingfish family led the honor parade of dancers and flags—American, Mesquaki, and the eagle feather staff—into the gym. As many as fifty dancers did several numbers, and then couple social dancing and contest dances for tots to teenagers followed.

After several hours of dancing, the grand finale was a special honor dance for Kurt. The immediate family of thirty or forty people, including in-laws, encircled Kurt and led the dance. As they went around the gym, most of the audience joined in. Each person shook the honoree's hand and gave him some money. After one round someone gave Kurt a cowboy hat for collecting money. When they finished the second round the family formed a half-moon and faced the crowd remaining in the stands.

Then the actual give-away began. During the next number the family group danced with large plastic sacks of gifts, which were placed in a huge pile near Kurt. The announcer read a list of thirty or forty people who were close to the family to come forward. The daughters gave them blankets and shawls, and the sons, grandsons, and Kurt formed a receiving line to shake their hands. Then the remaining gifts were laid on the floor, and everyone was told to take what they wanted. Another twenty or thirty people picked up gifts and shook Kurt's hand. When the gifts were distributed, the senior male dancers did a traditional-style dance to honor Kurt, and he chose the best senior male and female dancers.

A final "invented" modern ceremony was recently developed to celebrate the purchase of the settlement and the tribe's return to Iowa in 1857. Several tribal council members persuaded the tribal center's program administrators to create the first "Mesquaki national holiday." All tribal employees were given a holiday and encouraged to attend a celebration intended to be educational and culturally unifying. Whites were to learn that the settlement was not a traditional reservation. Mesquakis were to celebrate cultural practices that have been lost, like lacrosse, bone dice, and stick games. The event would also be used to hold "workshops" to teach kids history and discuss important issues like substance abuse and schools.

During the planning sessions they wanted Governor Terry Branstad to simulate the original historical signing. The idea was to make it a "living history event" that would be a good TV spot. The signing never happened, but a modestly attended celebration with dancing, a potluck, workshops, and "Indian games" did (TNH, July 24, 1992; DMR, July 21, 1992). Henry Blackhat Sr. gave a prayer and recounted the brave return of the Mesquakis and the generosity of Iowans to allow the land purchase. The ceremony was reminiscent of what other ethnic groups have done to promote their culture with the mainstream. The new holiday celebration was basically a public relations event, but it also expressed the tribe's growing political and economic autonomy.

Nevertheless, the new celebration received criticism from some tribal members. Poet-novelist Ted Pipestar chastised the planners in a scathing editorial for creating "a misconception that a 'pooling of money' from 'our ancestors' led to the establishment of our cultural sanctuary. That's a fallacy. It was Maminwanike who single-handedly made the decision to leave Kansas" (Marshalltown *Times-Republican,* July 18, 1992). Like Ernest TrueTongue, Ted has taken up the Oldbear discourse against an elected tribal council. He accuses "self-appointed tribal leaders" of failing to emphasize the sacred origins of Mesquaki history. If the celebration is to be truly educational, it must emphasize the importance of Maminwanike, the divine hereditary chief who led the people back. Without such an emphasis, Ted and a few others consider the new celebration a sign of cultural decline.

Living in a Racial Borderland: The Mixed-Bloods

Since journalists and scholars rarely explore the life of mixed-bloods, I decided to interview as many racially mixed couples as possible. Nearly all ten couples reported painful experiences with some family members. In some cases the parents objected to the interracial marriage. In other cases it was a sister or brother. White family members generally objected more often than Mesquaki family members. In two instances both sides of the family expressed displeasure, but two other teenage couples reported no anti-Indian or anti-white sentiments from any family members. On the whole, marrying outside the race seemed somewhat easier than it was in South Texas or in Mississippi (Foley, 1989; Foley, 1983). The mixed-marriage couples in those settings rarely felt accepted in either community.

In the Mesquaki case, only two of the mixed-race couples felt completely isolated from their racial community. Once the dissenting family members got over the shock, both communities generally accepted these marriages. In some cases it took dissenting family members years to visit the couple. Acceptance seemed to depend upon how a person conducted her/himself. One Mesquaki married to a white woman put it this way,

If you try to get along, you will be accepted. We attended church and oriented our kids towards the town and whites, but we went to some doings (adoptions and burials) too. The kids mostly hung around with whites, but they have danced in powwows many times. We still visit relatives on the settlement, but our life is mostly in town.

In a similar vein, a white man married to a Mesquaki woman said,

My wife takes me to ceremonies, and we join the senior center activities. I don't see many of my old white friends, but most whites leave us alone. We eat all the time at the Maid-Rite place. We get stared at now and then but that's about all. I guess some people just don't know no better.

This man and several others have adopted a live-and-let-live attitude. Such an attitude makes living on the racial border considerably easier. Mixed couples living in town generally orient themselves towards the white community. Of thirty children, only three went back to the settlement to attend adoption and burial ceremonies with their Indian parent. Most reported being able to live with white neighbors, go to church, and eat at the VFW and restaurants with little trouble. On the other hand, the parents tended to downplay the difficulties their children had in school. A number of young adults said their parents never realized how hard it was to be a half-breed. One young man said, "I got it from both sides. I got called an 'apple' and I got called 'Chief.' My parents never really knew what we went through. You couldn't come home bawling all the time."

Many other town "breeds" expressed some of the same frustrations, but, like their parents, most students knew some whites that accepted and dated them. They told the same stories that their parents told about overlooking occasional stares and nasty comments. In sharp contrast, most settlement mixed-bloods had mainly Indian friends. They generally considered themselves guests of the tribe and stayed out of politics. Such mixed-bloods were generally well accepted on the settlement, but others living on or near the settlement not involved in the ceremonies were not. They were considered "troublemakers." For various reasons these estranged families and their youth generally gravitated toward relationships with whites in town.

One such person is Bart Parsons, who now lives in town with his white wife and repairs cars in a garage behind his house. Bart, a tall, lanky man pushing forty, remembers the Sac and Fox school as follows:

It was like a nightmare. There was lots of prejudice towards half-breeds. In those days they didn't think white people belonged. They called me white trash and no-good Mukuman. It was odd. We used to have people over and took care of their vehicles, but it was one big stinkin' hassle 'till we changed to town school.

Despite many bad experiences, he remembers fondly hunting and fishing with "two civilized Indians," Ted Pipestar and Tom Warrior. But these friendships waned in high school because Bart "couldn't forget the past."

Like most whites, Bart remembers little discrimination and thought that white teachers "cut them (Mesquakis) a lot of slack." As race relations heated up during the 1970s, Bart found himself siding with the white motorcycle gang against "these guys who'd follow AIM into the tunnel of hell." But eventually the excitement of drinking and fighting lost its luster, and, like many of his peers, Bart remarried and settled down. "I've tried to let it all go. I've made my peace. I can go to most houses now. Mom still goes to some ceremonies." Somewhat wistfully, Bart added,

There's no fighting anymore. Now they come here to buy cars. My clients are half and half. Everybody pays. Nobody says or does things. This is the best its been for me. It must be like it's supposed to be.

So Bart, like other mixed-bloods who felt rejected on the settlement, has found his niche in the racial borderland.

One "town breed" who has done pretty well is "Ragin' Ron Sycamore," the founder of a popular local country-rock band. Ron and his brothers Keith and David remember feeling "caught in the middle, always being forced to take sides, almost getting into fights with full-bloods, being called names by some whites." Ron described his teenage years as a time of much confusion about his cultural identity. Although his parents oriented them towards their church and gospel singing, there were cultural connections to the settlement. Ron remembers spending summers with his Mesquaki-Winnebego grandmother and going to "doings" (ceremonies), hearing Indian stories, and dancing in powwows. But in the end, Ron says, his brothers and sister "tended to hang out with and date whites, except during the walkout, when we sided with the Indians."

Nevertheless, the connection with settlement life left Ron wanting to "make music with a message that helps my people and creates better understanding between whites and Indians." Another thing that feeds his desire to make ethnic music is racism. Ron and his brothers feel that local whites never accepted and supported their band the way they would have an all-white band. When we talked he was writing a "cowboys and Indian album that tries to get at the stereotypes of John Wayne movies with the Duke blasting a bunch of savage Indians." Although they have few intimate ties with the settlement, Ron still feels Indian enough to want to make a political statement with his music.

A friend and I went to see the band play, and Ron's hard-driving rockabilly and soulful ballads reminded us of early Elvis. Although the band has recently run into managerial, financial, and personal problems, Ron hopes to continue chasing his brass ring in Nashville. Ragin' Ron is not likely to give up his dreams easily. Meanwhile, most of the Sycamore children have settled into successful marriages and jobs. Living between two cultural worlds was a bittersweet experience for the Sycamores. Three of them, including Ron, eventually married whites, and they hope that their children will grow up in a more accepting white world.

No set of vignettes about the half-breed experience would be complete without what old-timers call a "blanket breed." Unlike settlement "troublemakers " and "town breeds," the blanket breed grows up Indian. I met several settlement breeds who were active in the clan ceremonies and considered themselves "traditionalists." One in particular, Jonas Cut-Cow, became a research colleague and friend. It turned out that we shared one experience that I had in common with several breeds. We were all abandoned by our white fathers. This mutual experience burst out of hiding one day when Jonas asked me, "Do you think I ought to look up my father?"

I was initially taken aback by this question. Did Jonas somehow know that I also came back here to find my father? I blinked and asked, "Did you know that my father was like yours and never claimed me?" He reassured me that no supernatural power was behind his question, but that he had guessed it from something I had said. Feeling reassured, I answered his question with more questions, "Can you take it if you meet him and he is ugly or dumb or hateful? Do you have him built up in your mind to be something special?"

In a matter-of-fact tone, he noted that his father was probably just a man like any other man. Jonas expressed little of the fear of rejection that kept me away for thirty years. He said ever so casually, "I just wanted to know if I got anything from him."

I retorted, "Do you mean wanna know if your white half is messing up your Indian half, right?" He chuckled and said there has always been something missing, this part that he does not know. I know the feeling, Jonas, and so must other abandoned half-breed children. But as we talked I could see that I was psychologizing his curiosity. He had none of the doubts about his cultural identity that some "town breeds" expressed. Jonas credits his sense of place and self to his family. Being traditional

Mesquakis, his mother and uncle took the missing father's place and brought Jonas up in the religion.

The one experience that seems to have left a mark, however, is talk about banishing the half-breeds. Over the years pure-bloods have called for the expulsion of all half-breeds from the settlement. Jonas remembers hearing several respected elders denouncing "my kind." That sent him running into the woods where he spent many anxious hours. He sprinkled tobacco around himself for protection and asked the trees, rocks, and sky to help him. Even today, he still worries that his family will be asked to leave when his mother dies.

On the other hand, white culture holds no great lure for this blanket breed. Town was "Just this place to go to get groceries." Jonas remembers a few white acquaintances and flirtations with white girls, but nothing he considers important. During five years at the University of Iowa, he met friendly liberal-minded professors and students, but a clique of Mesquaki students was his real support group. When I asked how the Iowa City experience affected him culturally, he replied, "It is just language. I have learned how to talk like a white. I am able to talk like a historian talks. It makes whites feel comfortable, but the real me is what I learned growing up, what my uncle Charlie and mom taught me."

Being the official tribal historian, many researchers, students, and reporters now seek out for Jonas for interviews. He has also given hundreds of history talks and is one of the few Mesquakis who rendezvous with white Buckskinners. By any standard, he is at ease communicating with whites. Unlike some blanket breeds, he was also at ease with being part-white because "I was always taught to respect both kinds of blood that flow in my veins." But for all of his facility with "white talk" and acceptance of his white blood, Jonas was a reluctant border-crosser. He always seemed more at ease with his people than with whites. He was always asking me what I really learned from our talks. Among other things, I learned that Mesquakis make white talk better than we make Mesquaki talk. They have to cross that racial border everyday, but most whites stay in their own cultural space.

White Wanderers and Wannabes in a Racial Borderland

During the research I also kept my eyes open for whites who had a little "border-crossing wanderlust." Such people have a longing to transgress the psychological border between the two cultures. I never wanted to explore the white-Indian border while growing up, but I did join the Peace Corps to see distant places. In retrospect, I was curious whether other whites who had joined the Peace Corps explored the white-Indian border more than I had. Of the four ex-Peace Corps Volunteers identified, only Mia Novaceck was still around.

Mia's parents — Gene, a retired postmaster, and Ivory, a long-time city clerk — anticipated her return from Gambia with great pride, so I was anxious to meet her. Mia, a 1980 honor graduate with a Grinnell College BA, turned out to be a slight-built, intense young woman full of future plans. After the Gambian experience, she wanted to do museum work and save the world from its cultural ignorance. She had my youthful fire and idealism, so I pressed to see how open-minded she was about Mesquakis.

Having gone to STC in the tumultuous 1970s, Mia remembers being

a cultural anachronism. I was political, voiced my views, discussed politics. I'd have voted Democratic. I'm more liberal now. I had a small group of friends. We were "bored jocks," academic types, drama types, mostly upper middle class, mostly college bound. Dave Letterman was our icon. We were trying to recapture the sixties. We listened to the Beatles, wore plaid flannel shirts, played soccer, weren't for marrying and settling down.

When she described the Mesquakis she said, "The girls were very clannish and it was hard to be friends with an entire group." Groups standing in the hall making smart remarks, throwing gum in each other's hair, and taunting were common. She did not remember any interracial dating or real friendships. According to Mia, serious drinking and pot smoking were common in both races. The Mesquakis apparently had a reputation of being tough, and some kids brought knives and pellet guns to school. She continued that a couple groups of white guys, one from the "social elite" and another from the "other side of the tracks," fought with Mesquakis regularly. She added that one white group even gang raped girls. That story evoked my own memories of a supposedly respectable group of farm boys who raped a girl from my country school.

When asked whether she tried to challege racist attitudes, Mia got very pensive. Like other liberal-minded locals, she was no crusader for Mesquaki causes:

No one was going to change it one way or another. It wasn't bad enough to say we had a problem and not good enough to say we didn't. The school and community didn't encourage us to change things. I don't like everything about Mesquaki culture, or white culture, but they have a right to their culture. Having their own school might help preserve their cultural identity.

Listening to Mia made it clear that she did not believe the usual stereotypes of Indians. She was quite critical of white racism and had a strong philosophical commitment to cultural pluralism. But her liberalism toward the Mesquaki seemed more abstract and philosophical than her feelings toward Gambians. She showed me pictures of Gambian neighbors and told touching stories about them. Unfortunately, she never had the same opportunity to know Mesquakis and life on the settlement the way she did the Gambians. Most Tama whites, myself included, grew up in our own little cultural world. It was hard to cross the white-Indian cultural border and just be neighborly.

One local white who crossed the racial border more than Mia or I did was Karen Johnson. Karen grew up on a Sioux reservation where her parents, Don and Jayne, taught school for ten years. She described the shock of transferring to South Tama County schools quite poignantly:

At first I was scared of white kids. They talked too loud and were always showing off. I hated them. They were obnoxious. I had problems looking teachers in the eyes like the Indians do. The Indians always excelled in teams, but in the classroom you were considered a show-off if you said much. Here it was the reverse — shine in classroom and your personal stats on the team were so important. On the reservation your school supplies were communal. You could borrow from others. Here I was considered a sucker for loaning my school supplies, but no one would lend to me. Most whites are me-oriented. Indians are team-oriented. If they are treated the way I was, it's no wonder they hate school. Indians aren't out to be the best dressed, best board-erasers. There was no question that the whites were the favorites.

Like most white outsiders, Karen eventually became well accepted when she excelled in academics and sports. Nevertheless, it bothered her that many white teammates on high school volleyball and basketball teams never saw Indians as equals and were "two-faced. Whites joked around, but down deep they were scared of them, and many would make fun of Indians behind their backs. It made me sick." I asked her if there were any white kids who wanted to help the Indians, and she replied,

Few whites have this attitude to help the Indians. Most think the Indians don't deserve it because they get all these special privileges like claims checks. They resent the nice cars and shoes and think they waste the government money. Most whites think it is baloney that we owe them for the past. I kept my opinion to myself, I'm not as gung ho about it. I told my friends to leave 'em alone.

She also expressed frustration that there were no school discussions about Mesquaki culture and race relations. Karen had grown up among the Sioux and had learned that Indians were human beings. She was beyond all the white stereotypes and resentments, yet she was no civil rights crusader in high school. She found herself alone in her views on white-Indian relations. So how does a young white woman caught between two races fit in socially?

Karen says she had white friends in all the social groups, but her closest friend was an equally talented Mesquaki student, Carrie Turner. Her depiction of visiting Carrie on the settlement illustrates the terrible power of the racial border that whites and Mesquakis create:

I was afraid they might think of me as a white show-off because of my all-state honors in drama and music and the basketball queen thing. I still don't like white values. Out there I feel bleached, white. When I drive through the settlement I know it puts people off. There is that tension. I get along with most Indians, but there were no Indian kids on the basketball team. Carrie told me that some might feel that way, but most won't. What bothered me was I knew I'd changed to something I despised. I wanted to write a book and do something for the Indians, go to the governor or something.

In her senior year the close friendship with Carrie came undone. Carrie crossed a cultural border of her own during a junior student time abroad in Thailand. She described how strange it felt to live in a world where no one was white, "I felt so at home in Thailand. It was like I had found my place. There was no pressure to be an Indian or a white."

This shy, attractive young Mesquaki woman had persevered in speech and drama contests to master her shyness. She was an honor roll student and everyone — family, counselors, teachers — was pressuring her to be a "super-Indian," a credit to her race. Like many academically talented minority students, she found herself somewhat accepted by whites and somewhat rejected by her group. Despite being caught in the middle, Carrie apparently made the best of a difficult situation. But upon returning from Thailand, her carefully constructed borderland existence was turned upside down. She suddenly felt the racism more than before, and she wanted nothing to do with old white friends and teachers. Her grades fell, and she shelved her plans for college and joined the Army. In retrospect, Carrie says that she lacked the self-confidence to handle all the pressures and regretted losing her friends.

Carrie and Karen have renewed their friendship as well as one can from a distance. For both, high school and all its interracial pressures are distant, unpleasant memories. Carrie is busy taking college courses and will finish her degree after service. She has no plans to return to the settlement to live. Meanwhile Karen is finishing a degree in anthropology and legal studies at Beloit College and expects to go to law or graduate school. The case of these two border-crossers illustrates what the racial border can do to friendships and intimate relationships.

One other kind of border-crosser is what Mesquakis referred to jokingly as a "wannabe." Mesquakis apply the wannabe label rather loosely to various whites they see trying to become Indian. One type of wannabe is the white "hobbyist" who puts on buckskins and "plays Indian" during weekend powwows and retreats. Another type of wannabe is much more dedicated to knowing, living with, and marrying into an Indian tribe.

Two young white men presently living near the settlement dislike being called wannabes because of the association with hobbyists. One retorted, "I think the wannabe term is funny. I just wanna be myself." The other said,

Indian people say there are some whites who are kinda like Indians. God lets 'em dance and sing like an Indian. Then there are hobbyists who do fake powwows. I thank God I am not one of them, and that the Mesquakis are teaching me the right way.

Both saw themselves as much more sincere and serious about learning Indian ways than hobbyists.

The first time I saw "Rock Island Red" or "Cowboy Red" beating on a drum and singing at a powwow, I thought he was a light-skinned half-breed. Someone in the crowd pointed him out as a good singer and he fit in too well to be a white. At first he was reluctant to talk to me, but one evening he called me and said "Come on over. I'm ready to talk," so I hopped in my car full of curiosity.

His small Toledo apartment was filled with drums and parts of dance costumes that he makes, and Indian music was blaring on the stereo. I began by asking him why he finally decided to talk with me. He smiled slyly and said he had checked me out with several Mesquakis. Later he confided that maybe I would tell his story in a way that would let the Mesquakis know how he felt about them. He was especially grateful to Greyson Kingfish, who had taken him into his family like an adopted son. Red explained that,

Dad made the mistake of taking me to a powwow when I was four. After that, every summer I went to the Mesquakis' Rock Island powwow. I'd sneak out of school on Friday and help Greyson do their work. When I got thirteen or fourteen, I started putting up a pup tent and staying over night. They fed me, talked to me, took me into their family. They'd start singing and I was instantly addicted. I'd tape songs and listen to them all year. I was a little off, but they'd joke and laugh and Greyson would squeeze my knee and tease me.

When Red got his driver's license he started visiting the settlement and staying with the Kingfishes. Eventually he was given an Indian name and he joined a drum group and played at powwows. He says he feels most at home around Mesquakis and hopes to live the rest of his life with them because

They are down-to-earth people, simple people. They know how to laugh and have fun and enjoy life. I'm walking around here humming songs. That's what gets me through the day. I can't explain it, but it pacifies me, the drum's like a heartbeat.

Of his own people he says that they make no effort to really know Mesquakis. He was quite critical of the BIA and called what whites did to
Indians a crime and more inhuman than Hitler. He recounted several
run-ins with local whites, and he thinks all locals are rednecks. Even his
"real dad doesn't know how to take me. He thinks the Indians stole me
away, that I'm wasting my life. My mom understands, she says that God
meant for me to be with the Indians."

So Red has very little to do with local whites, other than those he works
with as a Casino security guard. He sees his family occasionally, but his life
is centered around his Mesquaki friends, singing in a drum group, and
powwowing.

As we talked late into the night this strapping young ex-Golden Gloves
boxer recounted his bitter school experiences as a dyslexic learner. White
society's rules and regulations and social pressures helped drive him
towards the Mesquakis:

I wasn't accepted by white people even at a young age. I used to get made fun of
and got put in classes with retarded kids. I was the only white on an all-Mexican
boxing team, and I had a lot of black friends. I'd train in my gym in the garage
and they'd drive by and shoot bottle rockets at me and do cheap stuff.

Nevertheless, Red knows he is only a guest among the Mesquakis. Greyson has explained that he will never be fully accepted into the tribe, but
he still wants to marry a Mesquaki and settle down near the settlement.
He even hopes to die like an Indian. He wants to be buried in a pine box,
but added respectfully, "not dressed like an Indian. I know I can never
really be an Indian." So Cowboy Red wants the next best thing. He wants
to go out in his cowboy boots, jeans, and a beaded belt buckle with an
Indian blanket over him.

The other so-called "wannabe" is a tall, slender UNI graduate who was
initially drawn to the Mesquakis because of his interest in Indian art. Bill's
mother is a school teacher and his father an ex-farmer and foreman for a
city government. His mother is quite accepting of his lifestyle, but his
father thinks he is just "playing at being an Indian." His interest in Indians started in high school through an Indian friend and by going to
powwows. He was especially drawn to "museums and the real firsthand
stuff." Unfortunately, racist attitudes at UNI and dull college classes on
Indian art and culture left him unsatisfied with his knowledge of Indians.
So Bill began gravitating towards the Mesquaki settlement "to learn from
living craftspeople and a living culture." Initially, he met several traditional families and began taking pictures of people's family heirlooms.
He was especially drawn to the work of artist Leon GreyEagle.

After graduation Bill moved to Marshalltown to continue selling his

wood carvings, beadwork, and jewelry at powwows and buckskinner rendezvous. He continued to visit the settlement, and within three years was
actually living there with a friend. His story of endless relatives and friends
eating, sleeping, and using the house and his things reminded me of my
life in a tiny Philippine fishing village. Having been brought up in neighborly Iowa, I found it quite a shock when they considered me "stingy" and
"selfish" for not sharing everything freely. Bill had a somewhat similar
experience in a communal Mesquaki household. There was no privacy,
no private property, no organized household duties. Extended family
members who came visiting had a right to your things and space. Despite
these initial difficulties with communal living, Bill hopes to marry a Mesquaki and be as much a part of settlement life as possible.

After being around the settlement many years, Bill has gained the trust
of several families. His friend and mentor Leon GreyEagle has begun to
teach him what it means to be a good and spiritual person. Bill was quick
to add that Leon's teachings did not include any secret knowledge about
the clan ceremonies, but he was allowed to be a server and helper during
Leon's adoption. He has also attended some wakes and funerals, and
dances regularly in the powwow. He showed me his pouch of tobacco and
said in a reverential tone,

Leon taught me that there is great power in giving gifts to others, in trading
things, in not just killing an animal without giving thanks. Things return to you
when they are supposed to. I don't rush around trying to collect things anymore.
If I am supposed to have them, they will come to me.

The comment about how he collected things intrigued me. I had heard
several Mesquakis grumbling about Bill selling his art work as genuine
Indian artifacts. One tribal elder raged that he was going to have some of
the young men beat him up and throw him off the settlement. Before I
could confront Bill about these stories, he became very quiet and said, "It
is hard to admit these things but when I first came here." Then he confessed that he had tried to collect objects and to hear sacred stories
"before I was spiritually ready to have and know such things."

Later Bill also admitted making some objects that were not authentic
"to fool pompous art collectors and curators who claim to be Indian art
experts." Since he has never made much money off these sales and lives
quite simply in a small apartment in town, his primary motivation seems
to spring from being a bit of a maverick with an off-beat sense of humor.
He likes fooling the outsiders who come to "rip off" Mesquaki heirlooms.
But Leon made him see that he would never become a spiritual person
doing such things, so Bill has stopped tricking outside experts and collecting for himself.

Although very different personalities, both Red and Bill seemed like loyal white allies of the Mesquaki. One, an ex-boxer, has punched out local rednecks. The other, an artist, has fooled white art collectors. Both were highly critical of local whites for having little knowledge of and appreciation for Mesquaki culture. Both extolled the Mesquakis as less materialistic and more spiritual and humane than whites. They were drawn to what anthropologists call their expressive culture of music, dance, art, storytelling, and humor. Unlike the anguished liberal teachers and liberal white youths, these two experience little self-doubt or guilt about crossing the racial border. Their close friendships with prominent traditional families make them acceptable — as long as they understand that they are guests of the tribe and nothing more.

And where do anthropological border-crossers like me fit into all this? Lots of people questioned my sincerity and asked if I was going to disappear like most researchers do. One memorable discussion of this topic occurred with Jay WhiteHawk and Jonas CutCow. We were loafing around at the tribal center one day, and they began complaining that researchers came all friendly and full of questions but never returned. Jonas had one solution for the problem. He chipped in, "We oughta have our own pet anthropologist who stays and dances at the powwow. The Sacs and Chippewa have one with a Ph.D. and everything."

I protested that Bill and Red already dance at the powwows, and he retorted, "Ya, but they don't have Ph.D.s."

That got Jay going on the utility of white guys with doctor's degrees. He told this fanciful tale about about a dog he got from a Mexican who spoke Spanish to it. Unfortunately, the Mexican also screwed his dog, so Jay was stuck with one confused puppy. He continued, "She needs a psychiatrist, Doug. You are a doctor. Maybe you can help my dog out, give her some counseling."

Jonas and he went on telling dog stories, several with interracial themes, for example, the story of the rich white lady whose fancy pedigreed dog got screwed by a Mesquaki mutt at the powwow. At the time, these stories made me feel a little guilty about being an "anthropological drifter." So maybe I will have to come back to visit the settlement from time to time. It is the least I could do for my old pal Jay and his dog.

Chapter 6
Building a Modern Political Culture

Life on the settlement is punctuated by a great deal of heated political talk. For most local whites, Mesquaki politics is a wild, contentious, hopelessly factionalized affair. One businessman echoed a common sentiment,

They can't do anything out there without squabbling over it for a couple years. I hate doing anything with the tribal council for fear of getting caught up in some vendetta. That place will never prosper until they learn to cooperate with each other.

He is quite sure that Indians are inherently less reasonable and cooperative than whites. Indians are also supposedly much more susceptible to political corruption that whites. Most local whites willingly feed this view to the journalists who come looking for stories. After listening to such white commentaries and to Mesquaki political rhetoric, reporters serve up juicy stories about the corrupt, squabbling Indians. A series of articles by Bob Shaw (DMR, December 16, 21, 1984; October 5, 1986) illustrates nicely how contemporary journalists continue to portray Mesquaki politics.

In Search of "Backward Traditionalists"

Shaw writes about Mesquaki politics from the usual proassimilationist perspective. His final article (DMR, October 5, 1986) begins dramatically,

Like a timber wolf in a steel trap, the Mesquaki nation is caught. Fear of the "whiteman's progress" and the grip of ancient customs—including the ritual eating of dog meat, unknown to most outsiders until now—help keep the Indians locked in poverty.

He goes on to describe how members of the sacred bundle sect dominate the council and give all the houses and jobs to their relatives.

Shaw turns tribal politics into a melodramatic TV soap opera about the titanic struggle between the forces of good and evil. His portrayal of tribal politics fits into a long tradition of white commentary. In the 1930s and 1940s, the good guys were the progressive Youngbear faction who wanted to adopt white ways, and the bad guys were the conservative Oldbear faction who wanted to preserve Indian ways. In the 1980s, the good guys and reformers are the Mesquakis who want to build a casino. The bad guys are the corrupt, dog-eating, religious fanatics who run the tribal council and oppose the casino.

This caricature of "progressives" and "traditionalists" got a good laugh from several Mesquaki readers. Their favorite part, and mine, is when Mike Walkfar nearly pulls Shaw's leg out of the socket. I can see Mike telling Shaw in his dry, matter-of-fact way, "Indians generally consume terriers or collies, but never German shepherds, bulldogs, or hounds." Shaw, eager for a titillating story on bizarre Indian religion and politics, writes it all down as the gospel truth. As I read the article to Lone True-Blood, he almost fell out of his chair laughing at Mike's comments, "I guess whites will believe just about anything we tell 'em, huh, Doug?" I guess so, Lone. One has to wonder what white readers make of the alleged Mesquaki preference of Lassie over Rin Tin Tin.

The articles also use the well-worn poverty discourse of white liberals to portray settlement life sentimentally. Shaw serves up the usual tear-jerking story of a backward, poverty-stricken minority community. He gets various settlement residents to tell stories about the holes in their roofs and how they have hauled buckets of water for years. In this instance, the poverty portrayal is used to indict the traditionalists, who are against the progressives' high-stakes gambling schemes.

Finally, Shaw plays Mike Wallace and also goes after Mesquaki political corruption. He waves a federal audit under the noses of former tribal councilmen about their new houses and room additions. U.S. Attorney Evan Hultman, who has probably never seen the settlement, is cited as an "expert" on Mesquaki politics. Hultman willingly participates in Shaw's little melodrama and says authoritatively, "Favoritism is a way of doing business with them" (DMR, December 16, 1984). So Shaw gets everyone he interviews to paint his portrait of the corrupt, dog-eating conservatives who are holding back the tribe.

Local white commentaries on Mesquaki squabbling and political corruption are particularly amusing, given the history of political squabbling in my hometown. After many stories on Indian factionalism, the *Register* finally did a story on "white factionalism" entitled "So near, yet so far: Tama, Toledo seem to have agreed to disagree" (DMR, January 1, 1983). The reporter describes the two towns next to the settlement as "Siamese twins born joined at their outskirts in 1860 but forever looking askance at one another."

The article goes on to quote a number of old-timers characterizing these towns exactly the way I heard it growing up — and still hear it today. Tama was a dirty, rough little river town full of rowdy bars, and Toledo was a quiet, sophisticated town where the educated elite lived. They have always fought like cats and dogs and will never get together. Nevertheless, the article ends on an optimistic note that younger residents no longer care about the old rivalry and long for unity.

Days after the article surfaced, the local editor charged the *Register* with irresponsible journalism. He suggested it change its motto from "the paper all Iowa depends upon" to "the paper all Iowa defends itself from" (Toledo *Chronicle*, January 1, 1983). Some local residents agreed, and various Chamber of Commerce members decried it as an attempt to "tear down what we are trying to build." The mayor accused the reporter of "just bumming around trying to find the negative," and added that the two cities sponsored a host of joint programs. Others saw no point to an article that "opened up old wounds." Others claimed that the article misquoted them.

Reading about this hubbub made me wonder how my portrayal of racial conflict would be accepted. Whites are terribly sensitive about anyone recounting discord in their community. Apparently, the less said about conflict the better. In fact, the two towns squabbled for twenty years before finally combining their schools. They have also talked about combining city councils, police forces, and various services for forty years, but these services remain separate. In short, the original article is far more accurate than the townspeople will admit. So why do whites deny their own political squabbling and factionalism so vehemently?

Sociologist Dean McCannell's (1992) discussion of mainstream white attitudes helps explain why whites view Indian and white factionalism so differently. He argues that mainstream American whites, being the dominant political majority, think of themselves as the center of rationality. In contrast, those people living on the periphery of mainstream society, the nonwhite "minorities," are viewed as less controlled, objective, and rational. This is precisely how local whites talk about Mesquaki politics. Mesquakis are supposedly inherently irrational and quarrelsome. Constant talk about Mesquaki squabbling and corruption allows whites to downplay their own tendencies to factionalize, engage in political corruption, and be irrational and uncooperative.

Anyone who has paid attention to Watergate, Iran-Contra, the savings and loan scandal, and Pentagon-gouging should find Hultman's commentary on Mesquaki corruption amusing. White politicians are obviously excellent role models for ethnic politicians. Nevertheless, journalists persist in parroting the mainstream mentality that whites are more rational and incorruptible. If we are to get beyond such a shallow view of

Mesquaki politics, we must take a deeper look at Mesquaki culture. To this end, earlier action anthropologists tried to give a more cultural account of tribal politics (Gearing, 1970). Here is a sketch of how they understood the political secession dispute that has plagued the Mesquakis for a hundred years.

A Little Mesquaki Political History on Tribal Factionalism

By the late nineteenth century, the tribe had lost all its lands through a series of treaties culminating with the Black Hawk War Treaty of 1842. After refusing to stay on a federal reservation in Kansas, the Mesquakis returned to Iowa and purchased eighty acres on the Iowa River in 1856. There they eked out a subsistence living from hunting, trapping, summer gardens, and occasional day labor for local farmers. Missionaries came to Christianize them, and Indian agents tried to get them to take up farming and go to school. Some dissension over annuity payments and non-Mesquakis living on the settlement existed, but the hereditary monarch and council of clan elders generally ruled without serious factionalism. In 1882 the clan elders made a fateful decision that eventually caused a secession dispute. They chose Pushetonequa to be the hereditary chief over the apparent Oldbear heir, who was a young boy.

Pushetonequa actually ruled without controversy for thirteen years, but in 1895 Indian agent Horace Rebok cajoled and forced the reluctant chief to send Mesquaki youth to a vocational boarding school. As elaborated in Chapter three, Rebok's school definitely galvanized Oldbear opposition. The more white newspapers and Rebok praised Pushetonequa as a modern Indian, the more the Oldbear traditionalists saw him as a pawn in the whiteman's assimilation policy. Even today, one story on the settlement has it that Chief Pushetonequa greedily accepted the $500 annuity payment and sold out his people. Supporters of Pushetonequa claim that he had little choice. They claim that white authorities were threatening to imprison one of the chief's sons if he did not cooperate.

When historian Duran Ward arrived on the settlement in 1905, he found the Mesquaki political system in considerable turmoil (Ward files). The hereditary chieftainship was in dispute, and the tribe was badly divided. Two separate tribal councils existed — one run by Chief Pushetonequa and government sanctioned, the other run by John Tataposh and Oldbear loyalists. Ward quotes Pushetonequa as saying that Chief Poweshiek, who led the tribe after the Black Hawk War, was his father's brother and had passed the treaties to him. Moreover, Pushetonequa told Ward that his heart was made from the Creator's heart, thus divine blood flowed in his veins. The deposed Oldbear group claimed that Pushetonequa was no more than an orphan child taken in by the Poweshiek family.

They told Ward that he was a Sac without a drop of royal blood running through his veins. Moreover, the group added, Poweshiek had been a Mesquaki chief in name only and too influenced by the Sac appeaser, Chief Keokuk. The Oldbears complained that Poweshiek gave away tribal lands too easily and moved to the Kansas reservation without a fight.

In retrospect, the entire secession controversy seems to hinge on how strict the Mesquaki rule of secession was. Action anthropologist Charles Callender (ND) points out that the early accounts of the Mesquaki political system (Blair, 1911) are inconclusive. He argues that when the black bear lineage (the modern Oldbears) successor was too young or incompetent, the council selected a chief from another lineage within the bear clan. For example, Poweshiek of the brown bear lineage was chosen in 1842, as was his adopted son Pushetonequa in 1882. The creation story does not spell out whether only one bear clan lineage is divine. Given that ambiguity, both the Pushetonequa lineage and the Oldbear lineages apparently claimed divine origins.

Whatever the truth of these events, the Oldbear account of Pushteonequa's illegitimate secession eventually became the official written tribal political history (Waseskuk, 1978; Windsong,1978). Historically, Oldbear traditionalists have blasted the tribal council for not being Indian enough on various issues. In 1921 they attacked the white-sponsored powwow. In 1937 they tried to block the formation of a white-style elected tribal government. In 1957 they challenged the land reparations settlement as a sell-out of their sacred treaty. In 1972 they cried "sacrilege" when sacred trees were sold to white loggers. In the 1980s and 1990s they prophesized that gambling would bring disaster. Throughout history, the Oldbears have been outspoken, but their legal actions and search for the missing treaty has never been successful.

During this long, contentious debate over secession, tribal fortunes took a particularly bad turn from 1900 to 1937. Throughout this dark period of Mesquaki history, a string of Indian agents replaced the hereditary monarchy and clan system with their own council appointees. As in other colonial situations, the tribe was easier to rule and control when divided. Politically astute agents usually included elders from various clans and factions, but their meddling left Mesquaki political leaders ineffectual and powerless. It also left the more accommodating sons and grandsons of Pushetonequa in control of the council. Meanwhile, the deposed Oldbear faction refused to participate in the tribal council, which they considered illegitimate.

This state of affairs began to change when Indian Agency head John Collier, a liberal Roosevelt Democrat, tried to revitalize tribal governments through his Indian Reorganization Act. Put simply, tribes were to decide through open, democratic elections what form of political system they preferred. Some tribes went back to their traditional political systems, others chose to create entirely new political systems. In a hotly contested 1937 election, the Mesquakis chose a white-style elected tribal council with a written constitution by a vote of 87 to 85. On the positive side, this reform curbed the arbitrary power of Indian agents and reestablished the practice of Mesquakis choosing their council. On the other hand, leaders were now chosen by general elections rather than by clan elders. This signaled the official end of the hereditary monarchy, but not the controversy, which the white press played up as the good Youngbears versus the bad Oldbears.

Action Anthropologists Live and Write Mesquaki Factionalism

When action anthropologists arrived in 1948, they were inadvertently dragged into this Mesquaki political conflict. At the time, Jack Oldbear was actively pursuing a federal law suit, and Bertha Waseskuk was searching for secret treaties in Washington. The Fox Project fieldnotes suggest that the 1953 project leader Fred Gearing attended several Oldbear political meetings and developed close relations with traditionalists Bob and Bertha Waseskuk. Consequently, tribal chairman and progressive Ed Davenport became suspicious of the young anthropologists, and they in turn felt he treated them like "errand boys." They perceived him as an assimilated Indian who had a dictatorial, un-Mesquaki leadership style. When Gearing published his newspaper articles extolling Mesquaki traditionalism, the Davenport-led council apparently considered asking the project to leave.

But, after considerable agonizing, the student anthropologists were able to avoid a direct confrontation with the council. In their finest hour, they helped the Mesquakis stop the BIA from closing the tribal school. They also quietly launched a successful college scholarship program and a small handicraft industry. Having survived settlement politics, action anthropologists eventually wrote what is still considered the definitive account of modern Mesquaki politics (Gearing et al., 1960; Gearing, 1970). Unlike Shaw and many reporters before him, they never portrayed Mesquaki factionalism as a titanic assimilation battle between good, prowhite progressives and bad traditionalists. They quickly concluded that both political factions contained progressives and traditionalists. They also understood that progressives were not for giving up all Indian ways, and that traditionalists were not against adopting some white ways.

In addition, Tax and his students indicted the Indian service for destroying the traditional Mesquaki political system. To verify whether any old political practices survived, Walter Miller (1955) studied modern Mesquaki community organizations like the powwow, band, canning co-ops, sports teams, and veterans' association. Miller concluded that most contemporary Mesquaki organizations failed because they were modeled on white organizations. Invariably, strong, domineering leaders drove off many tribal members, thus these white-style hierarchical organizations collapsed.

The only Mesquaki organization that functioned well year after year was the powwow. Miller argued that it succeeded because its authority structure included representatives from all the clans. Moreover, its administrative leader was like an ancient peace chief who mediated conflict and never imposed decisions. In short, the only modern Mesquaki community organization that worked had a very ancient cultural character. This portrayal of the powwow committee as an ancient political organization makes little sense today, but Miller claimed it did in the 1950s.

Gearing (1970) eventually elaborated Miller's sobering study of dysfunctional community organizations with his own bleak portrait of a badly factionalized Mesquaki political system. He basically argued that the traditionalistic culture and personality of the Mesquakis was ill-suited to modernize their "structurally paralyzed" community. According to Gearing, modern Mesquakis were still being socialized to be gentle, circumspect, generous, and non-aggressive. As a result, the traditionalistic Mesquakis would have difficulty creating and functioning in a modern representative political system with a rigid hierarchy and strong leaders.

In retrospect, these action anthropologists wanted to fix the Mesquakis' broken political system. Since they believed the old system to be in ruins, they wanted to replace it with what political scientists of their era called a democratic civic culture (Almond and Verba, 1960). They saw themselves as "temporary advisors" and "therapists" who would help the Mesquakis develop a wide range of empowering modern "voluntary civic organizations." Consequently, they raised money to initiate and manage a variety of social and recreational and economic programs. Participation in these new community organizations was supposed to create more cooperative, civic-minded tribal members, thus ending the destructive factionalism the Indian service had created.

Their community projects never lasted long enough to build the new civic culture they extolled (Foley, ND), and their scientific theory prematurely declared the Mesquaki political system paralyzed. To better understand contemporary Mesquaki politics, we must abandon both the popular journalistic images of quarreling, corrupt Indians and the Fox Project's scientific theory of a dysfunctional, broken political system.

Another View of Mesquaki Factionalism and Politics

We must begin by acknowledging that Mesquaki society is still far more communalistic and religious than white society. The earlier presentations of traditional burial, mourning, and adoption ceremonies illustrate how closely linked Mesquakis are. Everyone shares the material and psychological costs of every death. Everyone participates in a variety of secular ceremonies as well. The one constant in Mesquaki society is the steady flow of people and food back and forth between households during various ceremonies.

In addition, the settlement has no private property with deeds of trusts and mortgages. Each enrolled tribal member has the right to claim and use a piece of land for his or her family home site. There is no specified minimum or maximum, but most people claim an acre or two for their homesteads. Not infrequently, family compounds develop with several houses and trailers on a few acres. If the family use and maintain the land, future generations of that family may continue to use the land. If the family abandon their land and residence, the tribal council eventually reassigns it to someone else. Larger tracts of tillable agricultural land are also assigned to families to keep using until abandoned.

The tribe provides each homestead plot with free sewer and water hookups and a driveway. The only utilities enrolled tribal members purchase from outside companies are electricity and phones. In addition, there is no local property tax to finance education, medical or alcohol treatment, indigent relief, food commodities, hot lunches, road maintenance, or garbage pickup programs. Each tribal service program is funded from a different federal grant, or from the general tribal fund. The general fund includes revenues from land reparations settlements, land rentals, and gaming revenues.

When additional federal money has been available to build houses, the tribal council has given enrolled members a free house. In the past twenty years, the tribe has built approximately fifty three-bedroom, one-thousand-square-foot frame houses. Usually, a housing committee creates a priority list of families based on need, which the council may or may not use to distribute the houses. As long as the houses are used and not abandoned, the original recipient can pass the house to a sibling. Oftentimes, other family members purchase a mobile home to place on the family site, or they may wish to split off from the family and develop their own site. In short, the tribe provides an impressive array of social services and free houses not available in the competitive, market-oriented, white community.

Finally, it is safe to say that nearly all Mesquakis are related through marriage ties or symbolic adoptions. I lacked the resources to do the usual community survey, but even casual observations quickly reveal the extraordinary movement of cousins, nephews and nieces, and in-laws between households. As the so-called white wannabe Bill found out, living in one individual's house means sharing food, clothes, vehicles, tools, and living quarters with many relatives and in-laws. Of course elders say that the old ways of sharing and cooperation have broken down. They lament the rise of consumerism and individualism and the decline of parental discipline and respect from the young. Traditionalist laments notwithstanding, the settlement is still much more communalistic than the neighboring white towns.

Lest I paint too romantic a view of tribal communalism or "communitas" (Turner, 1974), life on the settlement is not all peace and harmony. Mesquakis fight and argue over the same things that other people do. Despite their religion and close-knit families, they also get angry and drunk and do nasty things to spouses, girl/boy friends, in-laws, and neighbors. Numerous people told me stories about two family feuds that have gone on for years. These feuds have lead to much jealousy, gossip, and even a couple of revenge killings. Moreover, like any other group, some Mesquakis cannot stand other Mesquakis, and personality conflicts are not uncommon. Someone says something ugly about another person; that person punches out his or her critic, and a grudge is born.

Moreover, strong traditional religious beliefs may actually intensify the conflicts between groups or individuals. Most Mesquakis still believe in both good and evil spiritual forces. Consequently, they tend to judge the behavior of their political leaders from a religious perspective much more than whites do. I collected countless stories about prominent Mesquaki political leaders who allegedly misused their spiritual powers to get what they desire — another man's woman, his land, his house — with love potions and curses. Mesquakis seemed willing to believe that their leaders would stoop to using "bad medicine" or witchcraft.

In summary, ghost feasts, wakes, funerals, and adoptions create solidarity, but family feuds, personality conflicts, and the threat of bad medicine create suspicion and distrust. The intense, contradictory character of settlement life magnifies factional feuds such as the one over secession. Settlement politics is a Byzantine web of friends, enemies, and intrigues — a real cauldron of intense feelings that can get personal and nasty. Sometimes the tribe is its own worst enemy, and at times political factionalism has been disruptive and costly. The long secession dispute cost the Mesquakis control over their political system for years. The 1975 tribal school dispute cost the tribe many children who cannot speak Mesquaki.

Despite these setbacks, it is useful to take a more generous view of Mesquaki factionalism as a long, conflictful "discursive process." Faced with the powerful, hegemonic ideology of assimilation, the Mesquakis are constantly forced to debate each new adoption of white culture. Viewed this way, Mesquaki factionalism is actually a tribally led political debate or dialogue that moves the tribe forward. From this perspective, the ancient Mesquaki political system has never really broken down. The traditionalists and the progressives frequently argue openly about their differences before fusing various white cultural practices into their ever changing culture. Present-day Mesquaki talk about tribal political leaders illustrates nicely how this process of cultural fusion is taking place.

Political Talk and Petitions in a Cultural Borderland

Anyone visiting the settlement would be surprised by the harsh things that Mesquakis say about their tribal council. After listening to much settlement political talk, I finally realized that most Mesquakis expect their leaders to talk like whites, yet act like Indians. In traditional Mesquaki society, a moral leader is one who maintains the web of kin relations through political largess. Kin and friends actually have a right to jobs, houses, scholarships, and awards. There is nothing particularly corrupt about leaders rewarding kin.

On the other hand, settlement life is changing, and Mesquakis have begun to talk like the whiteman. They have gradually adopted the white notion of educational credentials and professionalism. They now criticize their political leaders for lacking educational credentials. Increasingly, they expect their leaders to possess formal, certified knowledge in various specializations. This introduces an entirely different notion of leadership and a new criteria for distributing tribal wealth. Impartial leaders are supposed to eschew kin and friendship affiliations. They are supposed to distribute jobs, houses, scholarships, and awards based on performance or objective standards of need. From this perspective, rewarding kin can be considered a form of political corruption.

Mesquakis have also borrowed a page from American political thought on direct forms of democracy. Tribal members who are dissatisfied with the elected leaders invariably initiate recall petition drives. Their petitions often denounce certain policies and leaders. They air their political differences through lively council meetings and scathing personal attacks on the councilmen. When Mesquaki politics really heats up, council critics will use outside federal audits to attack their political adversaries. The press loves to play up such audits and petitions as examples of widespread political corruption.

What most outside reporters overlook in these rhetorical blasts, petitions, firings, and audits is the complex fusion of white and Indian values occurring. Up to a point, it all looks like the lively town hall meetings extolled in the writings of Thomas Jefferson and Thomas Paine. But when the debate becomes too divisive some council members invariably stop coming to the meetings. Not infrequently a divided council may drift for months without a quorum or any decisions. Tribal government may come to a complete standstill until some peacemakers emerge and, somehow, create a political consensus.

Mesquaki politicians are often quick to use the white reformist discourse to attack opponents and win elections. But the political criticism of leaders usually runs a predictable course. Politicians and administrators are mercilessly criticized and ousted from office. Then when all the political rhetoric dies down, the tribe is able to create a consensus and make decisions. Even more important, Mesquakis rarely punish banished council members or administrators with criminal law suits. In Mesquaki society no one is ever really defeated politically or fired permanently. The ousted politicians usually retreat to private life and do a few years of penance. After a time, they return to work for the tribal enterprises or tribal center as if nothing had ever happened.

In the end, traditional practices of reciprocity tend to prevail over the rhetoric of professionalism and reformism. The so-called progressives are just as likely to give their relatives houses and jobs as the so-called traditionalists are. On the other hand, even traditionalists are increasingly professional in the way they run the tribal enterprises and social programs. As long as the communal basis of politics remains, Mesquaki leaders will continue to struggle with this fusion of modern professional norms and traditional norms of reciprocity. Moralistic denunciations of political corruption and scientistic theories of dysfunctional factionalism overlook the positive cultural changes. The discursive battles that outsiders call "factionalism" really signal a much broader, creative process of ethnic survival.

The Rise of Ethnic Indians and a Tribal Welfare State

After a hundred years of debate, most Mesquakis now accept the elected council and there is even talk of making the tribal council members a salaried position. For practical political purposes, the secession debate and the Oldbear-Youngbear factions have passed into history. Today, most Mesquakis say something like, "It is all mixed up now, you can't tell the Oldbears from the Youngbears." What they mean is that distinguishing between accommodating and antiwhite Indians is increasingly difficult. Vine Deloria's (1985) distinction between "traditional Indians" and "ethnic Indians" is useful here. Deloria argues that the 1960s civil rights era energized and politicized many young urban Indians to demand tribal rights and to revitalize their traditional cultures.

Like many other ethnic groups in the United States, the Mesquakis are responding to fundamental reforms in the American state. New laws and policies have opened up some space for Indian tribes to seek greater political and cultural autonomy. The Kennedy Commission report (1969) on Native Americans and the Indian Self-Determination Act of 1972 set BIA policies in a new direction. Old paternalistic policies have given way to Indian-controlled tribal governments, schools, health, and welfare agencies. With the passage of the 1988 Federal Gaming Act, Indian tribes were also encouraged to develop an independent, self-sufficient reservation economy.

As we saw in Chapter two, AIM and non-AIM Mesquaki activists responded to these national trends and initiated aggressive new civil rights demands. This new attitude is apparent in the protests, walkouts, pow-wow, cultural presentations, and writings described earlier. The ideological difference between the settlement's progressives and traditionalists has finally broken down. Now that the new college-educated leaders have the linguistic, educational, and economic capital to join the mainstream, they are demanding the rights and benefits due to all American citizens. They are also more openly espousing an ideology of cultural separatism. In essence, the tribe has become an assertive American ethnic minority.

If we take a longer historical view of this cultural and political transformation, it probably began around the turn of the century. Perhaps the first major turning point in modern Mesquaki cultural history occurred in 1902. At that time, the white medical authorities forced the tribe to burn the communal wickiups to avoid a smallpox epidemic (CutCow, ND). The authorities claimed that separate white-style frame houses for each family would help control contagious diseases. The new housing pattern, and the simultaneous implementation of day schools, fundamentally altered the way children were brought up.

The second important turning point occurred during World War II. Nearly every young male on the settlement went off to war, and many of the women worked in war plants. As the action anthropologists so ably documented, greater contact with the white world left Mesquakis more open to cultural change. On one hand, many Mesquaki veterans came home deeply discontent and disoriented. Unlike a number of other tribes (Bernstein, 1990), this postwar generation of Mesquaki males never took advantage of the G.I. Bill. Only two of fifty-two veterans used the bill to go to college or vocational school.

On the other hand, tribal leaders reacted to this crisis and requested Sol Tax and his students to help them educate the veterans' younger brothers and sisters. In response, the Fox Project worked tirelessly to raise $100,000 for a college scholarship program. Much of the money came from a New York foundation, but they also raised money statewide and talked Iowa colleges and universities into tuition waivers for Mesquakis. Although only five of eighteen scholarship recipients eventually returned to the settlement, the Fox Project helped initiate a post-war trend of Mesquaki youth going to college.

The third and final turning point in modern Mesquaki cultural history is the civil rights era. This epoch produced a plethora of political actions, laws, and social programs. The AIM movement, the Indian Self-Determination Act, and BIA scholarships for all Indian high school graduates created a unique set of political and economic conditions missing in the 1950s. The 1970s generation of Mesquakis were much more politicized than earlier generations, and they went off to junior college and college in record numbers. I was unable to do a systematic survey, but I would estimate that as many as 50 percent of the 1970s generation finished two or more years of college or junior college.

Once these "baby boomers" stopped raising hell in high school and college, they became the benefactors of a civil rights movement that precipitated much new empowering legislation. A sociologist would dub these middle-aged men and women the "new middle class" of Mesquaki society. We have already met this post-civil rights generation of civic leaders in the summer teacher training institute. They were pressing for educational reforms and urging their children to go to college. We have met others leading the school walkouts, writing books, and making cultural presentations. They, especially the women, were busy running the tribal school board, and recreational, community health, welfare, housing, and alcohol treatment programs. In addition, these women were keeping the tribe's books, programming the computers, and administering social service programs for the elderly and youth.

What follows are some vignettes of Mesquaki men and women who grew up in the 1970s and are active civically. These people all think of themselves as traditionalists or "real Indians." I should add that the label "traditionalist" is a very slippery term, and as an outsider, it was difficult for me to verify how active people were religiously. What I found interesting about the political talk of all these people was how they portrayed themselves as both progressives and traditionalists. They represent themselves as a new ideological synthesis in Mesquaki politics. They illustrate vividly how modern Mesquaki civic leaders are fusing white political and economic practices to their traditional culture. For lack of a better term, I have labeled them "progressive-traditionalists."

Progressive-Traditionalists Talk Politics and Religion

One of the most interesting "border crossers" I met was Lester Running-Wolf. Claude Windsong introduced him to me as someone who was also doing research. At the time, Lester was conducting interviews for a social work professor on family problems but said he was going to quit because "spying on my people makes me feel like a Crow scout." He said it in a way that made me curious, so one cold winter day I showed up at his house. Lester came out sleepy-eyed and led me to a room as he mumbled, "I don't usually let people come back here." Suddenly we entered a collage of bones, books, drums, rattles, and feathered headdresses surrounding a sleeping bag. I pulled up a box, and he stoked up the hot plate and threw some coffee grounds into a pot.

He began the conversation with a brutally frank admission about what people think of him:

Lots of people around here think I'm crazy, a drunkard, troublemaker, womanizer, fighter, too moody, over-educated, but I don't care. I've done stuff they'll never do like going to school, Viet Nam, my hunting.

To counter such talk, he recounted a ten-year quest to participate in and learn the traditional clan ceremonies. He was proud of being asked to be a lead singer but admitted that his involvement had been sporadic lately.

Lester has also pursued his spirituality in Drum Society ceremonies, and through other non-Mesquaki ceremonies. He recently completed an Arapaho Sun Dance ceremony and has two pipes blessed by Arapaho medicine men. He also holds sweat lodge ceremonies for settlement members in the woods near his house. Lester sees these activities as traditional and a way to get closer to the Creator. Nevertheless, some tribal elders frown on these ceremonies as "pan-Indianism" and his sweat lodge ceremonies as "untraditional" because they are not family-centered.

On the other hand, Lester also wants to be a part of the white world, so he has pursued white educational credentials vigorously. After a tour in Viet Nam, he came home even more angry and disoriented than during his troubled youth. Throughout the turbulent 1970s he veered in and out of the local barroom scene and college. He and his brothers, ex-Golden Gloves fighters, enjoyed their battles with the Rathman brothers. But unlike his brothers Lester went off to college and married a white social worker. The marriage eventually fell apart, and as the 1980s began he settled into a STC paraprofessional counselor's position. After counseling Mesquaki youth for several years, Lester went back to school and finished his MA in social work, then transferred into a PhD program in American studies at the University of Iowa.

Traveling back and forth between Iowa City and the settlement has limited Lester's involvement in religious and civic activities in recent years, but when I returned in 1993 he had dropped out of his doctoral program to be a tribal executive. He had traded in his hunting bow and jogging shorts for a shiny black suit and bolo tie and was one of three casino commissioners. As before, Lester remains a controversial figure. He said, "Some people want me out of this position." Then he added rather casually, "If the new council gives this job to their buddies, I'll just go back to school." He remains a staunch advocate of "eclecticism" and pursues Indian spiritualism as actively as he pursues white education.

Entrepreneurship is something that many of the 1970s generation emphasize. One of the most outspoken advocates for developing Mesquaki businesses was former tribal chairman Richard Moline. Richard, a veteran who finished a year of junior college, puts it like this,

The reason we need more businesses and industry here is so we won't have to work outside. That way we can set up jobs that are flexible enough to let people go to the ceremonies.

Like many others, Richard argues that the settlement needs its own small businesses and services "so the dollar turns over more here." As we sat there eating donuts and drinking coffee, I kept dissenting that money and industry might ruin the Mesquakis.

Richard countered forcefully that real political and cultural autonomy only comes from a self-contained tribal economy. He also wanted the tribe to create its own police force and court system. He was particularly proud of the council's control over the new gaming operations.

Bingo came to a multi-million dollar investment, and we did it on our own. I want to see us do the same thing with a casino. I like to rub that into their (whites') faces. I'd like to compete with them, beat them at their own game. After bingo and the casino dies out, we can just be who we are.

For many progressive-traditionalists like Richard, economic development activities will save traditional Mesquaki culture.

Unlike earlier traditionalists who were opposed to a bilingual-bicultural tribal school, Richard also wants a new K–12 tribal school that teaches their language and culture. Most progressive-traditionalists have seen their own children's language skills deteriorate, and some like Richard, who spent his grade school days in the city, have personally suffered. He confessed that "I understand and speak some Mesquaki but am not fluent like my mother." Richard and his wife Anna, a tribal bookkeeper and active in tribal education, want their school to offer language programs for young adults as well. Like many of this generation, they want the two hundred Mesquaki youth in the STC schools back in the tribal school.

Richard also reported being active in thunder clan ceremonies and sounded like an Oldbear conservative when he talked about mixed-bloods.

You got lots of people hanging around that shouldn't be. People don't tell the mixed bloods of our unwritten laws. We have to quit being so toleran t to survive in the twenty-first century. The only thing you can do is promote Indian blood.

He also worries that there are "too many single mothers who are not teaching the old ways."

For progressive-traditionalists, the old traditionalist credo that education, jobs, and money will ruin the Indian is no longer true. Not all of the new civic leaders would agree with Richard's views on mixed-bloods, but most expressed similar pro-business views. Many tribal members sounded remarkably like the local white Chamber of Commerce types. They were optimistic that the tribe could have modern business, jobs, and more money without jeopardizing the culture. Many women who grew up during the civil rights era share these perspectives, but they also brought up issues that question how the modern Mesquaki political system is evolving.

Women Talk About Politics and Gender Restrictions

Since the political views of women are rarely reported, I decided to talk with a variety of women active in civic affairs. In all, I interviewed twenty-seven women and talked to many others in passing. I wanted to spend even more time with Mesquaki women, but various people warned me that it might create gossip and illfeelings. There is such a long tradition of white male's exploiting Mesquaki women that I felt constrained about talking extensively with single and single-parent women. Hopefully, Mesquaki women writers and female anthropologists and reporters will provide more in-depth accounts in the future. Given how little is written on Mesquaki women, what follows is at least a beginning.

One ancient cultural practice that greatly reduces the pool of tribal council leaders is the way Mesquakis reckon gender roles. In Mesquaki society a woman is considered unclean when she is menstruating. The unwritten cultural rule is that women may run for political positions only when they have passed their child-bearing time. Since the creation of an elected tribal council, only two women, Audry Windsong and Hanna James, have ever been elected. These women, both from prominent traditional families, ran for the council successfully after reaching menopause.

One young professional woman who has spoken forcefully and openly about politics is Jane WhiteHawk-GreyEagle. Jane is another of the 1970s generation who settled into an active civic role. She and her husband Rick GreyEagle have been involved in the tribal school and various youth activities for many years. Jane, who finished two years of college, was also part of the management team that started high stakes bingo. She is presently a bookkeeper for the casino. She is anxious to finish her degree and work her way into a management position with the casino.

When I breakfasted with Jane and Rick in their spacious new double-wide trailer, both were working as youth counselors at the nearby Toledo Juvenile Home. Rick made me feel like I was among health-conscious Austin friends when he asked, "Decaf or caffeinated?" As I sipped on my decaf, we reminisced about campus life and political activism in the "sixties." When we shifted into Mesquaki politics, Jane explained the role of women the way many other women did.

The women's movement doesn't happen here. In our tradition women can't be leaders. It should be a man. For example it was OK for Mary Fernbreast and me to be on the bingo committee because we weren't the main leaders. It isn't that you lack the ability or skills. Nobody has ever pushed to change it. Our belief is so strong, traditionalists would say no. It's even OK to be a tribal director or planner, and more accepted, reserved, well-liked older women, who are no longer unclean, can be on the tribal council.

Jane was not interested in going against the religious prohibitions, but she was anxious to have a more business-oriented tribal council. She put it this way, "Our tribal council needs to be educated. You try to keep up with the elders. They have to have more business types. Other tribes are way ahead of us with young people in there." For Jane and most of the women interviewed, getting business-oriented types on the council was more urgent than getting women elected. No woman questioned or challenged the unwritten rule that menstruating women cannot be on the council. Several of the professional women were more interested in assuming administrative leadership roles. Jane hoped to someday be in a position of authority at the casino "to make sure that the management company doesn't get away with anything."

Another young professional woman, Renee GreyEagle, also hoped to become an administrator in the new tribal bureaucracy. Renee, a University of Iowa graduate in political science, was active in campus Native American affairs in the early 1970s. After a variety of administrative and grant-writing jobs in Chicago and Washington, D.C., she returned to a similar position in the white schools. Like other single-parent mothers she balances the demands of three children with a professional career. When asked how she saw the role of women in Mesquaki politics, she responded candidly, "Things are still fairly traditional here, but there are a growing number of women in tribal administrative positions, and most women work outside the home now."

Being a school administrator, Renee also saw more women than men being assertive about children's rights in the white schools. I observed the same pattern of female educational reformers in South Texas (Foley, 1988). Various studies suggest that women, as the primary care-providers and nurturers, often become active educational advocates (Delgado-Gaitan, 1990; Lareau, 1989). On the settlement, Claude Windsong has garnered much publicity as a strong educational reformer, but it is Mesquaki women who have quietly done the day-to-day work. According to various white educators, Mabel Moon and Lisa RockIsland represented the tribe on educational committees for years. More recently Anna First-ley, Iris Snowflake, and Pat Firstley have been even more outspoken educational critics of the white schools.

In short, Mesquaki women play an important, informal political role in educational reform, both on and off the settlement. Not only are women the most active advocates for children, they hold most of the certified teaching and teacher aide positions in both schools. They also hold the majority of positions on the new tribal school board. Most women wanted me to stress how little recognition they have received for these efforts. Others interviewed mentioned the role that women play in running the tribal bureaucracy and gaming operations. Women program administrators abound in both of these operations, but as Jane GreyEagle and others noted, males are usually in the top administrative positions.

Another young professional woman, Lonnie Firstley, urged me to emphasize that women were also the keepers of the tribal tradition. Lonnie is a University of Iowa social work graduate who works for the Department of Human Services in Des Moines. She lives with her parents so her mother and grandmother will pass the language and tradition to her young son. Lonnie added that women also preserve the traditions by being the sewers and makers of ritual costumes. Then with a twinkle in her eye she said, "You should also say that sometimes the power behind the men on the council is the woman. I know the men will not admit it, but it is true."

I had heard many stories about the outspoken Firstley women, so I could not resist kidding her, "Does that mean all the stories I have heard about Firstley women are true?" She let out a huge laugh, then sorted out some of facts from the fiction about her female relatives. In the end, her main point was that women hold many Mesquaki families together and command more respect that outsiders might imagine. She and her mother Anna told me enough strong women stories to counter any white stereotype that I might have had about "submissive squaws." She added, "Although feminism is kind of a derogatory term here because it's associated with lesbianism, lots of Mesquaki women have these ideas but don't draw attention to themselves."

Both Lonnie and Renee, along with others interviewed, portrayed Mesquaki women as gradually becoming assertive. They noted that more women were reporting abusive drinking and irresponsible husbands. As a result, separations and divorces were more common than in the old days. Very few studies of settlement marriages and family life exist, but common law unions are the dominant practice. Individuals begin to cohabituate and announce that they are husband and wife. Such free unions are not sanctioned by the state or some religious body. Nevertheless, the ideal is to be monogamous and stay together for a lifetime. I met a number of elderly couples who had raised families, but according to these women, separation and "divorce" is now as common in Mesquaki society as it is in mainstream society.

I interviewed eight single-parent mothers who had separated or divorced for various reasons. Several were struggling mightily to support their children by running back and forth between a casino job and a factory job. They had very little time and energy for a personal life, but seemed extraordinarily resilient. These women still lived on the settlement, maintained close contact with their families, and were bringing up their children the Mesquaki way. They were strong, independent women with a variety of careers and levels of education. Several other single-parent women had children with several men and lived in town in subsidized housing. Most of these women and their unenrolled mixed-blood children had drifted away from Mesquaki culture. They seemed much less independent and in control of their lives than women residing with their parents.

Judging from this small sample, single-parent mothers vary from strong, independent, college-educated traditionalists to abandoned, struggling, welfare mothers with few career options. Most of the women I knew were accepted, productive members of Mesquaki society. There seemed to be no particular stigma attached to being separated or divorced. A more extensive, in-depth study is sorely needed, however, to help dispel the sexist stereotypes of single-parent women as all being disoriented "welfare freeloaders."

One thing most women agreed on was that too many women and their children had drifted away culturally. Many women were highly critical of how easy it is for men to abandon their children. One mother explained that the white courts have no legal jurisdiction to garner wages earned from the tribal enterprises. As a result, Mesquaki males working on the settlement can evade white paternity laws that protect women's rights. When I suggested going to the tribal council, the women portrayed the council as a bunch of "do-nothings" who avoided "going against their relatives." Unfortunately, neither the white nor Indian legal system helps most abandoned Mesquaki mothers.

When I asked whether the tribal council should take up the cause of single-parent mothers, these women gave mixed reactions. Several argued that the problem was deeply rooted in male attitudes. They mentioned several former councilmen who had not enrolled their own illegitimate children. Others added that men generally held women responsible for taking birth control precautions. One college student put it this way:

If a woman gets in trouble out here, people think it is her fault. This is still a very patriarchal society. No, there is no real feminist movement to stop these things.

These women generally wanted the tribal council to pressure males to enroll and financially support their offspring. Several blamed the tribal council for being "spineless" and failing to punish Mesquaki men who dishonored their women. The older women interviewed said that alcohol abuse and child abandonment were less tolerated in the old days.

In the course of doing fieldwork, I met several men who echoed these same sentiments. Tom Warrior, who considered himself a good family man, was particularly outspoken on the issue of male irresponsibility. Tom admitted to a wild youth that produced several out-of-wedlock children, but he took pride in enrolling them all. He offered this theory to explain why others took little responsibility for their offspring:

Since World War II lots of Mesquakis have taken on white ways and have lost their sense of manhood. When there was hunting and warfare men had honorable roles and were much more responsible. They would never let their women and families just take care of them like nowadays as they drink and drift from job to job.

Unlike feminists who emphasize sexism, Tom emphasizes the breakdown of traditional culture and the male role of protector. I chided him that he was exaggerating, and he quickly listed a dozen males who had sired unenrolled children and added,

The women you talked to are right. If these people can't be responsible, the council needs to make them. The family is everything. Mesquaki men have always cared for kids, worked in the gardens, done housework more than the stereotype of the warrior suggests. A man who isn't involved with his kids is nothing. The problem is that we have drifted from the old ways. We are more like the whiteman now.

During a conversation with a mother and her college-bound daughter, they also began listing males who failed to enroll their children or who beat their wives. The mother blamed most of these problems on alcohol, but the daughter complained that many Mesquaki women just tolerate abusive male behavior. The daughter characterized Mesquaki men as "spoiled" because they are allowed to stay out late, date who they wish, and avoid many household chores. The mother responded that she knew some families who brought their boys up to wash dishes and clean the house, but her daughter forced her to admit that male privilege persists.

Ultimately, most women portrayed gender roles as evolving toward more equality. Not having studied Mesquaki families and gender roles intensively, it is difficult to say. I observed a number of males taking care of their children, but I rarely saw men doing other domestic duties considered "women's work." Only a careful survey of household domestic practices could quantify what these twenty-six women told me in passing. Kristina Nelson and associates (ND) have documented some of the family disfunctionality and male irresponsibility that concerns many Mesquakis. What is needed are more in-depth portraits of functioning, close-knit families.

Although I lacked the resources to do such studies, I was generally impressed with the continuing strength of the extended family system. Several single-parent women whom I knew received much financial and moral support from their families. Local court attorneys and welfare workers confirmed these casual observations. They noted that the Mesquaki extended family provided more of a safety net for abandoned mothers than among low-income white families. They perceived the tribal council as very reluctant, however, to involve itself in family matters. As many of the women and some men said, abandoned women must ultimately rely on their families.

The one family issue the tribal council has pursued is the placement of orphaned children. Under the Indian Children's Welfare Act the tribe can set up their own department of human services to administer protective family services. Under this act the court, in consultation with social workers, must make every effort to place homeless Mesquaki children with other Mesquaki or Native American families. In 1980 Claude Windsong initiated and ran such a program for several years, but the council allowed these services to lapse until reinstated in 1993 under Windsong's direction. The council remains reluctant to set up a legal and social service system that would adjudicate familial problems.

Another interesting aspect of women's reflections was the tendency to compare their lifestyles with whites. Most Mesquaki women agreed that Mesquaki girls were raised playing with boys outdoors, and as one woman explained proudly, "They can't play with them if they cry and come home to tattle, so they get tough." Several women said they were brought up a little more like white farm girls than town girls. One woman expressed that view this way:

We seem a little more like them [white farm girls]. We don't chop wood and haul water like our mothers used to, but we still help out at home a lot. It seems like the rich white girls don't do much but drive around and party.

When I asked if that made Mesquaki women less "feminine," many would agree with the following comment:

We wear make-up and dresses, too, but we are taught to be more modest and less showy than white girls. If you are too painted up, and your dress is too tight, people will call you a "whore."

Most of these women expressed pride in playing sports such as basketball, volleyball, and track. The sophomore Mesquaki girls, a particularly good group of athletes, held their own in practices with the boys. Adult women also participated actively in recreational and town league sports. The other related image that Mesquaki women expressed often was their reputation as being "tough" and willing to fight white girls. They sensed that some white girls, who they considered "prissy," feared them. Everyone told her favorite intimidate-the-white-girls-story.

Such tough talk leaves the impression than Mesquaki women are no longer the sheltered, shy girls I remember from the 1950s. The Fox Project fieldnotes and the recollections of older women bear this out dramaticallly. Everyone agrees that the young women of the 1990s are much freer to date, drive cars, stay out late, drink, smoke, and go off to college or military service than their mothers. When I asked if the women's liberation movement had inspired this new assertiveness, most women said no. They emphasized that Mesquaki women have always been stronger than the squaw stereotype allows.

On the other hand, they were quick to point out that Mesquaki girls are still brought up to be more quiet and reserved and less career-oriented than white girls. One college graduate spoke for many when she said, "White girls are brought up thinking they can do anything they want. They were freer to say and do things. They go after careers more than we do. They go out with who they want. It's a lot more traditional out here."

The achievement-oriented, middle class white girls seemed to be the implicit model guiding their reflections. Although many Mesquaki women now go to college and have careers, they perceive the college-bound white girls as more self-confident and assertive.

Others also mentioned the inequality they felt in the interracial dating scene. Most women felt that it was more acceptable for Mesquaki boys to date whites. Mesquaki girls are brought up to avoid white boys, and all experienced social pressures against cross-racial dating from both races. Several women reported being ridiculed as a "squaw" for dating a white. In addition, marrying outside the tribe is severely punished since the enrollment rule automatically disenfranchises a woman's mixed-blood offspring. Although much freer than their mothers, young Mesquaki women felt more constrained than white women or Mesquaki males in their choice of dating and marital partners.

To sum up, despite cultural restrictions against serving on the all-important tribal council, modern Mesquaki women have forged ahead politically as educational advocates, teachers, and tribal administrators. Mesquaki women are also beginning to speak out much more on issues concerning the family. Women have made their presence felt in the alcohol abuse program for dysfunctional families. They have also quietly lobbied male relatives on the council to help the many abandoned single-parent mothers. Several women activists expressed optimism that the council will eventually address pressing educational and familial issues. These women wisely see such issues as crucial for the survival of the language and culture.

The Enrollment Rule and the Politics of Racial Purity

Finally, we must ask whether there are any other blind spots in the tribe's shiny new civic activities and welfare state. One issue that most outside observers pick up on is the tribe's enrollment rule. A Cedar Rapids *Gazette* headline cries out that "Mesquaki Rules Shut Non-members Out of Their Indian Culture" (CRG, June 21, 1987). Reporter Rich Smith argues that the rule is sexist and generally discriminates against mixed-bloods. Some local whites delight in pointing out that Mesquakis are racist towards their "breeds." One white asked me, "You are an anthropologist, what is the difference between the so-called pure bloods and the KKK and Aryan nation types? Aren't the Mesquakis racists too?"

One obvious difference is that Mesquaki traditionalists have never advocated violence against those they consider less racially pure. As we saw in Chapter five, Mesquakis are both tolerant and intolerant toward their mixed-bloods.

Indeed, talk about who is a real Indian never ceases on the settlement. A relatively small number of families claim that they are "pure blooded Mesquakis." Others with known Pottawatami, Winnebago, Sioux, and white blood must constantly defend themselves as "outsiders." In the old days, half-breeds like Morgan, a brave band leader, proved themselves by their actions. If you were loyal and useful to the tribe, spoke the language, and practiced the culture, you were a Mesquaki. In eighteenth-century Mesquaki society one could overcome outsider status and become a part of families, religious ceremonies, war parties, and buffalo hunts. Being an outsider was not an inherited status that marked people forever, regardless of what they did.

Unfortunately, the question of who is a Mesquaki culturally has become entwined with the question of who is legally a tribal member. This confusion seems to start with the 1937 political reorganization. At that point the tribe developed an official government identity as the Sac and

Fox tribe of Mississippi. In the new tribal constitution only children of enrolled Mesquaki males can become "enrolled members" — if and when the father officially claims them. On the other hand, the offspring of enrolled female Mesquakis do not become enrolled tribal members unless the father is enrolled and claims them. Being enrolled as an official Sac and Fox entitles a tribal member to benefits such as voting, land claim payments, housing, educational scholarships, and health care. Enrollment in the tribe is a federal government category and has little to do with practicing Mesquaki culture.

The Fox Project fieldnotes contained many interviews of people grumbling about unenrolled outsiders. Today the sons and daughters of earlier critics are still grumbling about outside troublemakers. Occasionally, the complaining turns into a semiorganized political campaign. Important full-bloods preach against the outsiders before the tribal council. Enrolled pure-blood children call the mixed-bloods names and exclude them socially. Things are said during clan ceremonies. Rumors are spread that the outsiders are meddling in politics, practicing bad medicine, trying to cast spells. The outsiders are accused of not knowing their place as guests among the tribe.

A kind of pure-blood political discourse develops to ward off the crisis these outsiders allegedly create. These verbal campaigns against half-breeds are very reminiscent of the white temperance campaign against Mesquakis. Like prominent whites, prominent Mesquakis create a "moral panic" (Hall, 1978) to get rid of people considered outsiders. But prominent Mesquaki pure-bloods cannot exclude their outsiders as easily as whites can. To oust the half-breeds considered troublemakers, they would have to banish the good mixed-bloods as well. The good mixed-bloods practice traditional Mesquaki religion, stay out of politics, and accept a second-class citizenship without tribal benefits. They are no real threat to Mesquaki society.

Opposition invariably develops against the rhetoric of pure bloods to throw out all unenrolled "breeds." Someone stands up in council meetings and says they will ask their relatives to leave if others will. This usually slows the verbal attacks of the pure bloods. They are forced to admit that they, too, have unenrolled family members who cannot be banished easily. Even the so-called pure-bloods admit privately that no Mesquaki is racially pure. Everyone's family tree has marriages with outsiders. In the end, the tribal council wisely does nothing, the pure blood versus outsider rhetoric dies down, and many mixed-bloods continue to live peacefully among the tribe. Ultimately, the tribe is much more open about letting unenrolled outsiders live among them than Smith's journalistic account suggests.

On the other hand, contemporary Mesquaki traditionalists do systematically limit the participation of mixed-bloods in economics and politics. All unenrolled Mesquakis, wherever they live, are definitely second-class citizens. The current enrollment rule reduces the issue of membership in the culture down to patrilineal descent. Charles Callender's fieldnotes claim that a white agent put the patrilineal rule in the new 1937 constitution. The rule apparently made eighteen settlement children without enrolled fathers noncitizens. Conversely, half-breed children of enrolled males who grow up white in far-away cities may still receive tribal benefits. Now that the tribe has adopted a white-style elected council and written constitution, it would seem that the number of second-class citizens in Mesquaki society has increased. At times, the new bureaucratic enrollment rule actually punishes the cultural faithful and rewards others who live like whites.

In effect, a white-style elected tribal council actually turns out to be less open and democratic than the old hereditary monarchy was. In the old days everyone was a part of the political system through his or her family and clan, and everyone shared in the fruits of the winter hunts and the summer gardens. Today, the enrollment rule helps keep down the number of voters and severely restricts who can serve on the tribal council. Only Mesquakis who reside on the settlement and whose father and mother are enrolled can run for election. The combination of these two enrollment rules helps a relatively small number of pure-blood traditionalists maintain their political influence.

The political influence of pure-bloods is greatly enhanced by the way one gains social status in Mesquaki society. This communal society has few sharp differences in wealth and no class system of rich Mesquaki entrepreneurs and impoverished workers. I was struck by how little "keeping-up-with-the-Joneses" behavior exists on the settlement. The size of a person's car, brand of clothes, or splendor of house is of little importance. Mesquakis adorn their houses as modestly as they dress. They do not generally use consumer commodities to fashion their personal identities. Advanced educational credentials seems to be the one white practice that elevates social status. What does often bestow the social status needed to get elected is participating in the clan ceremonies.

At present, there is considerable debate over changing the tribal constitution. If the enrollment rules were changed, some fear that the tribe's economic resources would be drained. Mesquaki women with non-Mesquaki husbands might suddenly seek housing and other financial benefits. Others fear that a bloc of new voters living outside the settlement who have different lifestyles, interests, and agendas might gain power. Consequently, Mesquaki traditionalists usually justify a restrictive, inequitable enrollment policy with calls for preserving racial purity, hence traditional Mesquaki culture.

A Final Note on the Mesquaki Political Scene

I have characterized modern Mesquaki politics as an intense, rough-and-tumble scene filled with passionate petition drives and rhetorical flourishes about "do-nothing" politicians. Tribal council members are frequently assailed for being corrupt, yet expected to give their relatives new houses and jobs. They are hammered for being too secretive about tribal funds, yet few people inspect the financial printouts at the tribal center. They are ridiculed for a lack of common sense and educational credentials, yet the tribe keeps the pool of candidates limited by enrollment and gender rules. Finally, they are called lazy for missing controversial meetings, yet everyone knows that the Indian way is to avoid dissension while searching for unity.

All too often, white journalists make Mesquaki politics into an entertaining political spectacle that feeds white stereotypes about squabbling and corruption. Mesquaki politics does have its share of serious personal and group conflicts. But outsiders must realize that tribal politics has a deeply communal, religious, and familial character. All the passionate rhetoric and investigations are not necessarily signs of irreparable splits or stagnation. Such conflicts are best understood as a healthy, democratic dialogue over the future of the tribe. The story of the great gambling caper in the next chapter illustrates vividly how present-day Mesquaki politics makes major decisions. The tribe continues to debate each issue as if their way of life depended upon it — and, of course, it does.

Some Oldbear traditionalists continue to lament that the tribe is adopting white ways too fast. My portrayal of the gaming issue highlights the optimism of the post-civil rights generation of "progressive-traditionalists." These new leaders are creating a new, more autonomous civic-oriented, political culture and tribal welfare state with many social services. The more the tribal council does for the people, the more residents want an even stronger tribal government. Some elderly residents hope that the council revives the old tribal court and police force. They want the problems of youthful vandalism and drinking addressed more forcefully. Some single-parent women want the council to change the enrollment rule and address familial problems more.

Despite such social problems, life on the settlement has always been more peaceful and prosperous than the popular press stories on its grinding poverty. The cost of living on the settlement is extremely low. Anyone with a little initiative can get a job and stake out a family homestead.

Given all the tribal health, educational, food, relief, alcohol treatment, and recreational programs, no one has to go hungry or untreated. Given the constant round of tribal ceremonies, no one has to feel alone and abandoned. Finally, given the enormous safety net of close-knit extended families, no one ever lives and dies like the street people and runaway children of our society. The much-maligned tribal council can take some credit for maintaining some communal practices and creating a pretty good place to live.

Chapter 7
The Great Gambling Caper

When I returned to the settlement in the summer of 1993, a huge beacon announced the arrival of the Mesquaki Bingo and Casino. After years of contentious debate the tribe had finally gone into big-time gambling. The new casino runs 24 hours a day, 7 days a week, and employs 800 people. All able-bodied Mesquakis (200) not working in better outside jobs work for the casino. No one knows exactly how much profit they have made. Two newspaper accounts reported that the casino would make around $25 million a year (DMR, June 11, 1993; June 13, 1993). Many people connected with the casino continue to use that figure. Whatever the exact amount, its magnitude has astonished everyone. Typical weekday crowds hit three thousand, and weekend crowds often exceed eight thousand.

In the early 1980s the council wisely purchased an ideal site for the casino on Highway 30. A flat portion of that 200-acre farm also houses the new trading post/convenience store. Because this land sits on the edge of the settlement, it minimizes the impact of thirty to forty thousand gamblers a week. A multi-million-dollar gaming industry will obviously change settlement life, but no one is quite sure how much.

Before speculating on the impact of the casino, I would like to recount how the Mesquakis got into gaming. This story will complete the portrayal of cultural, political, and economic change in post-World War II Mesquaki society. The gambling venture adds a new economic base to the tribe's emerging civic culture and welfare state. The controversy over gaming illustrates vividly how Mesquaki-style democracy works. I should add that telling this tale is not easy. There were many versions of what happened. This is mine.

A Political Gadfly Comes to Town

No one person single-handedly initiated Mesquaki gaming, but Ed Long-knife certainly qualifies as an early and persistent advocate. His political enemies see this complex man as an opportunist and hustler, but I would characterize him as a political gadfly. His political activities go well beyond the gaming issue. I first heard about Ed in 1984 when townspeople were speculating about Mesquaki bingo. When I was a kid, Ed and his brother were outstanding Golden Gloves boxers, but there were always mysterious rumors about their departure. Ed's return after thirty years is the stuff of which legends are made.

People told all sorts of strange stories about the tall, gaunt stranger in a brown leather, flat-crown cowboy hat. The general theme was that "One of those wild Longknife boys blew into town with this shady gambling scheme." More than one person swore that Ed returned in a flashy Cadillac dangling diamonds and cash under the noses of his gullible tribesmen. Some folks claimed that the mafia sent him. Others said he had a rich white wife bankrolling him. Ed countered this unflattering speculation with a sly smile, "If I was rolling in money why would I be living in this trailer?" He laughs at such comments, but admits that he initially did want to be a manager in the bingo operation. He is also unabashedly open about the virtues of capitalism to uplift his people.

Ed generally sees himself as someone who works hard for the tribe's economic progress. He reasons that if he helps generate a great deal of money, he should be paid for his productivity because "that is the way capitalism works." For Ed everything boils down to the profit line, even academic research. One day after our interview concluded he joked, "What kind of book are you writing? How much is in it for me?" I gave him my usual spiel about academic books being labors of love, and a knowing smile came over his face. He laughed and joked, "You never know. Maybe somebody will make a movie out of it. If they do, I want a Cadillac for helping you. I have nothing to hide. I'll help you."

Several years later, Ed explained why Iowans were flocking to the new casino. He said, "It's simple. They want to see what is on the other side." That turned out to be the best explanation of why people gamble that anyone gave me. In retrospect, maybe Ed's joke about the Cadillac contained a grain of truth. Maybe people gave me their time to see what was on the other side, too. If you fed the little academic slot machine enough information, maybe it would crank out a good story, or even a Cadillac or two.

Anyway, there Ed Longknife was in 1984 chatting up the local merchants and promising that progress was at hand. Initially, some prominent whites were skeptical about whether he was on the up-and-up, and whether the settlement would ever progress. Nevertheless, they took him seriously enough to buy space in his new newspaper. They remember hoping that he would be a "progressive Indian," an Indian that "got that squabbling tribal council moving."

Several whites described his paper as "overly rhetorical, you know, yellow journalism," but they liked the general message. Ed reminded them a little of Ernest's fiery letters-to-the-editor. Like Ernest, he was going after the tribal council for doing nothing and for their graft and corruption, but there was a major difference. Ed was "practical and business-minded, not a dreamer who wanted to go back to being an Indian." He was unabashedly for adopting white ways and for economic progress. Chamber of Commerce types thought he was "just what these Indians needed." Having garnered some support in the white community, how did Ed sell the tribe on gambling?

Despite Ed's early arrival on the gambling scene, others actually initiated the idea with the tribal council. In the spring of 1983, Bill Baines from Hollywood, Florida had an option on 110 acres of land near the present casino site (TNH, March 11, 1983). Speculation on the settlement was that his corporation included Seminoles who wanted in on the Mesquaki gaming bonanza (*Indian Country*, October, 1984). Ed apparently arrived on the scene and initially wanted to work with anyone promoting gaming. But in a letter to the Mesquaki people, Baine's lawyer named two other Mesquakis as his official representatives (*Indian Country*, November, 1984).

By the spring of 1984, Baines, who managed a Winnebago bingo hall, had brought thirty tribal members to the Minnesota facility and had presented a plan to the council. In a news release the tribal director gave the impression that Baines was about to receive a contract because "ninety percent of the tribe favored the venture" (TNH, May 10, 1984). Meanwhile, Ed Longknife had become an advocate for John Browning of Dallas, Texas, who began competing with Baines for the Mesquaki contract. Ed apparently met Browning in California while doing printing for his high-stakes bingo operation with the Pomos.

Since the tribal council were already leaning toward Baines, they declined to visit Browning's California operations. In response, Longknife took Browning's case to the people. In a newspaper article he describes Browning as an honest man (*Indian Country*, October 1984). He applauded Browning for telling it like it is: "Yes, I intend to make money. But the only way we can make money is to make more money for ya'll first!" Browning was offering the Mesquakis a ten-year contract with a second ten-year option for 40 percent of the profits. He also promised to give Mesquakis job preference, respect their four-day mourning practices, and turn over the gaming facilities to the tribe when the contract ended.

With a referendum vote approaching, Ed continued to pressure the tribal council. Every issue of his paper attacked the council for its incompetence, corruption, and secrecy. The situation was ripe for such criticism because the federal district attorney had just completed an audit of all federal funds flowing into the settlement. His audit questioned $100,000 of federal expenditures and highlighted the following problems: (1) favoritism in granting new homes and home improvement funds, (2) no written property management system policy, (3) lack of adequate records for salaries and travel expenses, and (4) recommended prosecution of the Housing Authority Director for $10,000 in undocumented expenses. The BIA announced that it was investigating the situation but did not expect to file criminal charges (TNH, July 26, 1984).

The tribal council denied any wrongdoing, but opposition to the council was strong enough to generate a petition of 170 tribal members (TNH, March 3, 1983). In a bold move, Longknife also began taping and printing portions of the tribal council meetings in his paper. He urged the council to use the tribe's two-million-dollar tribal trust fund to fix houses and to distribute at least $200 to all enrolled members (*Indian Country*, December, 1984). Shortly after the paper's first edition, a Des Moines *Register* reporter arrived to photograph Ed holding up a copy of his newspaper. The *Register* articles went on to portray the present council as a monopoly of uneducated, corrupt, dog-eating religious traditionalists (DMR, December 11, 1984; November 5, 1986).

During the first referendum on bingo, Ed urged people to "vote no" on bingo "because the tribal council has got to show the people of the settlement that it can clean up 'its own house' and manage OUR finances better" (*Indian Country*, December 1984). Some settlement residents considered Longknife "self-serving" and a "rabble rouser." Others considered him "civic-minded" and "able to get a better deal for the tribe." Whatever the truth of these charges and counter-charges, Ed's approach was effective. One hundred and thirty-nine people voted against bingo and only sixty-five voted for it (TNH, December 12, 1984). In effect, Longknife had persuaded people to vote against any deal with Baines.

In response, Baine's supporters petitioned (116) the council to hold a referendum on their proposal, but that also failed. After two years of controversy, the tribe was at an impasse and sentiment was growing against any outside management company. Meanwhile, Ed continued to blast the council as an inactive monopoly of traditionalists. He entreated them to make per capita payments and fully disclose tribal funds and expenditures (DMR, November 5, 1986). He also urged the council to recoup at least $7 million dollars in improperly collected state taxes and interest from Tama County (*Indian Country*, May–June, 1986). Faced with a legal settlement that would have bankrupted Tama County, white enthusiasm for Ed Longknife cooled.

Ed's constant commentary eventually forced the council to call a general meeting "to clear the air and discuss major issues confronting the tribe." During the meeting, which was closed to outside reporters, the council brought out computer printouts on all the tribal accounts. They also conducted a straw vote of those present on several issues: (1) distribution of tribal funds (162, yes, 69, no); (2) 75 percent approval of enrolled members on all major expenditures (243, yes, 88, no); (3) monthly itemized statements on council expenditures (283, yes, 48, no). These votes show how strongly many Mesquakis felt about the tribal council being more open on financial decisions (TNH, March 13, 1986).

Although the council never instituted any fiscal reforms, they did start a tribal newspaper which published the minutes of council meetings, program reports, and some statements of financial expenditures. In effect, the Mesquaki News began serving some of the reporting functions of the now defunct Indian Country. In the end, neither Baines nor Browning received a contract for running a bingo hall, but Longknife had succeeded in putting the gaming issue on the tribal political agenda permanently. After a three years of debate, the council had to do something about gaming. What they did was far more conservative, however, than Ed Longknife's original plan.

A number of the "progressive-traditionalists" began agitating the council to hold a second referendum on gaming. Council chairman Henry Blackhat Jr. and several others pressed forward to create a bingo operation financed and run solely by Mesquakis. Six months later, in November, a referendum for a tribally-financed and run bingo hall passed 93 to 71 (Skywalker, March 28, 1990). Some Mesquakis grumbled that the low turnout was a sign of general confusion and frustration with the gaming issue. Nevertheless, the council of Henry Blackhat Jr. forged ahead. They sent a team of younger, college-educated Mesquakis to visit other Indian bingo halls.

The development team held many meetings and proposed an alternative plan for a low-budget, low-overhead operation in the tribal gym. This weekend "mom-and-pop" operation was supposed let the Mesquakis learn gaming without risking tribal capital. This is precisely what happened. The initial bingo operation in the gym laid the foundation for later expansion. Although a small operation, it apparently made more profit than critics generally acknowledge. Two Christmas bonuses totaling more than $500,000 were distributed to all enrolled members, and the council accumulated another $500,000 for construction of a new bingo hall.

Many local whites considered bingo's evolution from the gym to a large new facility a remarkable feat. An old friend and prominent merchant summed up the general feeling when he said,

I gotta hand it to them. I never thought they could run anything, much less a multi-million dollar business. Have you been out there? You can see the new building is first-class, and they started out with next to nothing in the gym. Now they are employing lots of people, paying off their debts, what more could you ask for?

Apparently a great deal more — if you live on the settlement and have a grand vision of Indian gaming. Ed Longknife argued long and hard for a 2,500-seat facility that would generated $12 million and a flood of jobs, houses, and prosperity. Since some Mesquakis had seen such operations elsewhere, they continued to snipe at the small tribally-run bingo operation. Nothing the management group did was right. Bingo was a flop because the tribe was not getting rich quick.

Several members of the management team remembered constant accusations of mismanagement and theft. They also expressed disillusionment over how little recognition they received. One person put it this way, "We had no personal life. We all worked very hard to make it a success even though the council and the people never gave us much support." Bingo managers worked sixty-hour weeks and were paid eight to ten dollars an hour with no fringe benefits. Such salaries were half the gaming industry standard.

In response to continuing criticism, the council authorized the management team to design a $2.5 million, 35,000 square foot, 1,500-capacity bingo hall. The actual construction of the hall was financed through a federal grant ($525,000), a federally-insured bank loan ($550,000), previous bingo profits ($750,000) and a loan from the tribal council's general fund ($250,000). In other words, the tribe launched their new bingo hall with very little debt to outsiders. Only 20 percent of the funds for the new bingo hall came from local bank loans. Such fiscal conservativism makes the 90 percent loans made regularly to local farmers look wildly risky.

The new bingo hall opened in July 1989, but in retrospect it is difficult to say exactly how well it did financially. The tribal council never made the annual audits public, and I was unable to review any financial records. Media releases reported an annual payroll of over $500,000 for 80 employees (*Skywalker*, March 28, 1990). In addition, the new bingo hall paid off the previously mentioned construction loans, sponsored several pow-wows, and gave money to indigent and widowed tribal members. More important, the Mesquakis gained six years of valuable business experience. For the young progressive-traditionalists the new bingo hall was a source of enormous racial pride. They relished confounding local whites who could not believe how clean, efficient, and secure it was.

Negotiating a Gambling Pact with the State

Despite these accomplishments, some Mesquakis continued to agitate against the bingo hall. For Ed Longknife and his followers, Mesquaki bingo was primarily a business venture, not some exercise in building cultural pride. They felt that the tribe had frittered away a golden opportunity to make some real money. They contended that a well-capitalized management company would have made the tribe a great deal more money. As a result, Ed urged the council to develop a state pact that allowed high-stakes gambling. He and his followers hoped that such a pact would bring a flood of investors wanting to develop a big casino.

Although the pact and a management contract was his primary focus, Ed also became active on many other political fronts. He applied for the tribal executive director's job unsuccessfully but was appointed to the committee supervising elections, the Housing Authority, and the Enterprise Development Board. From these important tribal committees, he continued to monitor tribal council meetings and to press for changes. This eventually brought him into direct conflict with the tribe's executive director, Claude Windsong.

Given a divided tribal council, the task of negotiating the gambling pact fell to the tribal lawyer and executive director. Consequently, those opposing the pact, which was considered too limited, sought to discredit the executive director. Rumors began to fly about collusion between the tribal lawyer and executive director. A petition with almost two hundred names demanded the director's removal for mismanagement of the Indian relief fund. Petitioners alleged that unqualified relatives were receiving relief funds while qualified people were being denied.

Meanwhile, Executive Director Windsong was encouraging the council to investigate and abolish the Housing Authority, which Longknife and his allies ran. At the time, the Housing Authority had HUD commitments for more than $500,000 to build rent-to-purchase houses. Tribal leaders against the HUD grants spread much misinformation about the HUD proposal, and the council eventually lost this HUD housing grant. This power-struggle between two of the settlement's more active politicians took a surprising turn when the press broke several stories on the executive director.

The Press Invents a Great Mesquaki Political Leader

A story in *Skywalker* magazine (April 4, 1990) portrayed Executive Director Windsong as a leader with great vision. According to Arthur Orduña, he was "that rare and most precious of human commodities: the right man in the right job at the right time who gave his people an incredible economic boost through bingo." This portrayal of a strong leader who single-handedly implemented bingo has little to do with historical reality. Apparently Orduña wanted to produce a genuine Native American hero and was captivated by Claude's storytelling prowess. Throughout the article he allowed Claude to wax on about various visions he had for the tribe. Claude spun tales about a settlement telecommunications center for the entire Midwest, the rerouting of the Avenue of the Saints Highway, and a joint car-building venture with Hyundai Corporation. The article ended with a lofty philosophical treatise on Aristotle's substantial form theory and the grave as a perfect sculpture!

Needless to say, the "great leader" image played poorly with those already petitioning for Claude's removal. Several petitioners argued that the article was another sign that Windsong held himself above the tribal council, and they vowed to cut him down to size. A true Mesquaki leader generally downplays his importance and power, and the article made Claude look like he was tooting his own horn too loudly. It set the stage for another media story that actually brought angry petitioners to a council meeting seeking Windsong's head.

Within two months after the Skywalker article a *Register* headline blared out "Mesquakie Tribe Would Buy Track, Build Casino" (DMR, June 8, 1990). I am not sure why such things were said, but I can imagine Windsong sitting in his office at the end of a long, tedious day. He is getting ready to head home and a reporter calls looking for a story. To lighten the day he asks somewhat facetiously, "Do the Polk county taxpayers want to be rescued by many, many Indians coming riding down the hill with wagons circled around the race track? We can do it. We have 1,000 horsemen."

That undoubtedly sounded like a great lead for a story, so the reporter presses on. Claude is feeling his oats and adds, "If they want to sell the place, they can give us a buzz, we might consider it. We'll make a deal with them. Since it is a losing proposition, why not convert it to a casino?"

As they say in the field of advertising: "Presto! A good story is born." The reporter made his story sound even more plausible by quoting a poll of Des Moines residents. Fifty-one percent favored selling the race track. A track board member was quoted as saying that a Mesquaki buy-out was a real possibility. A follow-up article fanned speculation with a lobbyist's admission that he was authorized to negotiate with the tribe (DMR, June 12, 1990). The article left the impression that many white taxpayers were waiting for the Mesquaki cavalry to rescue them. To quell such speculation, the Republican governor and his Democratic opponent quickly issued statements against such a sale.

Within two weeks an angry group demanded that the council fire

Windsong. Numerous references were made to a state audit of the Indian relief fund, but at this point the state audit had not been officially released to the public. Consequently, no evidence from the audit was presented to support the mismanagement charge. The most damning argument presented against Claude was that he had made unauthorized statements about purchasing the race track. A number of protesters shouted that he had embarrassed the council and the tribe and must go.

Since the petitioners had the council votes to dismiss Claude, those members supporting him absented themselves. After several hours of chaotic, one-sided discussion, Claude was fired without what whites call "due process." The audit did eventually come out, and several other staff members were also fired for placing their names or the names of relatives on the Indian aid roles. Record-keeping procedures were also apparently lax, and some money was misappropriated under Windsong's watch, but the tribal council never prosecuted anyone for criminal activities. Settlement opinion varied widely on the audit and whether any serious infractions were ever committed. Supporters of Windsong denied wrongdoing, and opponents declared him guilty.

The press, having started the whole story, ended it with two superficial articles that clarified little (DMR, June 21, 23). Several tribal members were quoted as saying that Windsong was unauthorized to speak for the tribe. They added that "statements about the race track might have exacerbated the situation." Others commented that Windsong was under investigation for administrative irregularities. The whole episode over the purchase of the race track was just one more media spectacle. It reconfirmed old racial images of corrupt, squabbling Indians rather than providing insight into Mesquaki politics. Unfortunately, the articles left the issue of Windsong's character and guilt unresolved. Within two months he had gone from a great visionary leader to a someone who was spinning unauthorized policies and mismanaging tribal funds.

The Tribal Council Grinds to a Halt

In the aftermath of the firing, Mesquaki politics became increasingly divisive. In November the tribal council added more fat to the fire when it refused to seat Richard Moline, who won a closely contested (81 to 79) election. The ostensible reason for not seating Moline was that the election board had failed to send out absentee ballots, thus making the election invalid. Those supporting Moline claimed that Longknife and his followers, who controlled the election board, had voided the election because their candidate lost. Longknife called such charges ridiculous and claimed that the board followed election procedures properly. A badly divided tribal council generally tried to avoid the issue. They made no move to seat Moline and gave no public reasons for their inaction (TNH, Feb. 7, 1991).

In response, 180 Mesquakis petitioned the tribal council. They called for the seating of Moline and the removal of two councilmen who supported Longknife's view of the gaming pact. By late March the beleaguered tribal council held another community meeting on the pact. The meeting was poorly attended and resolved little. Meanwhile, the *Mesquaki News* was no longer being published. Worse still, the council met infrequently because it often lacked a quorum. After Windsong's firing and the refusal to seat Moline, several councilmen stopped coming to meetings. To many Mesquakis the tribal council had gone into a shell and no longer functioned. By fall, 211 people submitted a second petition to remove the entire council (TNH, September 5, 1991). There was talk of requesting the BIA to intervene and hold new elections, but matters drifted until the regular fall elections.

Given the turmoil over gaming, the 1991 council elections were particularly heated, and four pro-casino candidates were eventually elected (CR *Gazette*, November 27, 1991). Richard Moline won the special seat a second time and was appointed tribal chairman. The new council quickly held a referendum on establishing a gambling casino that passed two-to-one (101 to 53) in a moderate turnout (DMR, December 30, 1991). Once again those against gaming claimed that the people stayed away from the polls because they were confused and disgusted with the bitter, protracted fight over gaming. Nevertheless, the new council quickly signed a gambling pact with the state that their lawyer and Claude Windsong had negotiated. For a brief moment a new unity seemed at hand. It looked as if the tribe was finally ready to enter the world of casino gambling.

Unfortunately, the 1991 election failed to magically unify the tribe. If anything, it set the stage for one final confrontation. On one side was the group of young progressive-traditionalists who had helped create a tribally-run bingo hall. Former bingo hall manager Henry Blackhat Jr., Tribal Chairman Richard Moline, and Councilman Rick RockIsland were a threesome determined to keep casino management in Mesquaki hands. On the other side, Ed Longknife and his followers had long advocated a large casino run by an outside management company. After seven years of arguing, the voters had put the two factions on the council to resolve the matter once and for all.

The Management Companies Come A-Courting

Sensing a new opening, management companies swarmed to the settlement. The courtship of the tribe actually started quietly that summer before the 1991 elections. At that time All-Star Casino got the jump on the other companies. All-Star was a large, successful management company listed on the New York Stock Exchange. They ran casinos for tribes in several states and were based in Minnesota (DMR, August 2, 1992). Kit Carson, who negotiated their Louisiana casino deal, began visiting the settlement that summer. Being from Nebraska, he knew the Mesquakis had an unusually favorable location. His first step was to sell All-Star on the idea of expanding into Iowa. The next step was to convince the tribal council to negotiate with All-Star Casino. A skillful deal-maker, he began busing Mesquakis to see All-Star's Minnesota casinos. Even more importantly, he zeroed in on unaligned councilmen and influential community leaders.

At that time the key swing vote on the council was Gordon Lightheart. Gordon was one of a handful college-educated traditionalists from the the 1950s era. He went to college on an athletic scholarship, worked for years in a white manufacturing company, and became a respected family man and clan leader. He was a soft-spoken advocate of economic progress and initially favored a small tribally-run gaming industry. Unlike Ed Longknife, Gordon never accused the management team of corruption publically, or the executive director and tribal lawyer of creating an unfavorable gaming pact. During the earlier controversies he quietly supported the bingo management team and avoided divisive political rhetoric. Although a traditionalist, he was less concerned with the issue of ethnic pride and proving the Mesquakis could run a casino than the threesome of Blackhat, Moline, and RockIsland. He also had less emotional attachment to the Mesquaki-run bingo operation. When Mesquaki Bingo failed to generate enough profits to buy land and build new houses, Lightheart began looking for a better alternative.

After Gordon visited All-Star's Minnesota casinos, his fears about an outside management company and indebtedness were allayed. He and other Mesquaki visitors were impressed with the scale of All-Star's operation and their rapport with tribal leaders. By the winter of 1992, at least a dozen more management companies came to the council hawking their wares. Apparently no one was more impressive than All-Star Casino. People previously against a large management company, like ex-Director Claude Windsong, also began praising their management know-how and strong capital base.

The threesome reluctantly agreed to negotiate with All-Star Casino, and the council initiated formal negotiations in March. All-Star Casino's first proposal included a grandiose plan for a large $30 million casino-hotel complex complete with an amusement and RV park. The bingo hall was to be closed and converted into a portion of the new casino. In return for a seven-year management contract at 40 percent of the profits, All-Star Casino would loan the tribe $20 million to build the complex and manage the operation.

During these negotiations, however, the threesome became increasingly dissatisfied with All-Star's proposal. They felt that giving up 40 percent of the profits was an exorbitant price to pay for management, and they feared that the huge debt to All-Star would keep them locked into their management contract for years. They also disliked the intrusion of a large hotel and a sprawling amusement and RV park. Finally, All-Star Casino's style offended their political sensibilities. They ridiculed their presentations "too slick," and their concern for preserving Indian culture "phony." They argued that closing Mesquaki Bingo and imposing an expensive scheme on a divided tribe showed little cultural sensitivity.

So the threesome began meeting with Darth Vinton's accounting firm outside the formal council negotiations. They were determined to develop a smaller scale, tribally-controlled alternative to All-Star Casino. Supporters of All-Star quickly accused them of "going off on their own" and of "trying to make an unauthorized deal with Darth Vinton." They were perceived as too headstrong and anxious to control casino management. Stories circulated about secret meetings at a local restaurant and political payoffs. People claimed that the bingo hall security cameras had tapes of Darth offering the bingo hall manager the casino management position.

The threesome's general plan was to use bingo profits and a BIA gaming loan to convert approximately two-thirds of the existing bingo hall into a small gambling casino. Darth Vinton, who owned a Minneapolis accounting firm, drew up a plan to convert the existing 35,000-square-foot bingo hall and buy the slot machines and equipment for $5 million. He also designed the accounting and security system and a plan to train the management staff. Under Vinton's plan, his yearly management fee was $500,000, and the tribe kept all the profits. He estimated that the tribe would need his services for approximately five years, but they had the right to terminate his services after two years.

While developing their alternative plan, the threesome and their followers were busy denouncing the pro-All-Star Casino councilmen for "selling out the tribe." They claimed that Ed Longknife was on All-Star Casino's payroll and had helped the company "buy off" the other councilmen. They also forced the council to suspend one pro-All-Star Casino councilman pending an investigation of some missing powwow money. That political move evened the vote to three for All-Star Casino and three against. Meanwhile, All-Star Casino negotiators met with several sympathetic Mesquakis and councilmen and hammered out a new contract proposal.

The new proposal scaled back the complex to a 100,000-square-foot, $20 million casino-restaurant without a hotel or amusement park. All-

Star also sweetened the pot by agreeing to loan the construction money to the tribe interest-free and to pay the remaining bingo hall debt with a $250,000 cash "gift." The bingo hall was to be saved, reduced in size, and run by Mesquakis independent of the casino. These were obviously concessions designed to win the threesome's support. The financial side of the management contract remained, however, essentially the same. All-Star Casino would run the Mesquaki operation for seven years at 40 percent of the profits and would rent the slot machines to the tribe for an additional $3 million a year. By June of 1992 All-Star grew restless and began putting heavy pressure on the council to sign the revised contract.

As negotiations with the tribe wore into the summer, All-Star cranked up its public relations campaign. I must admit, as I watched All-Star trying to get what it wanted, it was difficult to be dispassionate. All these casino management companies looked the same to me. They all needed tax-exempt Indian land to put up their neon money-making boxes. Four hundred years later, the whiteman is still grabbing Indian lands. In the old days, the whiteman offered a few paltry trade goods, then just took what they wanted by false treaties and force. Today, the whiteman must legally contract to use what is left of the tribal lands. He must convince the Indian that his management know-how and capital is indispensable.

The point man in All-Star's courtship was Kit Carson. I saw Kit's smiling face around the tribal center often that summer. One day he approached me out of curiosity and warmed quickly to the idea of a professor writing a book. He underscored that he too was a small-town boy who had a deep concern for Indians. I never claimed to have a deep concern for Indians, so he apparently thought that anyone writing a book about Indians must be concerned. I said jokingly that if he and his company cheated the Mesquakis I would write about it. He replied with great solemnity,

Oh no sir. We would never do that. All-Star Casino has an outstanding record with other tribes. We try our best to help the tribes preserve their culture. We are not just in this for the money.

I found his politically correct speeches painfully gratuitous, but Kit was a tall, slender, clean-cut type with a cherubic face. It was hard to dislike him when he did his boy-next-door routine.

Those leading the charge against All-Star Casino were far less impressed with Kit's boyish charm. Tom Warrior, the half-brother of Tribal Chairman Richard Moline, relished trying to catch that "slippery Kean" and the others in contradictions. At the time, Tom and the wives and sisters of the threesome were circulating an anti-All-Star Casino petition. They accused Kit of spreading lies about their petition and All-Star's contract. Those supporting All-Star claimed that the petitioners were spreading lies about their intentions and contract. The political rhetoric was so heated and extreme, it was difficult to assess the claims and counter-claims. Eventually, all these colorful personalities collided at the council meeting when All-Star Casino sought approval of their contract.

The Night All-Star Casino Got Some Signatures

That evening I rushed to the tribal center hoping to see the final showdown. In my haste, I forgot that council meetings always start an hour late. Lone Trueblood was on security, so we struck up a conversation. Lone said, "I hear the All-Star big shots are going to show up tonight. They're tryin' to get Gordon and them guys to sign the contract. You better get that pen of yours ready, Doug."

Lone was against All-Star Casino because its people were just too big and fancy and fast-talking. He wanted the tribe to run their own small operation. When All-Star's president Lance Larue strutted in with his entourage, Lone said, "You see what I mean." A couple of his management team were Indians, so Harry Blackhat Jr., who was standing nearby, grinned and said, "There's Tonto." Then Lone leaned over and confided, "Richard and them will never let All-Star get in here."

Meanwhile, All-Star's management team were busy shaking hands with their supporters. The real back-slapping began when the Lighthearts, Gordon and his three large sons, arrived. They came in shoulder-to-shoulder and looked a little like the defensive line of the Chicago Bears. Kit Carson, who was dressed in his red ribbon-appliqued shirt and beaded tie, was busy presenting the Lighthearts to Mr. Larue as Ed Longknife looked on. I was unable to catch Ed for a comment, but he must have been a little anxious. The contrast between his taunt craggy brown face and Kit's soft white boyish grin was striking. Meanwhile, the anti-All-Star councilmen were pacing restlessly, cracking jokes, and smoking furiously.

In contrast, Mr. Larue looked every bit his part. The cool, self-confident white company C.O. had come to pitch his contract. He and his troops seemed ready for any ambush the threesome might set. All-Star knew they still had a slim majority of the votes. Although intensely anti-All-Star Casino, Chairman Moline was unable to vote. Under the Mesquaki constitution, a chairman only votes when there is a tie. Nevertheless, there was an air of uncertainty. Legally a majority vote rules, but culturally the Mesquakis prefer a unanimous vote on important tribal decisions. Reaching a consensus is often difficult, but that is the Indian way. Even though Lance Larue was holding a winning hand, the pot of gold was still not his.

As all the protagonists filled the council chambers, Lone cajoled me, "You better get in there and get a seat so you can let me know what happens. I gotta stay out here and make sure nobody steals the place while you guys are talkin'."

I slipped into a seat near the door and began taking notes. Like most council meetings, this one went on for hours and was punctuated with sharp exchanges and long silences. Tom Warrior and others were asking a string of irritating technical questions. All-Star's management team had come to sign the contract, not spend hours picking it apart. After almost two hours of bickering Larue became impatient and began chastising the council.

Look, we don't want to do it on a three to two vote. We have invited you to see our operation, but we have been heckled that it's a bribe. But here is Running Rapids Casino. Isn't that a bribe? I don't know why we have to put up with this! We have spent a great deal getting here and negotiating. We've got a $7,000 bill from your lawyer, but he is making no substantive comments! Make a decision, and we will go away. We have got better things to do. If you want us to make a final presentation, we think we have got something to offer, but quite frankly I am sick and tired of this."

As a frustrated Larue fell silent, so did the council. Then Ed Longknife pleaded with everyone to not be hasty, to sit and talk this thing through, to grab this golden opportunity.

Larue seemed somewhat appeased, and he went on explaining how this was strictly business, how he had to make a profit, but "I assure you, there is no financial risk to you. There is no threat to your sovereignty." He explained how he had helped several other tribes build houses and schools, how they trusted him. Then he smiled and confided that his management team accused him of being too patient, "and after this, I agree. Your time has run out. This is my last trip down here." He was imploring the Mesquakis to act, to trust him, to give him what he wanted. And if they did not, he would find other more grateful, cooperative Indians to help. It was a classic great white father speech. I wondered how many French, British, and Americans had made this speech to the Mesquakis.

In response, the threesome claimed the other councilmen had never explained why they wanted All-Star Casino. More conversation ensued over All-Star's management skill and capital. More pesky questions. Larue was obviously exasperated, and he launched into another speech.

Look, we are not going to work with a divided tribe. Some councilmen are looking for another company. Are you afraid that a management company will make a profit? You don't need a lawyer. You need to find a business person that you respect to give you some advice.

Then Larue and his entire management team did what any good shopper would do in a Mexican market. They began folding up their papers and stood up as if they were heading for the door. Councilman Clark Kane quickly intervened, "Wait, I want to hear you."

Another pro-All-Star councilman entreated them,

Please, sit down. I'd like to apologize if you were shown disrespect. I am glad to hear that you are not mad. There's been lots of changes [in the contract], and I appreciate them. I don't like to look a gift horse in the mouth. I make a motion for All-Star Casino.

After hours of wrangling, the previously silent pro-All-Star Casino councilmen had finally spoken up for their management company. After more obfuscating questions the vote was taken, and All-Star was awarded the contract by a three-two margin.

Council Chairman Moline responded angrily, "I hope you guys understand what you just did." Then he tried unsuccessfully to get the other councilmen to pass a motion for a referendum vote on the All-Star Casino contract. As the meeting drew to an end, Larue was all smiles as Moline stomped out the door. As he was leaving, he vowed that he would never sign the contract.

The following week, the settlement was buzzing with talk about the signed contract and Moline's vow to stop it. Everyone knew that All-Star had its foot in the door, but no one knew whether the BIA would approve a split vote without the chairman's signature. Chairman Moline called the BIA in Minneapolis and urged it to sit on any gaming contract from All-Star Casino. Meanwhile, All-Star sent its negotiator Kit Carson to meet with the council to try and win over the threesome.

Kit was around most of the following week, chatting up the opposition. During the next council meeting, he showered praise on everyone for doing what was best for the tribe. Then he reiterated that All-Star Casino was shouldering all the risk and had no intention of taking tribal lands or destroying the culture. He claimed that All-Star's casinos were creating new hope, pride, and revived Indian cultures. It was a familiar speech that most of the visiting management companies used, and after praising the Mesquaki bingo operation he said, "Here's Lash's signed contract. Since the council voted on it, I'd like them [the dissenting councilmen] to sign it."

Ed Longknife entreated the tribal chairman to sign the contract, but the anti-All-Star forces waved their petition and called for a referendum. A long, heated exchange ensued between Tom Warrior and Ed Longknife on various issues and their respective motivations and character. Always the peacemaker, Kit Carson tried to end the acrimony with an uplifting statement about everyone working together, moving ahead, making money.

The moment he mentioned making money, Henry Blackhat Jr. perked up and asked point-blank, "If the tribe signs this, what's your percentage?"

I expected that to stop Kit in his tracks, but he responded with disarming aplomb, "If this is successful, I think I can make $2 million, and I think I will."

The conversation stood still for a moment, punctuated by a few knowing smiles. Then Kit defended making $2 million this way,

I've spent five years on this deal. I wanna work with this tribe. I do make money, but Dad gave 250 Indian kids toys. My grandmother taught in Indian schools and got nothing. I gave up three or four million in my deal with All-Star and the Coshatta. I'm the dumbest businessman you've ever seen.

Henry Jr. pretty much summed up the mood when he retorted, "If you're the dumbest businessman, how come you're making two million on this deal?"

Everyone else sat there in stunned silence. Even fiery Tom Warrior stopped asking pointed questions. It was one of those absurd moments when the truth was too outrageous for words. Kit was defending his obscene fee with comical stories about his family giving Christmas toys to Indian kids. It was all so matter-of-fact, so completely shameless. Surely this was the first time that Mesquakis had seen big-time greed up close. Here was an unctuous salesman making $2 million for producing nothing but talk and a signed contract. Everyone just sat there, and all I could think was, What a sorry-assed, white guy! Maybe it was his "culturally sensitive" beaded tie, but I lost whatever objectivity I had left.

During the lull after Kit's admission, Chairman Moline's Aunt Betty, an All-Star supporter, began cajoling her rebellious nephew to be reasonable and sign the contract. Longknife picked up on the familial mood and pleaded, "Come on guys and sign it." At that point a great anthropological insight hit me. I was witnessing an old-fashioned family squabble. And, like a troubled family, they continued arguing for a couple more hours. Every fear and suspicion anyone had told me privately came out. It was a remarkably open airing of what each side disliked about the other side philosophically and personally. Councilman Jack Windsong referred to the threesome as "these boys" and enumerated the errors of their ways, especially their mismanagement of the bingo hall. Gordon Lightheart's three sons challenged the threesome's unauthorized dealings with an outside company. They called Richard a dictator and demanded that he sign the All-Star contract or step down. The threesome angrily countered each denunciation and continued to call for more study and legal consultations. At one point a strong All-Star Casino supporter, Ryan GreyEagle, yelled out, "Quit stallin'! Sign the contract!" Exhaustion seemed to set in again, and the arguing tapered off. Suddenly Chairman

Moline got up and left without saying anything. He started wandering the halls, smoking, popping in and out, generally being elusive. Meanwhile, the squabbling Mesquaki family took a little break from itself. The bickering magically ceased. Some councilmen read papers. Others chatted with their relatives. One looked skyward, another dozed off. The audience of approximately fifty people went to the toilet, joked, and waited for the chairman to return.

I sat there in awe of the Mesquaki political process. After battling tooth and nail for hours, Tom and Ed were chatting like old friends. The Lightheart boys were joking around with Henry Jr. Blackhat and Rick Rock-Island. Aunt Betty was still cajoling her nephew Richard Moline to stop horsing around and sign the contract. For the past few hours these people had been blasting each other, and now they were laughing together. And next week they would be eating, joking, singing, and praying together at an adoption ceremony or ghost feast. Life would go on as if this spat had never happened. Some personal animosities and jealousies might linger, but the tribe will go on. It was an awesome display of direct democracy through petitions and endless dialogue.

The meeting finally started again with some small talk, and the three-some proposed yet another referendum vote. The other councilmen quickly voted it down without commentary. More silence. More heavy puffing on cigarettes. More sighs and murmurs. Ed Longknife captured the mood perfectly when he shrugged his shoulders and said ruefully, "We are hopelessly divided."

After some more talk, one of the Lightheart boys came right to the point and asked Chairman Moline, "Are you gonna sign?"

Chairman Molina responded angrily, "No! I told you!" and left again.

The remaining two of the threesome sat silently with their heads bowed. They were drinking coffee and smoking. They were waiting. They were not going to budge. Then Kit Carson breached the impasse with more sweet words, and called for another signing of the contract. He announced cheerfully, "One for the BIA, one for the tribe, and one for us," and the pro-All-Star councilmen signed without speaking. Kit closed the signing with this hollow sounding speech:

This should be a time for celebration. Henry, Richard, and Rick did what they think is right. This is still the best thing that could happen. We'll make this work. I'll be back on the thirtieth, and we'll all have a good time.

Ed Longknife led a subdued victory clap for the contract, and people slipped away exhausted and bleary-eyed. The council had finally aired what was being said privately. Neither side convinced the other, but such an open, passionate dialogue may have helped move the tribe forward.

Nevertheless, the council was still hopelessly divided, and what All-Star Casino had was more half-signed contracts.

More Companies Come A-Courting

That fact was not lost to others in the gaming industry. Word got out that tribal chairman Moline refused to sign the All-Star Casino contract. Chairman Moline went on the offensive in the newspapers (Waterloo *Courier,* June 15, 1992) and began openly inviting other management groups. More companies came running to give presentations and feeds. The variety of offers was mind-boggling. An all-Indian group from the Sioux's Magic Lake Casino made an impassioned self-determination pitch. They stressed racial pride, and a young Sioux woman, who ran their accounting department, entreated the tribe to borrow BIA money and run its own casino. They offered to manage the casino while training Mesquaki managers. Their fee was $55,000 a month.

The Running Rapids Casino group from Minnesota also came in with a contract tailored to undercut the All-Star contract. They had Hi-Vee Grocery cater a feed for 250 people, and after people had eaten they presented their contract. Their group proposed to put up $10 million to convert and expand the bingo hall for 30 percent of the profits over seven years. The building and indebtedness was approximately half that of All's proposal. They also advised the Mesquakis to buy the slot machines and equipment, which they claimed would save the tribe millions in rental fees. Lone and others quipped that this group looked like Mafiosi. I reluctantly agreed that the one called Angelo did look like a *Godfather* movie extra.

All-Star Casino also returned the following week to put on the biggest and most sumptuous feast. Three hundred and fifty people filed through the food line to get a plate of fried chicken and ham. Kit Carson was greeting people at the door and giving candy suckers to the kids. Following the feast they staged a festive "giveaway" filled with joking and speeches. All manner of prizes, from a color TV to jam boxes, clock radios, and fishing poles were distributed. Meanwhile, several of All-Star's Native American employees made speeches about All-Star's preferential treatment of Indians and respect for Indian culture. The white master of ceremonies also praised the pro All-Star Casino councilmen as "heroic" and "visionary." He lamented the lies and misinformation they were forced to endure. All-Star was putting as good a face as possible on the partially signed contract. Elsewhere the team went on the attack. In an article entitled "Squabble Threatens New Casino" (DMR, August 2, 1992). Lash Larue chronicled All-Star's many casino contracts with satisfied tribes and the Mesquakis' inexplicable, short-sighted squabbling.

When I left that summer, I was convinced that only new elections would bring tribal unity and a decision on gaming. To my surprise, within two months the tribal council voted unanimously to let Gambler's Inc. convert their bingo hall into a casino. After three months of frantic renovation work, the new casino opened in January 1993. That spring I sat at the university sorting through my fieldnotes, looking for a way to explain this miraculous event.

When I returned the following summer I was able to confirm much of what I suspected. Tom Warrior and others redid their petition for a referendum. The threesome had 218 people behind them demanding a vote on the All-Star contract. They simply refused to budge, and the one person capable of playing the role of an ancient peace chief, Gordon Lightheart, eventually did. He stepped forward with three other votes, and the impasse was broken. The united council began searching for a new management company beholden to no one. During the new negotiation there was no Kit Carson wowing people and no unauthorized meetings with Darth Vinton.

Within weeks the council chose Gambler's Inc. to convert two-thirds of the existing bingo hall to a casino, provide top management, and train Mesquakis for the mid-management positions. The money used for the conversion came from existing tribal monies or from credit extended by the suppliers. The tribe purchased all of their machines and casino equipment on installment contracts, which were paid off within six months. Gambler's management fee was 7 percent of the yearly profits, and their contract runs for five years. After two years the tribe has an option to buy out the contract for $2 million. In the end, the tribal council opted for a much smaller operation that gave them greater control and most of the profits.

Although some Mesquakis would disagree, the threesome's stubbornness and Gordon's capacity to make peace made this new deal possible. The more free-wheeling approach of Ed Longknife may have worked just as well, but as he said wistfully, "We will never know now." Many tribal members were simply too conservative and independent-minded to trust a big, rich white management company. They approached gaming the way Mesquakis have always adopted strange practices—with great caution and reluctance.

But never is a long time in Mesquaki politics. The temporary unity of the Gambler's Inc. decision has already faded. The 1993 fall elections solidified the power of Tribal Chairman Gordon Lightheart's group, but the loyal opposition persists. They accuse the chairman of giving his relatives all the cushy management jobs. They say that the new council's $2,500 per capita distribution ($3.5 million) to enrolled members is "chicken-feed" and "an attempt to buy off the voters." They ask why the council sits on millions and has not built everyone a new house and paved the settlement roads.

The opposition continues to mobilize people through petitions against the council. One petition stopped the conversion of the bingo space into casino space. Another petition blocked a new expansion plan to add a 140,000-square-foot casino-hotel complex with a large simulcast horse-racing operation. Ultimately, the council settled on a more modest 45,000-square-foot expansion that will be paid for out of profits saved. Nevertheless, speculation persists that the new council will buy out Gambler's Inc. and hire All-Star Casino to help finance and develop a huge casino. In short, the beat goes on. The forces for a small and big-time gambling continue to debate the gaming issue.

Many new imponderables loom on the horizon. The state gaming pact must be renegotiated within the year. The governor could reverse himself and open the state up for non-Indian gambling investors. The negotiations over a new state pact could end up in federal court. A buy-out of the Gamblers Inc. management company might lead to a court battle. The present tribal council has many difficult decisions ahead. With tribal expectations so high, a successful gaming operation must be maintained. If the council makes a serious misstep, it could be faced with more than talk. The tribal unity that finally brought the casino is sorely needed to face these problems. It remains to be seen whether tribal politics kills or fattens their golden goose.

Some Views on the Impact of the Casino

Politics aside, what of the economic and social impact of gaming on the settlement and surrounding towns? No detailed studies exist, but local whites were highly positive about the economic benefits to the area economy. Local real estate agents reported a miniboom. Rental occupancy rates were at 100 percent, and two new apartment houses were under construction. Ten new houses instead of the usual one or two were being built. Real estate values had risen 5 to 7 percent for the first time in years. Local gas stations, convenience stores, motels, and restaurants reported 20 to 30 percent more business. Local retails stores reported higher appliance, clothing, and food sales. Two new motels and a supermarket have also been built.

The primary impact has been in supplemental incomes to several hundred local white families. Wives, retired men, or men moonlighting at second jobs are all increasing the family coffers significantly. The casino pays better basic wages and fringe benefits than most local small-service or manufacturing companies. Only the top industrial companies in central Iowa—Maytag, Lennox, Fischer, and John Deere—have higher wages. Blackjack dealers, security guards, floor workers, office workers, and food service people make eight dollars an hour. Floor managers, shift supervisors, and office mangers make twelve dollars an hour. Various midlevel management people make $25,000 to $30,000 a year. All employees have a paid medical insurance package, many for the first time in their lives.

Given this kind of influx of wages and tourists, local whites are generally positive about the new Mesquaki Casino. They are hoping that the state does not open up gambling and take away the Mesquaki monopoly. Early fears about the arrival of criminal types and increases in drinking and violence have been unfounded. Most whites are quick to praise the operation's efficiency, cleanliness, prohibition of alcohol, and general orderliness. Indeed, the casino is such a safe, comfortable place to go that some local whites have their morning coffee there. Others like to see the entertainment, eat a meal, gamble a little, watch the gamblers. As the casino develops, it will probably become the liveliest spot in central Iowa.

In spite of all the positive feelings, some whites still grumble about the special treatment the Indians are getting. They resent that the casino runs tax-free and generates free houses, health, educational, and per capita distributions for Indians only. Others complain that the "Indians get all the lark jobs," and that "some of the Indian managers don't do nothin'." Nevertheless, the casino personnel manager reports few incidents between white employees and Indian supervisors. Most whites accept working for Indians quite well. My cousin Allan, who is a blackjack dealer, puts it this way,

They are strict about people doing their job, about drunks. It's a good place to work. One Indian supervisor kinda lords it over whites, but most are easy to get along with.

Conversely, one Mesquaki supervisor said, "I have even seen rednecks take orders real well. A couple have said nasty stuff, but most get along well. The ones who can't get along get fired."

One ironic twist is that most of the local police force, even the rednecks, moonlight for casino security. Several Mesquaki security men said sardonically, "We are all good buddies now." Several council members, white businessmen, and teachers expressed optimism that the casino was bringing the races together in a very positive way. One tribal councilman said hopefully, "Maybe it will soften them up. They will learn that Indians aren't such bad people." To a degree, I believe this is happening. The casino has been good for local race relations. Whites can no longer complain about the financial burden of Indians when the tribe employs so many whites.

But old racial attitudes die hard. The funniest story that whites were telling was what I call the "assimilation miracle." A prominent professional expressed it well for others.

You don't see any drunk Indians laying on the street anymore. This thing has given them a little pride. You go out there, and they are in their uniforms, all cleaned up, hair fixed, standing tall, looking sharp, smile on their faces. They are happier. This thing has lifted their spirits and given them a future. I never would have said we should save that reservation. I always figured they had to get away from it to make something of themselves. But maybe this thing will make them into something.

In this story having a job and earning money magically transforms the lazy, drunken, welfare-addicted Indians into happy, clean, smiling, self-assured workers. Capitalism has given them self-pride. Now that Indians are more like whites, maybe the dreaded "reservation" should survive after all. This is especially true when their tax-free lands are now benefiting whites.

The economic impact of gaming on settlement life is just beginning. As in the white community, the most immediate impact is on 200 Mesquaki employees. Many have twelve to fifteen dollar-an-hour midmanagement jobs. In addition, the initial $2,500 per capita payment from casino profits also added thousands to those families with several enrolled members. In only the second year of operation the tribal council upped the per capita payment to $2,500 three or four times a year, depending on casino profits. Further, the council now uses the casino's minimum wage and health benefits as the standard for other tribal employees. Some tribal employees at the center, school, and clinic experienced raises to bring them up to the casino's scale.

The council also has a wide range of plans to improve the general economic condition of the settlement. They have allocated almost $2 million to build 30 three-bedroom, two-bath, 1,500-square-foot houses. The plan is to build 150 houses over the next few years. This would house all families at a middle class level. The committee on housing was also allocating $20,000 remodeling grants for all existing homes. The biggest bottleneck in the housing plan is the settlement's antiquated sewer system, presently under expansion. A closely related plan is to expand the settlement's land base. Many Mesquakis feel that additional land is necessary to keep the homesites scattered and wooded. The council has spent approximately a million dollars to purchase an additional thousand acres. They are also exploring several other land purchases.

The council has other plans to pave the settlement roads and to develop a college scholarship program. The casino gives release time and tuition credit to employees for management, accounting, and law enforcement courses taken at the regional junior college. Some Mesquakis argue that the lure of easy casino jobs and money will deter promising youth from aspiring to university degrees. On the other hand, the casino's 24-hour-a-day operation affords many possibilities. With a flexible scheduling scheme the casino could provide workstudy opportunities for all tribal members.

Not enough time has passed to gauge the social and cultural impact of the casino. Fears and dire predictions do exist, however, on the settlement. Some Mesquakis complain that a number of tribal members are addicted to gambling. They claim this has led to greater instances of drinking and child abandonment. Others claim that the casino encourages a loose moral environment that has increased destructive relationships with outsiders. There are undoubtedly Mesquakis working at the casino with serious family and personal problems, but attributing that to the casino requires careful case studies. Some of the casino employees with family or drinking problems may have had them prior to the casino's arrival. Social impact studies are needed to confirm or disconfirm such fears.

One cultural impact often mentioned was that casino employees are restricted from participating in clan religious ceremonies. According to the casino commissioners, the casino has the same leave policy that bingo instituted in 1987. Anyone participating in clan ceremonies, funerals, wakes, and adoptions can request a leave with pay. This would include everyone hosting the ceremony — the immediate family of the deceased, singers, pall bearers, attendants, and cooks. Whether the gaming operation frequently grants such paid leaves is difficult to say without a detailed study of personnel records. One practice that seems to have been impacted negatively is the four-day mourning period. Traditionally, no tribal member is supposed to work during this period. My impression is that Mesquaki Bingo and Casino never shuts down for four days during a death. Many Mesquakis continue to work. Some do not, but their mourning leave is generally not compensated.

The other fear that many traditionalists have is that all the new jobs and money will slowly undermine the communal basis of Mesquaki society. They fear that the Mesquakis will become increasingly individualistic and consumer-oriented. At some point they will be too materialistic and secular to maintain their ancient religious traditions. The traditionalists see signs of familial breakdown everywhere. More and more parents no longer teach their children Mesquaki or the oral traditions. More adolescents are disrespectful and vandalize the tribal center and school. More women end up in town unwed and on welfare. Alcoholism is on the rise. Traditionalists often paint a very sobering picture of cultural decline. For them gaming may be the final death knell of Mesquaki culture.

On the other hand, the past few years has energized the tribe to pursue many new development opportunities. They have broken ground for a new health clinic. An alcohol treatment residential facility is also being requested. On the education front the tribe has a BIA commitment to fund the long-awaited new bilingual-bicultural tribal K–8 school. There are also plans afoot to expand that facility to a K–12 school. In addition, negotiations are underway for the regional community college to put a satellite or adjunct program on the settlement. Finally, the tribe is also seeking funds to build a museum and archives to initiate a massive reclamation of cultural artifacts. Compared to the pre-civil rights years, this is an astonishing burst of creative energy. If used wisely, the vast wealth from the casino may indeed underwrite greater political and cultural autonomy.

In short, the debate over gaming signals a major ideological shift in Mesquaki politics. Mesquakis who consider themselves progressives were primarily interested in economic issues. Those who consider themselves progressive-traditionalists expressed concern over economic and cultural issues. Meanwhile, Oldbear conservatives have been in the minority and on the political sidelines. Various clan religious leaders and outspoken social critics like Ernest TrueTongue and Ted Pipestar spoke and wrote against gaming (DMR, October 3, 1993), but the tribe ultimately chose gaming. The debate was really over how to manage the operation, not whether to have gambling. It would seem that the voice of Oldbear conservatives has grown weak. Yet something happened at the powwow which gives their view new life.

The Tale of the Strange Wind

Given the horrendous flooding throughout Iowa in 1993, the casino assumed control of the year's powwow. Only the casino had the money to relocate the powwow from its flooded site near the Iowa River. As with any major decision, some controversy ensued. Old-timers grumbled that the new site near the casino lacked the shade trees and bleachers of the old site. Conversely, Mesquaki business types hailed the new site's highway access and parking. Given the continuing rains, the new powwow committee decided to rent a huge bigtop tent and portable bleachers.

As always, the first two days of the powwow were slow. The weather kept threatening heavy rains, and crowds were sparse. But on the third day a large crowd arrived and something extraordinary happened. By three in the afternoon the sky looked dark and menacing. As luck would have it, I got a flat tire on the way to the powwow. As I sat at Elenbecker's station waiting for my tire, the ambulance, police, and firemen roared by. They were moving a little louder and faster than usual, so the old duffers at the station began speculating feverishly on what happened.

Then someone popped his head in and yelled, "The police radio just said that bigtop at the powwow blew over and hurt a bunch of people!" Someone added, "Oh Jesus, I hope they got all them people out before it went down." Visions of a major disaster ebbed as the messenger explained that most of the spectators had already left. When things got too dark and ominous, the powwow managers stopped the dancing early and told people to go home. Nevertheless, about twenty-five Mesquaki managers and performers were injured, some with broken bones and deep gashes.

When I arrived on the scene, the powwow management team was talking bravely about putting the tent up. But the people were badly shaken by what had happened. No one was saying much. By nightfall, all the families camping on the new powwow grounds had pulled down their tents and left. Some people were talking about the strange and powerful wind that came from the hills just east of the casino. That would have been counter to the storm which was rolling in from the west. That made no sense to me, so I kept listening to people talk.

Several people swore the east wind whistled across the casino parking lot and "picked up the tent like a naughty child." Lee Kingfish said frightened people came begging him to give them sacred tobacco, "I told 'em it's too late now." After the ambulances left, a black guy was still playing his boom box. Jonas CutCow went over and explained that a lot of people had been hurt and asked him to shut off the loud music. It was not a time for talking, so I just watched the Mesquakis pack up and leave quietly. I finally asked Jonas why the people were leaving, and all he said was, "They know it is time for the powwow to be over." I wanted to ask why, but it was obvious that they felt the collapse of the tent was a bad omen.

A few days later people talked more openly about the tragedy. The general gist was that the Creator had sent the tribe a sign. Religious leaders had apparently warned the powwow committee that the new site was too near an old battle ground and mass gravesite. Some said that the strange wind picked up the tent to "wake us up." The Creator spared the tribe a worse disaster so people might reflect on what was happening. The casino was getting too powerful. Money was talking too loud. The tribe was heading too far down the slippery slope of assimilation.

That was the question I kept asking progressive-traditionalists. Can you really have your cake and eat it too? Can you become big-time capitalists without destroying your culture? On these matters, the words of traditionalists weigh heavily. The Mesquaki are riding the restless tiger called modernity. Like many traditional peoples living in the belly of an empire, they are caught on the horns of a terrible dilemma. Their culture and language is changing at an increasingly rapid pace. Only the Mesquakis can decide whether they are changing too fast or too much. And, as in the past, only a dialogue between traditionalists and progressives can create the wisdom and unity needed to survive.

A Final Note on Cultural Survival

My portrayal of Mesquaki-white relations has highlighted tales that local people, journalists, and other scholars tell. These tales reveal the images each group invents about the other. For example, whites told stories about drunken Indians dying on the train tracks, and Mesquakis fought back with stories about white policemen putting Indians on the train tracks. Whites told stories about lazy Indian athletes, and Mesquakis countered with stories about the Booster Club favoritism of whites. Ultimately, this war of words helps produce a racial border that scars many people and inhibits racial understanding.

Fortunately, cultural and racial borders are never very impermeable. They are made to be transgressed. Some people in both races rejected the ignorance, fear, and envy that produces racial borders and stereotypes. Stories of several "border-crossers" show how some people blend elements from both cultural traditions. In fact, the Mesquakis as a group have fused many white cultural practices into their old ways. Despite the lamentations of traditionalists, this process of cultural fusion has neither destroyed nor assimilated Mesquakis.

With the help of empowering federal legislation, Mesquaki "progressive-traditionalists" have created a new tribal welfare state based on ancient communal and religious practices. Their vibrant communal society democratically debates every issue affecting the tribe. Some tribal members are also beginning to influence what is written about their culture. There is a new assertiveness in the texts of several Mesquaki writers and in invented ceremonies like the powwow. I labeled this assertiveness an "ethnogenetic process"; that is, the Mesquakis have become an "ethnic minority" that now demands basic American civil rights.

This is admittedly an optimistic view of contemporary Mesquaki society, one not always shared by traditionalists, who seem hypercritical of their leaders and the council. Their pessimistic discourse of cultural decline was so popular that I initally wondered if the tribe had lost its historical memory. But traditionalists were equally quick to recount proudly their miraculous escapes and survivals in a world full of enemies. They generally saw themselves as a tough, resilient, self-reliant people. So why does such a proud, historically conscious people have such a gloomy view of their own cultural evolution?

The obvious explanation is that the loss of the hereditary monarchy has left traditional Mesquakis full of sorrow. They consider the loss of divine leadership the most serious of many cultural losses. Traditionalists were always so melancholy about their lost past that they distrusted the incremental changes of the present. They were always very harsh and moralistic about the failings of their elected leaders, who lacked divine sanction. Nothing being created was ever as good as what was lost. Only the apocalyptic prophecy that someday the whitemen would be gone seemed to assuage their sorrow. Although many Mesquakis are no longer traditionalists, this fundamentalist discourse of worldly loss and divine deliverance remains very influential on the settlement.

To make sense out of the strange mixture of sadness and joyfulness, I began imagining the Mesquakis to be a little like my Irish ancestors. The Irish lack the Mesquaki prophecy that their tormentor will eventually disappear, but there are some historical parallels. Five hundred years of English domination has left the Irish an intensely religious, melancholy people who are noted for their creative writing, story-telling, humor, music, artistic expression, and political cynicism. I would like to think that Irish pubs and wakes are not so unlike Mesquaki "forty-nining" and wakes. Like the Irish, the Mesquakis are an intensely emotional, senti-mental, earthy people who live and die with much gusto and sorrow. Comparing Irishmen and Indians is probably hopelessly unscientific and essentialist in the postmodern era of anthropology. Nevertheless, that analogy helps me appreciate how human — how ordinary yet extraordi-nary — the Mesquaki are.

Epilogue

The Great Real Names Experiment

Since Tama is my hometown, I wanted to be especially open and responsive. To this end, I circulated a manuscript that used the real names of the forty main characters. The idea was to "dialogue" about the manuscript with these people and reach a mutual agreement. I was hoping that their comments would help me correct factual errors and soften my characterizations of people. Letting the main characters review the manuscript did not include the right of censorship, but I did offer several people the chance to print a rejoinder. After long, sometimes painful conversations, nearly all the reviewers gave me verbal permission to publish what I had written, with various modifications. Getting this kind of agreement seems noteworthy, but there were several important exceptions.

One prominent Mesquaki leader took great umbrage at his portrayal and called the manuscript "dog shit." He refused to engage me in a conversation to improve and correct whatever he disliked. From his perspective it was 90 percent wrong, and trying to work with me was a hopeless task. I was just some dumb white guy who had failed to get the facts, the real truth. So he threatened to sue me. Another prominent Mesquaki felt the manuscript was an invasion of privacy because it used people's real names. In addition, he felt that I tended to hide the identities of whites more than Mesquakis. Despite my good intentions to portray the evils of racism, I was a captive of my white upbringing. I still thought I had the right to waltz into the settlement and tell all about "Tama's Indians." Along the same line, one of my old high school buddies was deeply disappointed that I had not uncovered the real truth about Eddie Benson's mysterious death in the local jail. He said, "The white big shots must'a got to you, Doug."

When I told my publishers that one person had threatened a lawsuit, they became concerned. Then the Mesquakis who felt the book was an invasion of privacy called the University of Pennsylvania Press editor and urged the use of pseudonyms. At that point, my publishers put pressure on me either to get signed waivers to use people's real names, or to do what most anthropologists do and use pseudonyms. Initially, I was reluctant to abandon the real names for two reasons.

First, I felt the difficult process of talking with the main characters about their portrayals had worked well. I had come back to hear people's views, and in all but two cases we had worked through our differences. To me, these open, honest conversations were an agreement far stronger than any written contact. To go back and make people sign a piece of paper seemed like I suddenly distrusted what we had done face-to-face. The other reason for not using pseudonyms was that some Mesquakis wanted their accomplishments in the historical record. I felt that using pseudonyms would let these people down. In the end, however, I was unwilling to remake my verbal agreements into a legal, written agreement.

I decided that pseudonyms would not change the meaning of the story. One does not have to know the characters personally to appreciate the stories. In fact, had I fictionalized my characters more from the beginning, I would have been able to develop the complex characters one finds in fiction. I tended to leave out the negative side of those portrayed. Consequently, several reviewers complained that I glorified Claude Windsong, Ed Longknife, Ted Pipestar, Ernest TrueBlood, Jay WhiteHawk, Jonas Littletree, Gordon Lightheart, Richard Moline, and Tomas Warrior. The reviewers who accused me of glorifying someone were often political or personal enemies of the aforementioned. These critics invariably had less generous views of their leaders than I did.

So what is the lesson for other researchers in my failed attempt to use real names? In retrospect, I was probably naive to think I could write a more open manuscript about my hometown. I had two basic reasons, one very personal and one very philosophical, for imagining I could make this book different from most ethnographies. First, the research site is my hometown. Because I genuinely like the place and have old friends there, I imagined that I could win everyone's confidence and cooperation.

Second, I am deeply steeped in philosophical writings that champion the intelligence, rationality, openness, and sincerity of ordinary people. Antonio Gramsci (1971) is probably right that everyone is a philosopher, but that does not mean that ordinary people want to sit around with an anthropologist and "discursively redeem" the truth of his or her text. In retrospect, I may have been a little drunk on Habermas's notions of ideal communication (Habermas, 1984; Foley, 1990). Up to a point, I was able to win people's confidence and was generally well accepted. But some reviewers seemed mainly interested in maintaining a good public image or in discrediting their racial and political enemies. In conflict-filled communities, not everyone is going to be a high-minded philosopher anxious to dialogue dispassionately about some writer's truth claims.

One of the most fascinating things about the reviews was the incredulity it evoked in some reviewers. Several people told me I either had a "lot of guts" or was "pretty dumb" to think I could talk with people about the manuscript. Such comments threw the whole idea of dialogue and the discursive redemption of truth into question. One Mesquaki asked, "What will you do if someone doesn't want you to print what you said about them, but it really is the truth and other people here believe it?" He went on to say it was my book, so why would I let anyone else write it for me, especially if I had the "facts" to back up what I said. Another Mesquaki said what is the point of discussing what you wrote: "If I said, 'No, don't publish this.' would you stop?" His point was that I would publish it whether people liked it or not. I was, after all, a professor, an educated type who took for granted his right to speak about lowly non-educated types.

Of course this reviewer is right, up to a point. No amount of open "dialogue" over the text will completely abolish the power difference between the outside investigator and the community being studied. Ethnographers have long agonized over this dilemma and have tried to disperse their authorial power through various narrative techniques (Clifford, 1988) and collaboration with those being portrayed (Lather, 1991). All of these new techniques, including my community review, still preserve the author's right to speak and represent others, albeit in a more restrained way. Ultimately, the only foolproof way of reducing one's authorial power is to simply give up the right to speak for others. If social scientists, historians, journalists, and novelists would stop writing books, there would be no more misrepresentations, no more authorial abuses of power — and no more human reflections about the human condition. In the end, most writers believe that telling stories helps people see where they have been and where they must go. So writers from all fields are left searching for ways to disperse and limit, yet not give up their right to speak.

Fortunately, most of the reviewers did help me create a more dialogic ethnographic practice. They reaffirmed Gramsci's optimism that every person is a philosopher, and Habermas's high-minded notion that people really believe in and try to practice open communication. Most reviewers had the common sense to see my text as just a story, my story. They were willing to grant me the right to tell it my way, but not without arguing a little over its meaning. Most reviewers said what the following Mesquaki said, "It's your story. Tell it the way you see it." For me, this attitude is a powerful reaffirmation of the idea of a free society with free and responsible speech.

In the introduction, I make no grand claims that my story is an infallible, totally objective scientific study. I describe the text as a very personal encounter with my memories and old friends. I am not trying to pull academic rank on people and claim to be an all-knowing scientist. I did, however, try to collect varying opinons and differing accounts of events and be as truthful as possible. I used the techniques and ideas of anthropology to make sense of what I saw and heard. I think most people heard that attitude and voice in the text and responded in the same spirit. A few did not, and that is just the way it is.

Mesquaki Comments on the Heartland Chronicles

There is no way to convey all the comments without a long chapter. So I will report a few of the highlights, the main themes, the most critical and positive comments. I have chosen to group the comments by race because it provides the reader with a window into the differences between Indians and whites. Hopefully, these comments will give the reader another vantage point from which to judge the manuscript.

Perhaps the most critical comments came from an older traditionalist couple. The man, a former political leader, was disappointed in the emphasis on the new "progressive-traditionalists." From his perspective, many of these new self-proclaimed leaders were neither religious traditionalists, nor all that progressive and professional. This couple hammered me for not mentioning the criminal activities, infidelities, and rudeness of several of these "so-called leaders." They read the manuscript as hopelessly subjective about my old friends and buddies. Quite unexpectedly, an old friend who teaches at the high school made a similar comment. She accused me of slanting the book towards "your old buddies" and overlooking that "these so-called traditionalists do not bring up their kids with that old-time respect and discipline of real traditionalists."

The main point in the couple's commentary was that I greatly exaggerated the improvements in settlement life. For them the settlement has far too much youthful vandalism, drunkenness, and violence. They fault the new progressive-traditionalists for not developing a good police force and for not helping struggling families and abandoned women bring up their children the old way. They also regaled me with stories of various clan leaders' improprieties and asked how such flawed men could be spiritual leaders. Some of Ted Pipestar's writings ask the same unsettling questions. Such Mesquaki critics long for the return of deeply spiritual leaders and a more pure form of their ancient clan religion.

In retrospect, maybe the traditional culture and religion is collapsing more than I realized, and I may have glorified the progressive-traditionalists who confronted whites in the 1970s and developed gaming in the

1980s. But I remain impressed with the strong, intelligent, creative Mesquakis I portrayed. They were busy fusing white and Indian cultural practices and moving forward under difficult circumstances. That is the story I wanted to tell, not whether somone gave their relative a few bucks from the tribal coffers, or spent some time in jail. Those are not good things, not things to be condoned, but I was trying to capture the flow of tribal history, not make commentary on the character flaws of certain leaders. Future historians will record how impressive the survival of the Mesquakis and other native peoples has been.

The commentary that bothered me most was on my failure to uncover why Eddie Benson died in the local jail. I did try to talk to local officials about that case, but it was hard to get anyone to say anything. Maybe some white cop beat him senseless and he died from the injuries sustained. Maybe there is a smelly cover-up going on, but it was beyond my investigative powers to crack that one. In retrospect, I probably should have included more about the Benson case because it remains such a powerful symbol of racism for Mesquakis. Most local whites have conveniently forgotten that sad tale.

Another story that I took a little heat for was Jay WhiteHawk's great pig heist. Since he was an old football buddy, a couple of people thought I was trying to glorify his drunken exploits. One clan leader and one prominent white businessman grumbled that such stories set a bad example for the youth. They thought I was condoning drunkenness and violence. I did not tell Jay's story to condone his actions. All I wanted to convey was that Jay is a human being with feelings. Editor Hynek had no right to publish the sick stories he did about his mother's death. The real story here is that racism fueled his anger, and he did himself in with his fighting and drinking. Jay knows that I told the story to warn other Mesquaki youth, not to make him a hero.

Another story that one person objected to was the portrayal of Leon GreyEagle struggling with the death of his nephew Clyde. That reviewer told me that I had been insensitive to the widow. When I asked the widow what she thought, she said "This is really good. I am glad you wrote this because I was not there to see it." The reviewer claimed it was also insensitive to show Leon on the verge of tears since Mesquakis were not permitted to show grief in public. That did not turn out to be what embarrassed Leon. His main concern was that his joke about professors coming from buzzard droppings was a little too green. He feared that stuffy professor-types might not see that he was "just havin' a little fun with 'em." I must confess that I told Leon a fib on this one. I reassured him that my professor friends would love the story, but I do know some professors that are too full of themselves to get a laugh out of it. Fortunately, Leon relented and said I could keep it in the book.

Most Mesquaki reviewers thought the manuscript was a realistic portrait of contemporary events. It showed the tribe fighting for their civil rights and moving forward. One woman said,

I really liked it. It's contemporary. When you give our kids something to read, it will give an accurate picture of what we are trying to do. The tribe is a social service agency that has a multi-million dollar budget, and the system will break down without more professionalism. The Casino has escalated everything, and the tribe isn't ready. It is a real interesting time of change, and you captured that well.

Over and over again, Mesquaki reviewers said that the manuscript's main redeeming quality was its portrayal of racism. One individual expressed that sentiment in the following way:

In every study we've been a stepping-stone, but you don't step on us too hard. That is just the way it is. Of all the studies, what have we gotten, really? I think your story about racism will be of some benefit, but you will probably get somethin', too. It's a story that needs to be told. It's a good book. But people don't come here to study us out of the goodness of their heart. They are just followin' their chosen profession. We knew what they were doin', so we didn't keep 'em off the settlement. To get our story known, we have to help the outsiders who come.

What pleased me most about the Mesquaki reviews was that no one blasted me for revealing cultural secrets or for romanticizing or stereotyping Indians. The following comment about portraying selected aspects of Mesquaki culture was fairly common:

I think it is ok to a certain point to let whites know things about our culture. It will bring a little more understanding. I try to explain these things like adoptions and funerals to whites, but it's hard. The other thing is that you show us as real people. I didn't expect this kind of book. This has names and shows how people are thinkin'. I thought it was going to be more dry and boring, but once you started readin' it, I couldn't put it down. It was full of humor and real people. The way you describe Lone and Claude and others is really how they are. You talk about a person from all sides, what you see, what others say, that was something.

Another person also emphasized the book's use of humor and stories to portray the cultural difference between Mesquakis and whites:

I liked the whole thing. It's humorous. Indians really like those stories about dogs and buzzards. The whites, when they go broke, they kill themselves. Heck, I've been broke a thousand times. Even the serious stuff, we laugh about.

This individual went on to say that "The reporters always seem to go to the wrong people, but you dug around, you go deeper, at least you talked to everyone, different sides." But later in the conversation he said I could have dug deeper into what the cops do, the Benson killing, and discrimination in sports. I had done a fairly good job but did not get the whole story. He ended with a comment that I cherish because no one else said it so directly

What I like best about this book is you came back home to write it. You remembered all this stuff from when you were a kid. Have any other whites ever bothered to do that?

The topic that garnered the most varied response was gaming. Most of the reviewers felt the way the following reviewer did:

The Casino stuff was ok. A lot of this told what happened. You gave a history, the views of the people who ran it. You portray the big versus small thing pretty well. That has always been the issue. But some people will probably disagree. They'll say only their way is the right way, but I didn't think you took sides.

In sharp contrast, another reviewer said,

This thing on the gaming sounds like a big fairy tale, how we got such a good deal for getting rid of All-Star Casino. You make Moline and Warrior and Lightheart sound like heros. It's Longknife that set those people straight.

Several traditionalists felt I had given the casino too big a part in Mesquaki life. They grudgingly admitted it had to be written about, but just did not find that chapter interesting. They had heard it all for years and were sick of what gaming was doing to the settlement. For them the casino meant creeping materialism, fewer people at the clan ceremonies, family against family, and too many abandoned children. The only thing that redeemed the chapter was the story of the Creator blowing down the tent to warn the tribe.

Another topic that evoked some interesting difference of opinion was the brief section on women's views. All the women reviewers were enthusiastic about that section and felt it dispelled white stereotypes of Indian women as subservient squaws. Mesquaki men were somewhat less glowing. The men still tend to think that it is the woman's fault for marrying an outsider or for being unwed mothers. In their view, women are told not to do these things. They know tribal law and custom, so they must take responsibility for their mistakes and not complain. Nevertheless, many Mesquakis acknowledge that the tribal council must begin to address the problem of abandoned mothers and enrollment. Several reviewers pointed out that a new committee to revise the constitution is wrestling with those issues.

White Comments on the Heartland Chronicles

Generally, white reviewers were more interested in the portrayal of Mesquaki culture than in the stories about racism. Nevertheless, the white
response to the portrayals of racism was better than I expected. When
South Texas whites reviewed my book about racism in their town, they
accused me of glorifying the Chicano civil rights movement. Several
threatened to sue and/or beat me up. They saw me as a real traitor to my
race, a pathetic, bleeding-heart liberal. There was no such outpouring of
anger and denial from whites in my hometown. Perhaps people were
being nice to their hometown boy. Or perhaps I was able to write this
book with more balance and a less accusatory tone.

For whatever reason, only a few Tama whites reacted as defensively as
South Texans did. Only one white reviewer thought the book would really
upset locals. Others said not to worry, the hateful rednecks would never
read this or any other book. One teacher said that

the book shows the town as basically redneck with a few liberal teachers. That is
about the way I'd portray it. I think most people around here would have to agree
with that, but maybe some will get mad about it.

Another retired white politician added:

It is pro-Indian, but every time I was about to get you for that, you'd mention
something good about whites. All in all, I thought you tried hard to give it some
balance, show some good whites, too. I think you showed how both sides saw each
other. There's still lots of misunderstandings. You captured that real well.

I was also pleased that no white defended what Mayor Carnal did in his
court, or what John Hynek wrote in his scandal sheet. One woman said,
"That is just the way it was. The mayor did some pretty nasty things to
Indians." Another man said,

Hynek wrote some mean stuff about Indians, it's true. He was just out to make a
buck, to sell newspapers. Now I can see it wasn't right-like that story about the
woman who froze. That should'a never been written about anybody.

On the other hand, one woman felt that I was a little condescending
toward whites, that I sounded like I was superior. One Mesquaki reported
that another white reader had told him, "This guy is on a real ego trip.
The whole book is very condescending towards Mesquaki culture." So
despite all my attempts to portray both sides generously, a few reviewers
thought I was looking down my nose at them.

Generally, however, most whites accepted what they called a "pro-

Indian" tone. Most said it was true that the Mesquakis had it rough, but many were quick to add that most locals still think they get far too much government aid and cry racism too often. Too many whites even resent the gambling windfall, regardless how much it adds to the local economy. During these exchanges I told the reviewers over and over that the book is pro-human, not pro-Indian.

White reviews were also fascinated with my portrayals of Mesquaki leaders. Several whites said they were surprised at some of the things Claude Windsong had done for his people, "I thought he was just this big mouth who always complained." Of Ernest TrueBlood another said, "I never realized that Ernest believed those old religion things. I guess he had some good reasons for all the letters he wrote." Another was surprised to know that Ted Pipestar's life as a literary figure was not all roses, "I can see that he gets caught in the middle out there. It must get rough when he criticizes the council for stuff." Another felt Ed Longknife was a bigger player in getting gambling than he realized, "I heard he was out for himself, but he seems to have pushed them to finally do something." In general, local white readers seemed to come away with positive views of the main Mesquaki characters. In addition, several women reviewers were effusive in their praise of the section on Mesquaki women.

My favorite white reaction to the manuscript was from a businessman who had initially told me what a horrible place the settlement was and how much he wanted the Mesquakis to assimilate:

I gotta admit, you changed my mind on a few things. I never realized there was so much of their old ways left out there. I knew a little about the burials and wakes, but that stuff on adoptions was really interesting. And I never did understand all the Oldbear versus Youngbear stuff. I can see now that they are fighting to save their old ways. Maybe we should just leave them alone to be what they want to be. We do the same for the Amish. Why not the Indians? I was also pretty shocked by all that stuff on prohibition. I never realized that we went that far. Now I don't entirely agree with all you wrote on sports. They have to come to practice if they want to play. They probably do get picked on, but it isn't entirely the whites' fault. The two cultures are just more different than I thought.

This individual went on about a number of other points, but the upshot was he really did have more respect for Mesquaki culture and wanted to be a better neighbor.

Another topic that fascinated white reviewers was the Mesquaki prophecy,

I never knew they thought they were going to get all their lands back someday. No wonder they got such a chip on their shoulders. I can see why they fight so hard with all that history and that prophecy thing. That deal sure surprised me.

Many white readers were also impressed with the adoption ceremony and reminisced wistfully that old-time white wakes used to be like the Mesquaki wakes. Others thought the account of the gaming helped make sense of why it took so long to decide. For most whites it was a very simple decision: put up a casino and make lots of money. They never thought of gaming as a threat to the traditional culture. They found the differences between those advocating big-time and small-time gaming interesting, and the story of the tent blowing over amazing. Several echoed the following comment, "I guess they just don't think of it the way we do: as a business deal."

That white reviewers focused on cultural differences pleased me. I emphasized the huge cultural gulf between whites and Indians to explain the racial conflicts. Some Mesquaki friends wanted me to rub the townspeople's noses in their racism more, but I opted to show that each group has its reasons for believing what they do. Regrettably, the average white is still woefully ignorant about Mesquaki culture and history, and she or he consumes a steady diet of media stereotypes and racist train track stories. In addition, the local schools and media, for all their good intentions, do precious little to change white attitudes. So my hometown, like the rest of America, still has a long way to go, but I did find many whites of good will living there.

One final story that needs some commentary is the one about my riding the bench my junior year. Several whites thought I was sore over getting beat out of a spot on the basketball team. There I was, squawking and belly-aching about discrimination just like the Mesquakis do. One prominent businessman kidded me, "I heard you were madder at Willis than you were at the town!" That small-minded comment irritated the hell out of me. First off, I never came back to get revenge on my hometown. Secondly, I never told the story to get back at Willis or, as one Coach Levi-hater imagined, the coach who benched me. I told this story to illustrate how difficult it is for any outsider to join the little cliques that control social life and sports in small town high schools. That is especially true for outsiders who seem as different and strange as Mesquakis do to whites. If you are in the wrong social class or race, the so-called town big shots can make your life so miserable you will feel like dropping out.

These, then, were the highlights of what the forty reviewers said. I returned to Texas feeling that most reviewers had not held back, that our conversations had been open and frank. But one never knows. For whatever reason, some reviewers may have told me what they thought I wanted to hear. They may have chosen to be silent to avoid any conflict or ill feelings. One thing of which I am sure — the review was a good learning experience for me, and this final version is better than the original manuscript.

More Mesquaki Story-Telling About the Researcher

As Mesquaki reviewers discussed the text, they spun several stories I must share. The first good story was apparently a tribal elder's way of telling me that I had a great deal more to learn about Mesquaki politics and the gambling issue. After politely going over the politics chapters in some detail, correcting a point here and there, Mr. Z suddenly started telling me a story about the scorpion and the frog. Having been through such storytelling episodes before, I knew a zinger was surely coming.

It seems that a scorpion came to Frogville and found himself unable to cross their river. So he found himself a friendly frog and asked him for a ride across his river. At first the frog said, "No, you'll bite me and I will die."

The scorpion replied, "Don't be silly, I won't bite you. I want to get to the other side of the river. I need you to help me."

After a time the frog relented and said, "OK, hop on."

When they got to the middle of the river the scorpion bit the frog. The baffled frog asked, "Why did you bite me? Now we are both going to die."

The scorpion replied, "Because I am a scorpion." Then they both began to sink, and that is the end of the story.

I waited a moment, and the elder continued in a hushed voice that an evil force had come to the settlement. He said the trusting frogs were being corrupted, that family was turning against family. The elder reeled off all sorts of names, dates, and sums of money exchanged. I sat there feeling a little overwhelmed and glad that I had no more time left to verify and retell his story.

The other two good stories that surfaced during the interviews had to do with burials and spirits. I had numerous conversations with Mesquakis about burials, and they were always fascinated with whites who wanted to be buried the Indian way. So one day Lone, Claude, Leon, and Jonas were sitting around the tribal center discussing this strange white longing. One comment led to another and someone came up with the idea of the tribe buying a lot next to the settlement for burying such whitemen.

That brilliant idea provoked another, and someone said, "Yea, we could get one of these big augurs that digs holes for light posts."

Another person chipped in, "Yeah, and then we could bury one after the other on top of each other. First there would be Michelson, then Sol Tax, then McTaggart, then Rock Island Red and Bill, then that Foley character."

Someone else added that they could mark the spot with a giant telephone pole, and everyone present thought that was a splendid idea.

In the same vein, I had many conversations with Mesquakis about where our spirits or souls go after death. According to Mesquakis, all

Indians go West to a place where there are no whites. Whenever clan leaders told me this story, I protested and demanded my civil rights to visit old friends in the Indian spirit world. Most Mesquakis were amused by my protestations, so one elder apparently took it upon himself to set my mind and spirit at ease. During our discussion of the manuscript, he suddenly began describing how spirits whiz through the universe across time and space. In a very comforting, serene voice he said:

Don't worry, Doug, we'll be seein' each other out there. Our trails will cross. I'll be whizzin' somewhere, and so will you. We'll meet in some other galaxy and talk about old times, how your book sold, what my relatives are doin' now, who's shackin' up with who.

I will not go into all the detail, but he painted a beautiful, surrealistic picture of a place full of friendly spirits and good storytelling. I gotta admit, this is probably my favorite Mesquaki story because it almost set my skeptical white mind to rest. It seems fitting that we will all meet again in some strange, beautiful place. With these two stories, my Mesquaki friends tried to counsel me on spiritual matters. They probably did more for me than I will ever do as a shrink for Jay WhiteHawk's poor dog.

Another Lesson from a Guardian of Mesquaki Culture

Since one of the primary characters in the manuscript was Claude Wind-song, I was anxious to get his response. My portrayal of his ups and downs politically was meant to be a tribute to his persistence and dedication, but nobody likes someone showing their defeats. A couple of weeks after I had given him the manuscript, I saw Claude at an adoption ceremony and he said, "I won't be able to talk to you about your book next week. I'm going out of town."

After I asked him where he was going, he replied laconically, "Tokyo, Wisconsin." I paused and looked for some sign that he was pulling my leg. I knew that he had a Indian child welfare conference in Wisconsin, so maybe there was a Tokyo, Wisconsin. There is, after all, a Moscow, Idaho. Claude put on his most dead-pan face and strung me out for what seemed like an eternity, then he cracked a little smile. I started roaring with laughter, and he let me enjoy the moment. Then he suddenly turned serious. He stared at me the way only Claude can stare and asked, "What are you laughing at? Are you laughing at these people?"

It would seem that the joke had turned sour. Claude had put me through these paces before, so I steeled myself and said with conviction, "No. I would never make fun of these people." I tried to convey that he should know better and shifted the conversation back to a lighter topic.

Claude had said what he wanted, so he relented and smiled. It was always like that with Claude. Sometimes he wanted to sting you and get your attention. Once he had made his point, he would retreat quietly.

A few days later I showed up on Claude's doorstep to talk about the manuscript. He was at home slouched before the TV, obviously tired, and apparently feeling very philosophical. He went on quite a while about what happened at the powwow, saying that it was a "spanking from the Creator. A warning to wake people up because the tribe was getting weaker and weaker." We talked briefly about the manuscript, and he seemed generally positive, even said I had done a good job. That seemed too easy, so I pleaded for another meeting to go over the manuscript in detail.

When I returned at the agreed time a couple of days later, Claude was not there. I worried that he was avoiding me. Eventually we had a conversation by phone, and he asked me if I knew what happened at the powwow. I equivocated and said, "Well, some people said it was a sign from the Creator."

Claude sensed he had me doing the academic shuffle, so he pressed forward,

You don't know what you are talking about, Doug. You are walkin' on a tightrope, and you are about to fall off; so you better grab your family jewels so you don't get hurt when you fall. Why don't you just write that a big wind blew the tent down. That is all it was, a big wind. That is what you believe, don't you?

Claude was in my mind, working on me, making me feel unsure of myself. One day it is, "You did a good job." The next day it is, "You don't know what you're talkin' about." One day the wind is a sign, and the next day it is not. It was vintage Claude. Once again he had gotten my attention. He wanted me to write what I was going to write with great care. If nothing else, at least write with a little humility. Understand that you are nothing in the Creator's scheme of things. A nice well-meaning white come to write your book, but really nothing. If you can understand that, maybe you will write something worthwhile. Claude was still being a guardian of the tribe's cultural tradition.

I took this last lesson as seriously as the first, and as before, I went to see Lone TrueBlood. After four years, I am not sure if I went to see him because he is my pal, or because he is the hereditary chief. Maybe a little of both. For whatever reason, I just wanted to hear his reassuring laugh. As always, Lone did not disappoint. A man of few words, he bellowed at what Claude had said and told me not to worry. Still, I could not get this scene out of my head. Driving home to Texas I kept thinking about what kind of researcher-wolf I was. Was I the wolf in McTaggart's book, or the wolf in the movie *Dances with Wolves?* Did I mistake dung for green corn dumplings and eat dung? Or did I get close enough to dine on the beef jerky? Probably a little of both.

Some Final Reflections on Why I Came Home

In the introduction, I said the irony of Indian gambling and the evils of racism brought me back. After years in the civil rights trenches of Texas and Mississippi, I really did want to do a similar study of my hometown. But each time I regaled Ted Pipestar with my noble political reasons for this study, he politely asked why I really came back. So one day I told him my other noble reason for the study. This reason stems from a growing uncertainty that anthropology is a science. As I explained in an earlier fable about Dracula's scientific castle, postmodern philosophers have sown enough doubt to make some anthropologists want to write novelistic studies. At any rate, I droned on to poor Ted, explaining that studying my hometown would help me move in that direction. I claimed that writing for friends and loved ones would up the emotional ante and force me to write a more personal, engaging ethnography.

But Ted seemed unmoved by my passionate quest for the perfect ethnographic text. He has never bought into the academic game, so such a pursuit must have sounded a little crazy. Sensing his skepticism, I shifted gears and launched into a tirade about the deadly effects of academic socialization. I proclaimed that the catch-22 of being a "scholar" was that your professional voice destroys your personal voice. You read an endless stream of books and articles to keep up with the latest academic jargon. You train eager young graduate students to speak anthropologese. You review the articles they write for journals to make sure they can ply anthropological metaphors and models cleverly. You become a gatekeeper dedicated to propagating the academic discourse, and in the end Ryan GreyEagle's kindly academic bull snake eats you.

Eventually, writing dull scholarly articles makes you start dreaming about writing fiction. You imagine that fiction has none of the abstract models and ponderous jargon that crushes your personal voice. The solution to academic writing seems so simple. All you have to do is become more literary. But wiggling out of a pact with the academic devil was much harder than I thought. The concepts of history and culture proved to be stern taskmasters. Making all historical events and cultural patterns dramatic and entertaining is impossible. In the process of finishing this book, I gave up any fantasy I had about making ethnography into "good literature."

What I ended up doing was sprinkling a scholarly study with enough dry, matter-of-fact Iowa wit, stories, and vignettes of people to make it more personal and less pedantic. Many local reviewers found the narrative style engaging and easy to understand. After the reviews, I knew I had not lost people in a pool of academic jargon. But the comment on my narrative style that I cherish most came from an anthropologist living in Michigan. She said I was "the Garrison Keillor of anthropology." Since I love Keillor's yarns about the Midwest, that is the best thing anyone will ever say about my work.

At any rate, after reading the first few chapters, Ted was not particularly impressed with my great quest to write in a personal, midwestern voice. He asked me why I told my story in such ordinary, colloquial language. He wanted me to write about what anthropologists usually write about. He wanted detailed technical accounts of Mesquaki "social structure" and "kinship." There I was listening to the postmodern poet tell me to stick to an older-style scientific narrative! The least my study could do is sound authoritative and objective and leave the subjective stuff to literary folks. He felt that the manuscript was a little like a soap opera and was punctuated by too much gossip and rumor. As we talked, all my literary pretensions about our "dialogic encounter" went up in a chuckle. We were like the proverbial ships passing in the night.

My encounter with Ted turned out to be the final cork-popper that made me reflect more deeply on my personal motivations for coming home. As I said in Chapter one, I was drawn back to Iowa for all sorts of sentimental reasons. I have powerful, positive memories about growing up on a farm, about my first true love, glorious athletic victories, loving family Fourth of July picnics. At times I have lost my bearings in the world beyond my childhood world. So coming back was an opportunity to see myself anew. Being back among youthful memories created a "double consciousness." I met the old me in my recollections. I saw more clearly how I have changed — sometimes for the better, sometimes for the worse. I was tempted to gush on about all that in the book, but elected to channel those feelings into the stories of others.

Having said all that, I must, nevertheless, end these Chronicles with the most compelling personal reason why I came home. This story should illustrate what probably lies at the root of much social science writing. Hopefully, it will make the "science" of anthropology less strange and imperial for non-academic and literary types. Like Jonas CutCow, I grew up never knowing my father, but, unlike Jonas, I felt like a bastard. My family never rubbed it in, but other whites did. That is just how whites were in those days. The worst of it was I never knew why he left, or why he never made me one of his truck stops.

Around ten years ago, when I finally stopped feeling sorry for myself, I decided to lay this memory to rest. Now that I was a big-time researcher, surely I could unravel the mystery of my past while studying race relations. So during the fieldwork I located his relatives in nearby Colo, Iowa. They said lots of surprising things about my father. His brother summed it up this way, "Well, you didn't miss much. He could work like hell when he wanted to, but you couldn't depend on him." And what I remember most is that this hard-drinking Irishman apparently always wanted a son who played basketball.

Tom Foley died before I ever met him, but many good things still came out of that research. His family turned out to be very nice people. I have several lovely pictures of Grandpa Foley and Bridget Kelly fresh from Ireland. But the real breakthrough was hearing Mom's side of it. My training in collecting life histories finally proved useful. We spent many hours around the kitchen table before she died. She told me the whole sad tale of her fake wedding shower, the retreat to Denver, and the lonely boarding house. The "wedding" and "divorce" preserved the family honor, but it took a lot of years for us to talk and bury the hatchet. It was the first time that I truly appreciated her. And when several Mesquakis remembered Hazel and her tavern fondly, it left me proud. It must have been hard to be an independent woman in those days.

So there you have it, a more personal reason for this study — the search for myself. The working through of both positive and painful memories. Maybe "social science" boils down to one person trying to understand him- or herself enough to understand other people. Maybe social science storytellers are not all that different from literary storytellers. Perhaps knowing Mom better was absolutely crucial for understanding abandoned Mesquaki mothers and grieving Mesquaki men. Of course, understanding another culture takes much more than simple empathy. It takes endless hours of listening to people and observing, constant recording and reflecting, a grab-bag of theories to ply. But knowing yourself always seems like the biggest part of understanding others. In this case, exploring my memories and missing past probably influenced greatly the stories I chose to tell. One reviewer told me this manuscript was "real heartfelt." She got that one right.

References

Almond, Gabriel and Sidney Verba (1960). *The Civic Culture*. Boston: Little Brown.

Almquist, Rex (1972). "Educational History of the Iowa Sac and Fox: Present Problems in School and Community and Implications for Social Work." Unpublished MA thesis, University of Iowa.

Anzaldua, Gloria (1987). *Borderlands/La Frontera: The New Mestiza*. San Francisco: Spinsters/Aunt Lute.

Basso, Keith (1979). *Portaits of "the Whiteman": Linguistic Play and Cultural Symbols among the Apache*. Cambridge: Cambridge University Press.

Berkhofer, Robert F. Jr. (1978). *The WhiteMan's Indian: Images of the American Indian from Columbus to the Present*. New York: Vintage.

Bernstein, Alison R. (1991). *American Indians and World War II: Toward a New Era in Indian Affairs*. Norman: University of Oklahoma Press.

Blair, Emma Hunt, ed. (1911). *The Indian Tribes of the Upper Mississipi Valley and the Region of the Great Lakes*. 2 vols. Cleveland: Arthur H. Clark Co.

Brunel, Adrian (ND). Untitled report on Mesquaki teenage girls. Fox Project fieldnotes. National Anthropological Archives, Smithsonian Institution.

Busby, Alli (1886). *Two Summers Among the Mesquaki*. Vinton, Iowa: Herold Book and Job Rooms.

Caldwell, Joseph (1910). *A History of Tama County, Iowa*. Chicago: Lewis Publishing Co.

Callender, Charles (ND). "Changes in the Fox Culture Between 1820 and 1955." Unpublished paper, Fox Project Fieldnotes, Smithsonian Institution.

Clifford, James (1994). "Diasporas." *Cultural Anthropology* 9, 3: 302–338.

—— (1988). *The Predicament of Culture: Twentieth-Century Ethnography, Literature, and Art*. Cambridge, Mass.: Harvard University Press.

CutCow, Jonas (ND). "Green Corn Dance to Annual Pow-wow: A History of the Annual Mesquaki Pow-Wow." Unpublished paper.

—— (ND). *A History of the Mesquaki People*. Unpublished manuscript.

Delgado-Gaitan, Concha (1990). *Literacy for Empowerment: The Role of Parents in Their Children's Education*. London: Falmer Press.

Deloria, Vine, ed. (1985). *American Indian Policy in the Twentieth Century*. Norman: University of Oklahoma Press.

Dumont, R.V. (1972). "Learning English and How to Be Silent: Studies in Sioux and Cherokee Classrooms." In Courtney B. Cazden, Vera P. John, and Dell Hymes, eds., *Functions of Language in the Classroom*. New York: Teachers College Press, 344–369.

Eckert, Penelope (1989). *Jocks and Burnouts: Social Categories and Identity in the High School.* New York: Teachers College Press.

Edmunds R. David and Joseph L. Peyser (1993). *The Fox Wars: The Mesquaki Challenge to New France.* Norman: University of Oklahoma Press.

Erickson, Fred and Gerald Mohatt (1982). "Cultural Organization of Participant Structures in Two Classrooms of Indian Students." In George Spindler, ed., *Doing the Ethnography of Schooling: Educational Anthropology in Action.* New York: Holt Rinehart and Winston, 132–174.

Ferguson, Lee, ed. (1981). *Race Relations in Tama County.* Report prepared by the Iowa advisory committee to the U.S. Civil Rights Commission. Washington, D.C.: U.S. Government Printing Office.

Foley, Douglas E. (ND). "Charles Evers and the Black Civil Rights Movement in Mississippi." Unpublished paper.

—— (1990). *Learning Capitalist Culture: Deep in the Heart of Tejas.* Philadelphia: University of Pennsylvania Press.

Foley, Douglas, Clarice Mota, Donald Post, and Ignacio Lozano (1988). *From Peones to Politicos: Class and Ethnicity in a South Texas Town, 1900–1987.* Austin: University of Texas Press.

Foucault, Michel (1972). *Power/Knowledge: Selected Interviews and Other Writings, 1972–77.* New York: Pantheon Books, 1977.

Gearing, Frederick O (1970). *The Face of the Fox.* Chicago: Aldine.

Gearing, Fred, Robert McC. Netting, and Lisa R. Peattie (1960). *A Documentary History of the Fox Project, 1948–1959.* Chicago: University of Chicago Press.

Goddard, Ives (1990). "Some Literary Devices in the Writings of Alfred Kiyana." In William Cowan, ed., *Papers of the 21st Algonquien Conference.* Ottowa: Carleton University Press, 159–171.

Gramsci, Antonio (1971). *Selections from the Prison Notebooks.* New York: International Publishers.

Habermas, Jurgen (1984). *The Theory of Communicative Action: Reason and the Rationalization of Society.* Boston: Beacon Press.

Hall, Stuart, Charles Cricher, Tony Jefferson, John Clarke, and Brian Roberts (1978) *Policing the Crises: Mugging, the State and Law and Order.* London: Macmillan Press.

Hill, Thomas (1974). "From Hell-Raiser to Family Man." In James P. Spradley and David W. McCurdy, eds., *Conformity and Conflict: Readings in Cultural Anthropology.* Boston: Little Brown, 186–200.

hooks, bell (1992). *Black Looks: Race and Representation.* Boston: South End Press.

Joffe, Natalie F. (1940). *The Fox of Iowa.* New York: Appleton Century.

Jones, Ben (1931). "The Economic, Legal and Educational Status of the Mesquakie (Fox) Indians of Iowa." MA thesis, University of Iowa.

Jones, William (1907). *Fox Texts.* American Ethnological society #1. Leeden: E.J. Brill Reprint; New York: AMS Press, 1974.

Katz, Michael (1989). *The Undeserving Poor: From the War on Poverty to the War on Welfare.* New York: Pantheon.

Krupat, Arnold (1989). *The Voices in the Margin: Native American Literature and the Canon.* Berkeley: University of California Press.

Lareau, Annette (1989). *Home Advantage: Social Class and Parental Intervention in Elementary Education.* London: Falmer Press.

Lather, Patti (1991) *Getting Smart: Feminist Research and Pedagogy with/in the Postmodern.* London: Routledge.

Leemon, Thomas A. (1972). *The Rites of Passage in a Student Culture: A Study of the Dynamics of Transition.* New York: Teachers College Press.

Lingeman, Richard (1980). *Small Town America: A Narrative History, 1620 to the Present.* Boston: Houghton Mifflin.

Lurie, Nancy (1988). "Relations Between Indians and Anthropologists." In Wilcomb E. Washburn, ed., *Handbook of North American Indians.* Washington, D.C.: Smithsonian Institution, 4: 548–556.

MacBurnie, Allison (1974). "Education and the Mesquakie." Unpublished PhD dissertation, Iowa State University.

MacLeod, Jay (1987). *Ain't No Makin' It: Leveled Aspirations in a Low-Income Neighborhood.* Boulder, Colo.: Westview.

Mead, Margaret (1970). *Culture and Commitment: A Study of the Generation Gap.* New York: Natural History Press/Doubleday.

McCannell, Dean (1992). *Empty Meeting Grounds: The Tourist Papers.* London: Routledge.

McTaggart, Fred (1976). *Wolf That I Am: In Search of the Red Earth People.* Norman: University of Oklahoma Press.

Miller, Walter B. (1955). "Two Concepts of Authority." *American Anthropologist* 57: 171–289.

Michelson, Truman. (1925). "The Autobiography of a Fox Indian Woman." *Fortieth Annual Report of the Bureau of American Ethnology.* Washington, D.C.: U.S. Government Printing Office, 295–349.

—— (1925). "The Mythical Origin of the White Buffalo Dance of the Fox Indians." *Fortieth Annual Report of the Bureau of American Ethnology.* Washington, D.C.: U.S. Government Printing Office, 23–289.

—— (1925). "Notes on Fox Mortuary Customs and Beliefs." *Fortieth Annual Report of the Bureau of American Ethnology.* Washington, D.C.: U.S. Government Printing Office, 351–496.

—— (1925). "A Select Fox Bibliography." In "The Mythical Origin of the White Buffalo Dance of the Fox Indians." *Fortieth Annual Report of the Bureau of American Ethnology.* Washington, D.C.: U.S. Government Printin g Office.

Nelson, Kristine, Terry L. Cross, Miriam J. Londsam, and Margaret Tyler (ND). "Native American Families and Child Neglect." Unpublished paper, School of Social Work, University of Iowa.

Owens, Mary (1904). *Folklore of the Mesquakie: Indians of North America.* London: Folklore Society.

Phillips, Ruth B. (1991). "Clothed in Blessing: Meaning in Mesquakie Costume." *Annals of Iowa* 51,1: 1–25.

Philips, Susan U. (1983). *The Invisible Culture: Communication in Classroom and Community In the Warm Springs Reservation.* New York: Longman.

Pipestar, Ted (1980). *Winter of The Salamander.* San Francisco: Harper and Row Press.

—— (1990). *The Invisible Musician.* Duluth, Minn: Holy Cow! Press.

—— (1992). *Black Eagle Child: The Facepaint Narratives.* Iowa City: University of Iowa Press.

Polgar, Steven (1960). "Biculturation of Mesquakie Teenage Boys." *American Anthropologist* 62: 217–235.

Powers, William (1988). "The American Hobbyist Movement in North America." In Wilcomb E. Washburn, ed., *Handbook of North American Indians.* Washington, D.C.: Smithsonian Institution, 4: 557–561.

Pratt, Mary Louise (1992). *Imperial Eyes: Travel Writing and Transculturation.* London: Routledge.

Rebok, Horace (1900). *The Last of the Musquakies.* Dayton, Ohio: WR. Funk.

Roosens, Eugene E (1989). *Creating Ethnicity: The Process of Ethnogenesis.* Newbury Park, Calif.: Sage.

Rosaldo, Renato (1989). *Culture and Truth: The Remaking of Social Analysis.* Boston: Beacon Press.

Saldivar, Ramon (1990). *Chicano Narrative: The Dialectics of Difference.* Madison: University of Wisconsin Press.

Samuel, Raphael, ed. (1981). *People's History and Socialist Theory.* London: Routledge.

Taylor, Colin (1988). "The Indian Hobbyist Movement in Europe" In Wilcomb E. Washburn, ed., *Handbook of North American Indians.* Washington D.C.: Smithsonian Institution, 4: 522–547.

Torrence, Gaylord and Robert Hobbs (1989). *Art of the Red Earth People: The Mesquakie of Iowa.* University of Iowa Museum of Art, distributed by the University of Washington Press.

TrueTongue, Ernest (1986). *The Larry Andy People Fun Book.* Tama, Iowa: Mikona Publishing.

Tyler, Steven (1986). "Post-Modern Ethnography: From Document of the Occult to Occult document." In James Clifford and George E. Marcus, eds., *Writing Culture: The Poetics and Politics of Ethnography.* Berkeley: University of California Press, 122–140.

Vidich, Arthur J. and Joseph Bensman (1968). *Small Town in Mass Society: Class, Power, and Religion in a Rural Community.* Princeton, N.J.: Princeton University Press.

Vizenor, Gerald (1990). "Trickster Discourse" *American Indian Quarterly* 14, 3 (summer): 277–287.

Ward, Duren (1905). The Ward Files. Iowa City: State Historical Society of Iowa.

Waseskuk, Bertha (1978). "Mesquaki History — As We Know It." In Gretchen M. Bataille, David M. Gradwohl, and Charles P. Silet, eds., *The Worlds Between Two Rivers.* Ames: Iowa State University Press, 54–61.

Willis, Paul (1981). *Learning to Labor: How Working Class Kids Get Working Class Jobs.* New York: Columbia University Press.

Windsong, Claude (1978). "The Lion, the Fleur de Lis, the Eagle, or the Fox: A Study of Government." In Gretchen M. Bataille, David M. Gradwohl, and Charles P. Silet, eds., *The Worlds Between Two Rivers.* Ames: Iowa State University Press, 74–83.

Zielinski, John M. (1976). *Mesquakie and Proud of It.* Kalona, Iowa: Photo-Art Gallery.

Index

University of Pennsylvania Press
Series in Contemporary Ethnography
Dan Rose and Paul Stoller, General Editors

Camille Bacon-Smith. *Enterprising Women: Television Fandom and the Creation of Popular Myth.* 1991

Robert R. Desjarlais. *Body and Emotion: The Aesthetics of Illness and Healing in the Nepal Himalayas.* 1992

John D. Dorst. *The Written Suburb: An American Site, An Ethnographic Dilemma.* 1989

Douglas E. Foley. *Learning Capitalist Culture: Deep in the Heart of Tejas.* 1990

Douglas E. Foley. *The Heartland Chronicles.* 1995

Deborah A. Kapchan. *Gender on the Market: Moroccan Women and the Revoicing of Tradition.* 1995

Kirin Narayan. *Storytellers, Saints, and Scoundrels: Folk Narrative in Hindu Religious Teaching.* 1989

Sally Ann Ness. *Body, Movement, and Culture: Kinesthetic and Visual Symbolism in a Philippine Community.* 1992

Dan Rose. *Patterns of American Culture: Ethnography and Estrangement.* 1989

Paul Stoller. *The Taste of Ethnographic Things: The Senses in Anthropology.* 1989

Lawrence J. Taylor. *Occasions of Faith: An Anthropology of Irish Catholics.* 1995

Edith Turner, with William Blodgett, Singleton Kahona, and Fideli Benwa. *Experiencing Ritual: A New Interpretation of African Healing.* 1992

Jim Wafer. *The Taste of Blood: Spirit Possession in Brazilian Candomblé.* 1991

This book was set in Baskerville and Eras typefaces. Baskerville was designed by John Baskerville at his private press in Birmingham, England, in the eighteenth century. The first typeface to depart from oldstyle typeface design, Baskerville has more variation between thick and thin strokes. In an effort to insure that the thick and thin strokes of his typeface reproduced well on ppaer, John Baskerville developed the first wove paper, the surface of which was much smoother than the laid paper of the time. The development of wove paper was partly responsible for the introduction of typefaces classified as modern, which have even more contrast between thick and thin strokes.

Eras was designed in 1969 by Studio Hollenstein in Paris for the Wagner Typefoundry. A contemporary script-like version of a sans-serif typeface, the letters of Eras have a monotone stroke and are slightly inclined.

Printed on acid-free paper.